THE KINGDOM OF AFGHANISTAN

A HISTORICAL SKETCH

THE KINGDOM OF
AFGHANISTAN
A HISTORICAL SKETCH

BY

G. P. TATE, M.R.A.S., F.R.G.S.,

Member of the Asiatic Society, Bengal, Survey of India.

Author of "Seistan : A Memoir on the History, Topography, Antiquities, and People of the Country"; "The Frontiers of Baluchistan : Travels on the Borders of Persia and Afghanistan"; "Kalat : A Memoir on the Country and Family of the Ahmadzai Khans of Kalat";
&c.

WITH AN INTRODUCTORY NOTE

BY

THE RIGHT HON'BLE SIR HENRY MORTIMER DURAND,
P.C., G.C.M.G., K.C.S.I., K.C.I.E.

GYAN

Published by

Gyan Publishing House
5, Ansari Road
Daryaganj, New Delhi-110002
Phone: 011-47034999, 9811692060
E-mail: books@gyanbooks.com

Distribution Network
gyanbooks.com
India, USA, Canada, UK, Australia, France

ISBN : 978-81-212-3665-2 (PB)
First Published, 1911

2nd Impression 2020

Printed at: Gyan Press, Delhi.

The book at your disposal is the edition of an old book originally published long back. The Text quality of this book may not be at par as compared to our other books but many readers approached us to reprint this important book so that it could satiate their hunger. We request all the readers of this book to help us to improve its quality by providing the necessary text of those pages which are not properly visible. Your valuable support in this case will be highly appreciated and acknowledged and our future readers will be benefitted immensely.

THE KINGDOM OF

AFGHANISTAN.

A HISTORICAL SKETCH

BY

G. P. TATE, M.R.A.S., F.R.G.S.,

Member of the Asiatic Society, Bengal, Survey of India.

Author of "Seistan: A Memoir on the History, Topography, Antiquities, and People of the Country"; "The Frontiers of Baluchistan: Travels on the Borders of Persia and Afghanistan"; "Kalat: A Memoir on the Country and Family of the Ahmadzai Khans of Kalat"; &c.

WITH AN INTRODUCTORY NOTE

BY

THE RIGHT HON'BLE SIR HENRY MORTIMER DURAND,

P.C., G.C.M.G., K.C.S.I., K.C.I.E.

PRINTED BY BENNETT COLEMAN & Co., & PUBLISHED AT THE "TIMES OF INDIA" OFFICES,

BOMBAY & CALCUTTA.

LONDON AGENCY: 99, SHOE LANE, E.C.

1911.

INTRODUCTION.

I HAVE been asked to write a short introduction to this book, and have much pleasure in doing so.

Afghanistan is a country which should be of interest to thinking Englishmen, for its history during the last hundred years has been closely bound up with the history of our Indian Empire; and whatever may be the course of future events in Asia, the Afghan tribes, with their warlike character and rugged territory, will always have an important part to play.

Having seen something of them, in peace and in war, and learned to admire their many fine qualities, I hope that they may long retain the independence to which they are so passionately attached, and that our future relations with them may become more and more friendly. However this may be, it is very desirable that Englishmen should know as much as possible about them and their past.

Mr. Tate has many special qualifications for the work he has undertaken. His long service on the North-West Frontier, and his evident sympathy with the people among whom he has spent so much of his life, must make what he writes valuable to all students of Afghan affairs.

The book contains here and there passages in which I do not entirely agree; but this is inevitable in all such cases. Mr. Tate has certainly brought to his work not only knowledge and sympathy but much care and research.

A book of the kind is really wanted, and I hope it may meet with the attention it deserves.

H. M. DURAND.

PREFACE.

DURING a period of many years of service on the outskirts of Afghanistan, I was brought into contact with all classes of the inhabitants who are now British subjects, and after the Ghilzai and Hazara rebellions against the late Amir, with refugees who had retired for a season into the districts adjoining Afghanistan. On other occasions also I came into touch with chiefs and common folk who were the subjects of H. H. the Amir. In this way an appetite was created for a fuller knowledge of that country and the people, which was sharpened by the fact that it was impossible to enter the country. I very soon found that, besides Elphinstone's Caubool, which, although a classic, does not satisfy modern requirements, it was not possible to obtain in any one book, a general and connected account of the Afghans. In the course of time, as I had concentrated my efforts in this direction, I discovered that a very great deal of valuable information can be found in books, published but out of print, or difficult to get at; and also in the works of many oriental authors, the texts of which, either manuscript or printed, can be obtained. I have ventured to collect between two covers and to present in a connected form, the record of the most important incidents in the history of the Afghans and their relations with neighbouring States, avoiding details which would obscure the narrative without adding to the value of the result. An exhaustive account of Afghanistan and the races, which are grouped under the name Afghan, could not be achieved at all satisfactorily, except in many volumes, and it would be a task beyond the powers of an individual author.

The narrative will disclose the help I have received from my friend, W. Irvine, Esq., I.C.S. (retired); but I am constrained to make a special acknowledgment for the encouragement I have received from him, and also for a very great deal of active and effective assistance in prosecuting my researches in this direction ; and lastly for the labour he has voluntarily undergone in aiding me with valuable information gleaned from sources, which, but for him, would have been inaccessible to me—at any rate for some time to come. Any merit, which this narrative may possess, will be due largely to his valuable and cordial assistance.

With regard to the map of Afghanistan, attached to this book, it is as well to state explicitly, that it is intended to be no more than a key to the positions of the more important localities and places mentioned in the text and to the geographical situation of that country with reference to the dominions of neighbouring powers. Many very excellent maps of Afghanistan are to be found in the various atlases published recently. It would not be possible to improve on those maps without making inroads on information which at present is withheld from publication.

G. P. TATE.

Mussoorie, 7th June 1910.

CONTENTS.

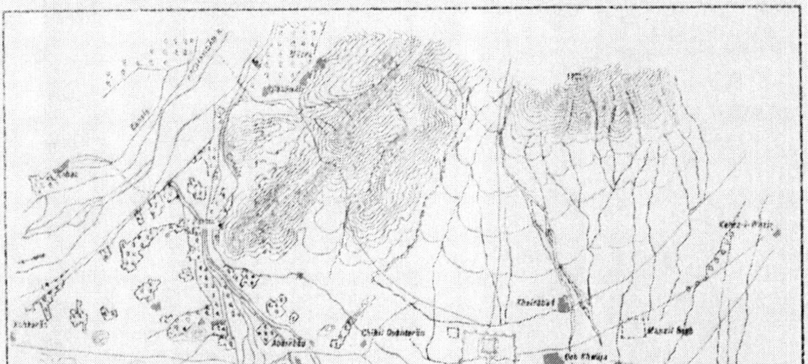

No.8885 500

THE THREE CITIES OF KANDAHAR.

THE KINGDOM OF AFGHANISTAN.

CHAPTER I.

THE COUNTRY OF AFGHANISTAN.

BETWEEN the Russian Dominions in Asia and the Indian Empire of Great Britain, Afghanistan is placed, like a nut, between the levers of a cracker. The notoriously unwholesome quality of the kernel, however, will perhaps continue to preserve it from being shared by its powerful neighbours. The disorganised condition of Persia relieves the Ruler of Afghanistan of all fears of military aggression, but it is not unlikely to be the cause of considerable anxiety to His Majesty the Amir. The progress of modern ideas, and the aspirations of the Persians in the direction of some form of constitutional government, which apparently has terminated the old established despotism of the Shahs, must, in course of time, filter across the border into Afghanistan ; and the democratic nature of the people would seem to render them peculiarly susceptible to the movement, which has reformed the governments of the Kingdom of Turkey (the head of Islam) and Persia. The restrictions placed upon trade by the late Amir, and, therefore, to the influx of foreigners into his country, may possibly have been designed as a precaution also against the introduction of modern ideas among his subjects, which would greatly increase the difficulties with which the rulers have always had to contend in the administration of that State.

The rivalry (that has happily, of late years, subsided) between the great powers which are the neighbours of the Afghans has led to the careful demarcation of the boundaries of that State, with the exception of a short and unimportant length on the west and east. The generally accepted area of 243,000 square miles, therefore, may be regarded as correct. While, however, a fairly accurate general knowledge exists with regard to the geography of Afghanistan, very little is known as to the number of the inhabitants the country supports. From observations made in Seistan, in 1904, there is reason to believe that an average density of 50 souls to a square mile, is not an excessive estimate, or (say) 12,000,000 souls for the population of the country. The richer lands in the wider valleys drained by the principal rivers of the country carry the densest population. In the more elevated and poorer districts, there are fewer inhabitants, and they are to a certain extent migratory. Those who are able to avoid the rigorous winter descend to the lower levels on the approach of that season. Above these districts, again, are others to which shepherds resort in the spring, and in which, during the summer, a considerable population is to be found. These tracts are vacated as winter draws on. The flocks are driven down to warmer districts, where fodder is procurable and in which during the early spring (the lambing season), the climate is not too severe for the young stock.

The name Afghanistan was invented in the 16th and 17th centuries, as a convenient term by the Moghal government in India, and since then it has become current in the mouths of foreigners. The Afghans speak of their country as Wilāyat and less commonly as Khurassan, although Afghanistan covers less than a third of the area of that ancient Division of Asia. As late as the 14th and 15th centuries, the country from Kandahar to Kabul, including the Valley of the Helmand, was still known as Bakhtar Zamin, the country of Bakhtar, and in 1832 Sir Alexander Burnes was told that the country from Kabul to Balkh had also been known by the same name. In this name, perhaps, may be found a corruption of the older form of Vaerkerata, which scholars, versed in the ancient languages of Persia, say, was the name of a Province which appears in the Avesta. In this name, Bakhtar, may also be found the origin of the name Baktria, and the Paktyan land of ancient European writers, which was governed by the Asiatic Greeks till their declining authority, was extinguished by the inroads of hordes from Central Asia.

The great range of the Hindu-Kush divides Afghanistan into two unequal parts, about a third part lying to the north of the water-shed. The country generally consists of narrow valleys sheltered by giant spurs, and ridges of inferior elevation, which descend from the parent range. The latter is a double range pierced by streams which flow alternately north and south, and drain the trough between the ridges. The Heri-Rud, the River of Herat, drains the western end of this trough.[1] Within the present limits of Afghanistan, permanent snow covers only the loftier summits of the range or collects at the heads of the most elevated valleys, which descend on either side; but the heavy snowfall of winter, on the whole range, and rain which falls at certain seasons replenish the rivers which rise high up on the slopes of the mountains. The southern ridge of the Hindu-Kush is pierced by the beds of the principal rivers of Afghanistan, and the northern ridge is broken by torrential streams which descend towards the Oxus; but only the more important of these actually join that river. The beds of these streams and rivers are followed by the routes which cross the lofty saddles of the range, and the lowest of these passes is the Khawak, considerably over 11,000 feet above sea-level.

The two ridges culminate in the vicinity of the mass of Tirich Mir, close to the eastern boundary of Afghanistan, the highest peak of which attains to an altitude of 25,426 feet above the sea. Westwards from the junction of the ridges, the Hindu-Kush throws off minor ranges or great spurs, and continuously decreases in height; and to the north of Herat, the mountains disappear under the sloping glacis which descends towards the Turkoman Desert. A broken chain of low hills, links the southern water-shed of the Heri-Rud, and the Hindu-Kush,[2] with the mountain system of Northern Persia.

The Kabul, Helmand, the Heri-Rud, the Murghāb and the River of Badakshan to the north of the Hindu-Kush are the principal rivers of Afghanistan. The Arghassan, Tarnak, Arghandāb, which swell the discharge of the Helmand; the Rivers of Khāsh, of Farah and Kushk,

---

[1] Geography and Geology of the Himalayas: Col. Burrard, R.E., F. R. S., and H. H. Hayden, B. A., F. G. S., 1908: Part III, pp. 122-123.

[2] The soldiers of Alexander, the first of all Europeans to cross the range, named it the Parapamisus. That eminent scholar, the late Sir Henry Rawlinson, derived this name from Paru-parae-sanna. and which, he wrote, was the cuneiform title of the range read in full. Jour R. Geogr. Soc. Vol. XLII, pp. 501-2.

Hindu-Kush is not a modern name. It appears to have been current in the 14th Century, when Timur crossed from Andarab, "by the Pass of (the) Hindu-Kush, and the ice-bound road (or path) of Jarkārān" (Charikār ?) into the valley of the Kabul river, on his way towards India. In a 17th Century Indian Chronicle (Bādshāhnāmah) the variant Hindu-Kuh, is to be found.

Hindu-Kush is probably a corruption of Hindi-Kash or Kesh—the boundary of Hind, *i.e.* India. Before the Christian era, and afterwards, there was an intimate connection between the Kabul Valley and India. All the Passes of the Hindu-Kush descend into that valley; and travellers from the north as soon as they crossed the watershed, found a civilization and religion, the same as that which prevailed in India. The great range was the boundary in those days and a barrier that was at times impassable.

Hindu-Kuh—the mountains of Hind—was similarly derived

the streams which water the district of Sabzawār and which terminate in the Lake of Seistan; the other streams which nourish the districts of Andikhui, Shibarghān and Hazdanahr (Balkh) are the minor rivers of the country.

Of these the Helmand is the first in rank draining an area of about 100,000 square miles, and with a discharge in the summer (taken in Seistan) of 70,000 cubic feet per second in ordinary years. This river also ranks the twelfth in the list of the rivers of Asia, having regard to the area drained by it and its tributaries, and eleventh with reference to the population it supports.[1] The Kabul river draining an area of 35,000 square miles, and a discharge about 30,000 cubic feet per second in the summer, ranks next to the Helmand. The river Helmand is crossed near Girishk with difficulty by travellers from Herat.[2] The waters of the Kabul river flow swiftly to meet the Indus and the fords are deep and unsafe. Recently, however, it has been spanned by a suspension bridge near Jalālābād, and permanent communication between one bank and the other has been insured; the numerous canals which irrigate the valley of Herat deplete the waters of the Heri-Rud, but the Murghāb has always nourished the famous oasis of Merv, and a dam across the river-bed maintains a good supply of water in the irrigation channels which fertilize the soil. This work was destroyed by the troops of the Amir of Bokhara towards the close of the 18th century, but it has been restored by the Russians and the Tsar's private domains in that district are a valuable property on which great results have been achieved by irrigation. The rivers of Andikhui and Shibarghān are exhausted by the canals which are supplied with water by them, which have always rendered those districts fertile. The rivers of Khash, Farah, of Sabzawār, and the Harut Rud are torrents. They rise in the mountainous district of Ghor and the Zamindāwar, and are subject to sudden irresistible floods, rendering them inpassable for a time. These streams contain no flowing water for some distance above the lake of Seistan into which their floods are discharged. The principal tributary of the Helmand is the Arghandāb,

[1] Geography and Geology of the Himalayas, Pt. III, p. 120.

[2] The column detailed to Girishk under Brigadier Genl. Sale, in 1839, crossed the Helmand in the month of May. The troops crossed with some difficulty on rafts made of rum kegs. "It was, at one time, contemplated to swim over the Cavalry horses; but it is said there would have been great risk, as the water was deep, and the stream rushed with such violence, that some few who tried it riding barebacked were carried more than a mile down the river." Major Hough's narrative:—Major Abbot, on his journey from Herat to Simla in 1837-38, crossed the Helmand at this place on an elephant. Captain Edward Conolly at an earlier date found that boats, which ferried passengers and goods to the opposite bank, were provided at this crossing.

and its name is derived from the swiftness of the current when in flood. It is said to become impassable when the depth of water in its channel exceeds three feet. In 1839 a cavalry reconnaisance from Kalat-i-Ghilzai visited the Maidan district on the banks of the Arghandāb, and the tired horses were ridden girth-deep into the stream and slaked their thirst in its clear swift waters. The country on either banks was found to be cultivated and studded with towns and villages. The district of Mālistan, in which this river has its source, is famed for its temperate climate in the summer, rich pastures, and an abundance of springs. The waters of the Tarnak and Arghasan barely suffice for the demands of the agriculturists in the country round Kandahar, and in the valley of the last-named stream. The district of Ghor, in which the rivers of Khāsh and of Farah rise, has always been famous for its strength and inaccessibility.

The Kabul river and its tributaries, the Panjshir and Kunar, rise at great elevations upon the slopes of the Hindu-Kush. At Dakka (below Jalālābād), close to which their united waters pass out of Afghan territory, the elevation of the valley is under 1,300 feet. The Helmand, at the point where it is crossed on the road from Kabul to Bāmiān, is about 10,500 feet above sea-level. The lake which it forms in Seistan is 1,600 feet above the sea. The rivers of Herat and the Murghāb rise at elevations of about 9,000 feet. Herat itself is 6,000 feet below the source, and Bālā Murghāb is lower still. Kabul is under 6,000 feet, Kandahar a little more than 3,000 feet ; Balkh (about 40 miles from the left bank of the Oxus), at the foot of the Hindu-Kush, is 1,300 feet, and Khāmiāb, the frontier post of Afghanistan on the left bank of the Oxus, is only 900 feet above the sea. No less than one hundred and four peaks, attaining altitudes from 20,000 to over 25,000 feet above the sea[1] break the sky line of the ridges of the Hindu-Kush; but these are situated outside of the modern limit of Afghanistan on the east. Within the boundaries of that country, the summit of the range is considerably below 20,000 feet. The differences in elevation, which the country exhibits, are very considerable[2] and are accompanied by corresponding differences in climate, scenery, and produce. In the highest inhabited valleys, the moderate temperature of a short-lived summer provides a single crop of cereals for the inhabitants. In the low-lying valleys, a warmer climate, a rich soil, and an abundance of

[1] Geography and Geology of the Himalayas, Pt. I, p. 31.

[2] In Switzerland the lowest levels are on the Lago Maggiore 614 feet and at Basel on the Aar 914 feet above sea level. The Monte Rosa attains to an elevation of more than 15,000 feet above the sea.

water are congenial to rice, the lemon flourishes, and the plantain was introduced by the famous Baber, who founded the Moghul dynasty in India. With the exception of Kafiristan and the northern slopes of the Hindu-Kush, where the forests which once must have clothed the mountains have escaped complete destruction, the country may, with justice, be described as treeless, except where, in the valleys, fruit trees take the place of natural vegetation.

There is no part of Afghanistan where snow never falls. The rainfall is very small, and except on irrigated lands, there is an absence of moisture, and the climate of the country is very favourable to human existence. The inhabitants of those lands suffer from ailments, due to malaria and damp. [1] The district of Hazdanahar (so called from the 18 water-courses which exhaust the water of the River of Balkh) in which Balkh stands, the country round the Cities of Kabul and of Kandahar and the small district of Girishk on the right bank of the Helmand, are notoriously unhealthy in the summer. Owing to neglect of the elements of sanitation, and owing to vicious habits diseases are rife in the towns. The dry atmosphere, and bright sunshine during the greatest part of the year, combined with the migratory habits of a large proportion of the inhabitants, and the isolated position of the principal centres of population in Afghanistan with respect to neighbouring countries, have preserved the inhabitants of that country from the pestilences which scourge India so frequently. [2]

Years of scarcity are not infrequent, but severe distress is confined to those districts in which cultivation depends chiefly on the rainfall. It rarely becomes very general or developes into a famine. The rivers, which are fed by the snowfall on the Hindu-Kush, provide an unfailing but variable supply of water, which is conveyed to the lands on either bank by open flood water canals, and in suitable localities, under-ground springs are tapped and their waters led by means of Kārezes to lands often many miles distant from the heads of these

---

[1] In the vicinity of Kabul, the sub-soil water is about 6 feet below the surface of the land. At Kandahar it is about 4 feet, and in the vicinity of Herat from 10 to 12 feet below the surface.

[2] In the 15th century an outbreak of pestilence—probably of plague, almost depopulated the City of Herat, at that time the capital of the wide Empire, ruled by Shah Rukh, the son of Tamerlane. The disease attracted notice on the 6th February 1435, by which time it had become established. It raged for four months. A local chronicler has recorded the mortality in that period at 1,000,000 souls in the city itself and the surrounding country. An outbreak of pestilence in 1685 was general, and as it was considered worthy of being recorded, the mortality must have been very great. The year 1828 was marked by another visitation, and Herat was again afflicted.

works. Wherever it is possible to do so, the inhabitants surround their villages and towns with orchards and vineyards,[1] and the banks of the irrigation channels are adorned with fruit trees, poplars and willows. The Tajiks are famous horticulturists. Expert judges profess to recognise more than thirty varieties of grapes alone. All stone fruits attain to perfection. The melons (of many varieties), grown in the country round Herat and Kandahar have always been celebrated for their flavour. Dried fruit of all kinds used to be imported in very great quantities to India; and the value of this branch of trade is said to have exceeded that of all other exports not excepting even the export of horses, at a time when the imports of horses into India from Australia was in its infancy, and when Afghanistan supplied India with animals suited for all kinds of work. Wheat and barley are the staple crops; but rice and other cereals are cultivated successfully in suitable localities. The chaff, after the wheat and barley have been trodden out and winnowed, forms the principal supply of food for horses, camels, and live-stock generally during the winter, and for the greater part of the year. The silkworm is raised in the valley of Herat, and silk is manufactured there, not, however, to the same extent that it was when Herat was the capital of Khurassān. Sir Alexander Burnes is credited with the introduction of the potato into Afghanistan in 1837. The soil is a light loam, impregnated with saline constituents, but wherever water is available for irrigation, it yields a good return to the husbandman. The animals owned by the latter supply the manure which is necessary, but as the quantity is not great, it is reserved for those lands which can be irrigated. Shepherds are encouraged to herd their flocks on outlying fallow lands during the winter, and the manure which collects within the folds is valued by the owners of the soil. The national agricultural implement is the spade, and the universal pattern of plough, which is used everywhere in the east, is also employed to till the land. In constructing irrigation channels, a shallow brass or iron dish containing water is used as a guide for the eye of the person in charge of the work and serves the purpose of a level.

The theory usually prevalent in oriental countries that the soil is the property of the State, is considerably modified in Afghanistan owing to the turbulent character of a large part of the population occupying the land; and among the latter some very curious primitive customs

[1] The vines are grown inside parallel trenches, and are trained up the slopes of the banks into which the soil is heaped between the trenches. The plants are in this way sheltered from the cutting winds, and additional protection is afforded by means of high walls enclosing the vineyard.

are in force regarding the distribution of tribal lands whether among the various families of the tribe or among individuals in the latter. The underlying principle is probably to attempt to maintain a rough equilibrium of prosperity between the occupiers of land unequal in quality, so as to prevent some members of the community becoming rich on good holdings, while others starve on poor soil. The periods for which the shares are held extends to several years, but the details of the system vary among the tribes observing it and in different districts. Some extend its application—each male, female or child receiving a share, including the houses in their villages in the redistribution; and on the other hand among the certain tribes of the Ghilzais, unmarried men are said not to receive any share at all, the right being apparently restricted to the heads of families. In some districts the distribution is effected by lot, if a majority of those interested in the operation wish it.

About 43,000 square miles of unproductive desert exists in the extreme southern portion of Afghanistan. The river of Khāsh and the Helmand flow through this inhospitable region, but the restricted areas on their banks, which might be cultivated by means of irrigation, are insignificant in comparison with the expanse of desert on every side. Although no one knows how much of the remaining area of 200,000 square miles is capable of cultivation, yet it is possible to make a rough estimate which may be not very far from the truth, by taking as a guide the proportion of cultivable land, which is known to exist in those districts (once a part of Afghanistan), which have been transferred to the Indian Empire, from the Kuram Valley on the north to Sibi on the south. Ten per cent. of the whole area of Afghanistan may perhaps represent the area which might be cultivated. Of this, however, only ten per cent. again may be actually under crops in any year, owing to a variety of causes, of which the varying quality of the soil, the precarious supply of moisture supplied by nature, and the nomadic proclivities of a large proportion of the population are the more important.

The mineral resources of the country are as yet unexplored; and as it is a task which can be successfully carried out only by foreign experts, progress in this direction must be slow. Some minerals such as silver, lead, antimony and iron have always been worked in a very unskilful and desultory fashion; and traces of gold have been discovered in the neighbourhood of Kandahar. The dislike of foreigners and of their interference, whether it is due to hostile relations with foreigners in the past, a dread of sinister designs on their country and cherished liberty, or to an unconfessed knowledge of their own barbarity, on the part of the Afghans themselves, offer an unsurmountable barrier to the exploration of the mineral resources of the country, and to development in other directions. The last thirty years of peace between India and Afghanistan cannot but have had an effect on this exclusive attitude. India offers now, as it always has done, a field for the enterprise of the Afghans, whose hands can wield indifferently a cloth measure, a spade, a sword or a rifle. Numbers of the poorer classes of the population enter India every winter, when all avocations are suspended in their own country, either for trade or seeking for employment. The needy tribesmen wander as far afield as Assam and Burma in search of work, which the natives are too well off or too indolent to undertake themselves, and for wages which apparently offer no temptation to the natives for exertion. The Afghans have crossed the sea to Australia with camels, and some have amassed money there in other occupations. A very few individuals have even returned to their homes accompanied by white women, whom they have induced to take a step, the ultimate result of which can never be known. Such intercourse with countries beyond their borders cannot but have an effect favourable to the increase of knowledge, and that desire for the amenities of civilized existence, which is such an incentive to progress.

The future of Afghanistan lies in Afghanistan; and though the ignorance of the mass of the population will retard the development of the natural resources of their country; of late years, it is evident that the government, and probably the more thoughtful among the population, have realized the fact. Recent small importations of machinery for industrial purposes is a very hopeful sign of this movement. The absence of fuel is a serious hindrance; but it has led to a search for coal, hitherto apparently without much success, which will probably lead to other discoveries, and finally may attain the desired end.

Lastly, owing to the poverty of the country and scanty supplies, the difficulties of transport and communications, and the intractable character of the inhabitants, in whom an aptitude for guerrilla warfare has become an inherited talent, the words of King Henri IV of France, by which he described Spain of his day, are almost equally appropriate as a description of Afghanistan of the present time:—It is a country which it is impossible to conquer, a little army is beaten there, and a large one starved.[1]

---

[1] Life of Louis, Prince of Conde—Earl Stanhope.

CHAPTER II.

Claim of the Afghans to be descended from Dispersed Tribes of Israel.

THE origin of the tribes who call themselves Afghans has attracted a great deal of attention, owing to the fact that they claim to be the descendants of Jews, who had settled in Ghor; and the various clans refer their origin to some one of the three sons of Kais, the chieftain of that community, who is said to have been the 37th in descent from Saul, King of Israel. Owing to intercourse with the Jews settled in Arabia, so the story goes, Kais was induced to visit the Prophet Muhammad, who won the Jewish Chief to Islam, and bestowed on him the name of Abdur Rashid, and the title of Pahtan. This last is a mysterious word which cannot be traced to an origin in any known language, but it is believed to mean either or both, the rudder, or the mast of a ship. So say those who have committed the genealogy of the Afghans to paper. The conversion of Kais is not mentioned in the history of Islam.

The so-called genealogy of the Afghans was compiled at a time when all the races of Mankind were believed to have been the offspring of the first man and woman created by the Almighty and the eponymous ancestor of every tribe appears at some stage in the genealogy, which there seems every reason to believe was concocted in the 15th century A. D., probably when the Afghans began to attain to power in India. The main feature in it is the alleged Jewish ancestry of all the tribes, and this belief must have been very strong for the retention of the legend, when the tables of descent were compiled. All that can be said at present is that the legend has preserved the memory of a fact which has dropped out of history. It is not improbable that there may have been a Hebrew Community in Ghor.

The Jews of Bokhara delivered to Dr. Wolff a tradition to the effect that 'when their forefathers belonging to the Reubenites,

Gadites and the half tribe of Manasseh were removed by Tiglath Pileser ' (B.C. 738) ' they were brought to Hala (Balkh), and Habor (Samarkand) and Hara (Bokhara) and to the river of Gozan (that is to say, the Amu, (called by Europeans the Oxus), from Palestine'. If this is a genuinė tradition, it would render possible the presence of an independent community of professing Jews in the adjoining fastnesses of Ghor and the Firuzkoh. This tradition described the dispersal of the Hebrews by Chingiz Khan[1] and they fled into Sabzawar and Nishapur in Khurassan and dwelt there for some centuries till they at last returned to their former seats along the Oxus, and claim to have been kindly treated by the famous Tamerlane.

In February 1896, on the southern boundary of Afghanistan, men pointed out an almost obliterated mound and a hollow, which they said were the remains of a fort and tank constructed by the Bani Israel, who had come from the west and passed on towards the north. Both the mound and hollow needed to be carefully pointed out, so time-worn were they. It is, as far as can be ascertained, the only instance in which the tradition of the exiled Israelites—the Bani-Israel of the Afghan legend, has been found to be associated, with a definite site or remains. There is, of course, that famous shrine in the Lamghan district on the Kabul River, dedicated to the Saint Mihtar Lam, who is said to have been buried there and who is supposed by some to have been none other than the Patriarch Lamech.

The persecution of the Hebrews in Persia, set on foot by the Sassanian Monarch Firuz, in 490 A.D., scattered them over Asia. European travellers and authors in the 12th century mention the existence of independent communities of Israelites in Eastern Persia and in Afghanistan and in India.[2]

The silence of local historians as to the existence of any Hebrew communities cannot be regarded as proof to the contrary ; for those writers were more eager to embellish their pages with the record of high political affairs and the marchings of vast armies, led by potent sovereigns, than to treat of humbler events ; but the existence of an independent community and a ruling chief could hardly have escaped notice, except by reason of the fact that they had forsaken their religion and had adopted Islam or an earlier Pagan religion instead.

---

[1] Life and adventures of the Revd. Joseph Wolff, D D., LL.D., Vol. II, pp. 12-13

[2] The mystery that shrouded the fate of those Israelites, who never returned to their native land, inspired the journey of discovery, undertaken by the Rabbi Benjamin of Toledo and by Petachya of Prague. The former discovered a community of professing Jews, 4,000 strong, belonging to the tribes of Dan, Asher, Zebulon, and Naphthali who maintained their independence in the mountains of

The district of Ghor is an unexplored part of Afghanistan, and no European has set eyes on the ruins of the comparatively modern capital of the Ghori Sultans. It was also the last stronghold of an ancient religion professed by the inhabitants when all their neighbours had become Muhammadan. In the 11th century A. D. Mahmud of Ghazni defeated the Prince of Ghor, Ibn-i-Suri, and made him prisoner in a severely contested engagement in the valley of Ahingarān. Ibn-i-Suri is called a Hindu by the author, who has recorded his overthrow; it does not follow that he was one either by religion or by race, but merely that he was not a Muhammadan.

Although the Afghans firmly believe the legend of their Jewish origin, yet indications exist which support a contrary opinion. Afghanistan has been the ante-chamber of India for centuries of time beginning with ages of which no knowledge exists. Through this country have passed those successive immigrations of nations which have spread over the plains of the Punjab and Upper India, from which the present-day population of those tracts has descended. Some part of these immigrants may have drifted over the barrier of the Hindu-Kush, as bands of fugitives, but the great movements must have followed the easier route round the western end of those lofty mountains, the immigrants travelling deliberately, encumbered with their families, and driving before them their herds of cattle and live stock. The valley of the Helmand and of its tributaries provided easy routes for this advance, and further to the east, the well trodden paths, which follow the courses of the Kuram, the Tochi, Gomal and Bolan Streams admitted the immigrants to their ultimate destination in the valley of the Indus and further to the east. It is reasonable to suppose that some part of the immigrating nations must have remained in Afghanistan,

---

Nishapur. Their Prince, a Hebrew, in 1153 acknowledged the Sultan of the Saljuks as his Suzerain. Petachya found a race of dark skinned Israelites in India, who had preserved merely the observance of the Sabbath, and the rite of circumcision. History of the Jews. H. Graetz, Vol. II.

Edrisi in the 12th century compiled a treatise on geography, and he gives a curiously circumstantial and accurate description of the old town of Kandahar, where he says a whole quarter in the town was occupied by infidel, *i.e.*, professing Hebrews, for Edrisi was a Muhammadan. The existence of such a community is not confirmed by well known authors, such as Al Baihaki (12th century), and the author of the Tabakat-i-Nasiri (13th century), both of whom were natives of Khurassan and might be expected to have known of the existence of such a community. There were, however, two cities both named Kandahar and both with the same letters, one was in the Southern Afghan country and the second in the Peninsula of India. Whether the latter town was in existence in the 12th century is uncertain; if it was, perhaps that was the town intended by Edrisi, who may have confounded it with the other town of the same name in Afghanistan. In the Indian town of Kandahar a community of professing Hebrews might very possibly have been in existence.

and that from them are descended the semi-pastoral tribes who call themselves Afghans. These may have come to regard, in course of time, the Jewish Princes of Ghor as their overlord and, as time passed, themselves as members by blood of that community. At the present day there are confederacies of tribes called by one name, the members of which belong to a variety of tribes who have been drawn together by common interests, and who now call themselves by the general name of the group to which they belong—Brahui, Imak, Durani, and so on. The spread of Islam, which for some six centuries had put an end to the recurring immigrations, on a large scale, of nations from Central Asia into the countries to the south of the Oxus, has in a great measure obliterated all knowledge of their origin among those who follow the teachings of that religion.

The name Afghan appears in chronicles of the 11th and succeeding Centuries A. D., when they had passed under the rule of the dynasty founded by Sabaktakin (on the ruins of the Empire of the Samanis), and whose capital was Ghazni, now a town of second-rate importance in Afghanistan. At that time the Afghans appear to have been located in the country to the south and east of that city, on the banks of the Indus river, and in the narrow valleys and glens of the Roh. This name was applied to the mountainous and unproductive tract, with which we are now very familiar as the home of those unruly people, the Afridis and the Waziris. It is composed of great spurs which descend from the western water-shed of the Indus ; and the name was given to all the country from the Safed Koh, south of the Kabul River to Cape Monze, overlooking the Sea of Oman. The mountains to the north of the Kabul River and between the Kunar and Jhelum rivers also, were at one time regarded as forming a part of the Roh. Later, when the Afghans had risen to importance in the country to the west of the water-shed, the country up to the Helmand River was supposed by them to be a part of the Roh. In the 11th century, the Afghans were notorious for their turbulence and as bad subjects, and the famous Mahmud Sultan of Ghazni, the son of Sabaktakin, was forced to take order with them, and the difficult character of their abodes or fastnesses (in the Roh) is mentioned.

Up to the first quarter of the 13th century, the countries to the west of the Roh were occupied and controlled by a civilized population. Then took place the collapse of the barriers that Islam had opposed for almost six centuries to the inroads of barbarians from Central Asia. Religious schisms had weakened the faith of the professors of Islam, and political rivalries had still further relaxed the bond of unity between them that had prevailed at an earlier period.[1] The hordes of Chingiz Khan beat down the ill-concerted and desultory opposition offered by the world of Islam, and for a time the fabric of society and civilization was overthrown by the onslaught of the Mongols. The fair Province of Khurassan was depopulated and devastated. For three hundred years and more, wandering hordes of Mongols, Turks and later of Uzbegs rendered life in it too strenuous for the barbarous Afghans, who were pushed about the country or projected into India. It was not till the 16th century and the early part of the following century that the Uzbegs were forced beyond the Hindu-Kush and the vacant lands that existed in all districts were available for the Afghans to occupy.[2]

These conditions which lasted for nearly 300 years have left their impress on the population, which is now composed of three races, each of which differs from its neighbours in many very important respects: in physiogonomy, in character and in their mode of life. These are the Hazara, the Tajik, and the Afghan tribes. The Hazaras are Mongols—relics of the invasion of Chingiz Khan, reinforced afterwards by later arrivals from the banks of the Oxus and the country beyond. The physical traits of the Hazaras have rendered them easily distinguishable. They are addicted to the heretical form of belief of the Ali Illahi sect. They do not coalesce socially or politically with either Tajik or Afghan. They are located to the west of the road from Kandahar to Kabul; and they occupy that tract to-day in which the Huns settled and where they had their centres of government in the 6th century A. D. The Hazaras are hardy, strongly built and industrious, and the ranks

---

[1] The political ambitions of the Caliph-an-Nasir, caused him to fall out with his (at one time) any, Muhammad, Khwarazm Shah. The Caliph was powerless for open enmity with a potentate whose Empire reached from the Jaxartes to the Persian Gulf, so he invited Chingiz Khan to attack the Khwarazm sovereign, and sent an embassy to the pagan chieftain to urge him to take this course, which a few years later extinguished the Caliphate itself. The Caliphate, Muir. pp. 582-3.

[2] Some time in the 13th or 14th century the Mongols expelled the Momands and Khallils from their possessions in the valley, from Kalat-i-Ghilzai, towards Kabul, including Ghazni, Shashgau, Haftasia and Haidar Khel. The tribes then wandered down the valley of the Kabul, and seized the lands they now occupy turning out the Dilazaks, who were driven across the Indus into Chach. The Wardak clan deprived the Hazaras subsequently of the lands they had taken from the Momands and Khallils to the north of Ghazni.

A similar probable cause also decided the Yusufzais to abandon their homes in the country between Nushki and Quetta. They wandered northwards through the Zhob Valley, and after a long period passed in moving about Afghanistan and northwards towards the Hindu-Kush, in the first quarter of the 15th century; they finally settled down in their present abodes.

The Parni tribe, who came into collision with Timur at the close of the 14th century, in the upper part of the Lohgar Valley, were impelled southwards. These are a few instances that will illustrate the vicissitudes the tribes suffered before the rise of the Safavi, and Moghul Empire of Delhi gave them an opportunity of a less strenuous existence.

of servants and labourers throughout the country are recruited from them. In consequence of this they are to be found all over Afghanistan, and have even provided the Indian Army with useful soldiers.

The Tajiks display to-day all those qualities, which distinguished the agricultural population in the valley of the Oxus, who were known to the Chinese as the Ta-hia. They live in houses and form orderly village communities. They are appreciative of the benefits of education and of the amenities of civilized existence; and in their households they maintain a higher standard of comfort to that which prevails among the Afghans or Hazaras. They are everywhere regarded as the people of the soil; descendants of the ancient race which owned the land. In spite of centuries of misgovernment and oppression at the hands of predatory barbarians, they have clung tenaciously to agriculture, and engage in commerce as well. Wherever there is arable soil and water to irrigate it, there always is to be found a remnant of this ancient race. Called by different names in different localities, whether they be known as Dehwār or Dehkān (inhabitants of villages), Tajik, or Farsiwān (Persian-speaking—Persian is their mother-tongue); they are one people and in all probability they represent the original Iranian or Aryan race among whom Zoroaster published his doctrine; among whom the Greek colonists of Alexander settled, and to whom a thousand years later the soldiers of Islam offered the alternatives of the Korān, the Poll-tax, or the sword. While the Mongol Hazara holds aloof, the Tajik and Afghan are drawn together by common interests; and the former first calls himself an Afghan and owns to being a Tajik afterwards.

The Afghans pride themselves on their nomadic proclivities, and on those qualities, which they complacently regard as military virtues, but which others may stigmatize, with good reason, as brutality. The Afghan is frequently spoken of as a Pat-hān, and in the latter some have professed to recognise the name of a people mentioned by Herodotus [1] and other writers of antiquity. In some parts of the country, the term Pat-hān appears to be restricted to those tribes who are cultivators of the lands they occupy. Afghan is applied to the tribes collectively, and also to the pastoral tribes among them. These affect to despise the Tajik as men of peace, civilians, in fact—and this attitude towards the arts of peace attaches a stigma to those tribes of Afghans, who themselves engage in agricultures.

[1] The Paktues, and Pakthas of the Vedas. The Afghans call themselves Pakhtān (pl. Pakhtāna), from which the change to Pahtāna and again to Pathān is easy.

Differences of religious dogmas of Islam—the Shia and Suni schools of thought tend to keep the Tajik apart from the Afghan. The Tajik is usually a Shia—the Afghan always professes to be a Suni of a bigoted type. In the Kuram Valley there are, however, tribes which regard themselves as Afghans, but which profess the Shia doctrines. They are, however, the exception, and of not great importance. The ignorant and arrogant Afghan cannot, however, do without the despised Tajik, whether as agriculturists or administrators. They intermarry, but the Tajik wife ranks below other wives belonging to Afghan tribes. Some of the greatest men in the history of the country have been the offspring of such mixed unions, the ability and prudence for which they have been distinguished having been inherited from their Tajik mothers.

An Afghan tribe is theoretically constituted from a number of kindred groups of agnates, that is to say, descent is through the father, and the son inherits the father's blood. The groups comprising the tribe are divided into a multiplicity of sub-divisions, which it is almost impossible to follow; but for practical purposes, four are in common use—the "Kaum" or main body, the "Khel" or "Zai," representing both the class (a group generally occupying a common locality), and the section, a group whose members live in close proximity to one another and probably hold common land; and lastly the "Kahol", a family group united by kinship. Affiliated with many tribes are to be found a number of alien groups known as "mindun" or "hamsayah." In such cases the test of kinship does not apply, and such groups, families, or individuals are united to the tribe by common good and common ill. In other words, common blood feud is the underlying principle uniting a tribe, but the conception in time merges into the fiction of common blood, *i.e.*, connection by kinship.

Among the Afghans, heredity is not a fixed principle, but the unfit is passed by in favour of another who is better able to lead the tribe in war and to manage its affairs in times of peace. Individuality has a greater field for its expression among Afghans than among other races.

Social or class distinctions are lightly esteemed by them.[1] In every tribe, however, there are families who claim a superior social

---

[1] As free-born, all Afghans are on an equality with, though not as rich, perhaps as their chiefs. Honours and property can only be inherited by sons borne by free women—the son of the handmaid inherits the disabilities of his mother, and is regarded as spurious. A bare subsistence is all he is entitled to.

Baluchistan District Gazetteer, Vol. V.—Quetta, Pishin, 1907.

status, the reason for which is no longer apparent. Among the rest all are on an equal social level, and even the office of malik does not give the holder of it any superiority over the rest of his countrymen. The office is filled by election, and depends on the goodwill of the electors. With regard to the supreme chieftainship of a great tribe, consisting of many sub-divisions, the dignity is hereditary in some particular family, any member of which, however, can be elected as the chief, the choice depending on the characters of the available candidates. In time of peace the eldest son of the chieftain usually succeeds his father ; but in times of peril it not unfrequently happens that some person who has displayed pre-eminent courage and ability is acknowledged as their chieftain by the tribesmen, although he may not belong to the family in which the office has become hereditary.

The bold and warlike character of the Afghans has always preserved them from being crushed by the despotic use of power by their chiefs or kings. Innovations are liable to be fiercely resented and opposed by the armed strength of the tribes concerned. The petty and selfish ambitions of the chiefs, tribal feuds and jealousies have always enabled an adroit Ruler to maintain his authority, and by acts of well-timed daring even to assert his supremacy, over the chiefs and people of Afghanistan. The great Ahmad Shah, and his equally famous minister, were compelled to regard the wishes of the people, and their policy and schemes were liable to be frustrated by his stiff-necked subjects, when they were not in accordance with popular feeling. The ruthless determination displayed by the late Amir, Abdur Rahman, with regard to the establishment of the supremacy of the crown, and in order to break down opposition to his plans for raising his country in the scale of civilization, placed him far above his predecessors. Having subdued the tribes by removing those persons whose influence was likely to prove dangerous, he was able to control the irresponsible priesthood of Afghanistan—a measure which no preceding Rulers of the country would have dared to attempt.[1]

The progress of modern ideas which promises to remodel the conservative and despotic monarchies of Turkey and Persia into some form of constitutional governments cannot but affect Afghanistan i course of time ; and it is easy to understand the interest which events

[1] The support of the Duranis and Tajiks enabled him to do this succesfully. The latter are always ready to support a stable government. Their interest lies on the side of law and order or as close to these conditions as it is possible to attain in Afghanistan. The Duranis had their ancient feud with the Ghilzais and no common interests with the Hazaras. The Triumph of the Barakzai Amir was shared by every single Durani, as they attained to supremacy over all the other tribes in their country period.

in those countries are reported to have created among the Afghans, who appear to be peculiarly susceptible to a movement which has revolutionized the Muhammadan Empires of Western Asia, by reason of their democratic nature and the practice of managing their domestic ffairs by means of tribal and family councils.

The history of the Afghans is practically the story of the two great confederacies led by the Duranis and Ghilzais. At present the former are supreme in Afghanistan, but the latter possess the more brilliant record. They have given kings to India and Persia, and have ruled as kings in their own country. The memory of these achievements has led to sanguinary struggles against the supremacy of the Duranis. The bravery and the numerical superiority of the Ghilzais has, however, been rendered of no avail, owing to a fatal absence of co-operation. Owing to the extent of country over which they are spread, local interests have caused the interests of the clan at large to be lost sight of, some tribes holding back, while the others were asserting their pretensions in arms. Owing to their position at the head of the Passes, which lead to India, they have been intimately connected with that country. The Ghilzais are both agricultural and pastoral in their mode of life, according to the position of the lands they occupy. The Duranis have been associated with Persia, owing to their situation in Afghanistan. Theirs is apparently a better military organisation than that of their rivals. They are more equestrian or nomadic in their habits than the latter. The histories of the less famous tribes contain a great deal of interesting information, but do not illuminate the obscurer portions of the history of their country. With some important exceptions, such as the Momands, the Yusufzais, the Afridis and Khataks, the tribes have adhered to one or other of the confederacies led by the Ghilzais and the Duranis.[1]

---

[1] The Duranis are divided into two groups known as the Panjpai, or Panjpao and Zirak. The former consist of the tribes of Nurzai, Alizai, Ishakzai, Khwagani and Maku. The Zirak division, of the Popalzai, Alakozai, Barakzai and Achakzai. The Sadozais belonged to the Popalzai clan, the present Muhammadzai Dynasty to the Barakzai clan. The Popalzai are located to the north of Kandahar, but are to be found in the country towards the Helmand. The Barakzais to the south of Kandahar, towards the Helmand and in the Arghasan valley. The Achakzais were a branch of this tribe from which they were separated, it is said, by Ahmad Shah. The Achakzais inhabit the country between the Kadanai and Lora rivers, the western edge of the Pishin district and the Khojak and Toba hills, in the Baluchistan Agency.

The Nurzais towards Seistan, Khāsh and Farah. The Alizai head-quarters are in the Zamindāwar country. The Ishakzais (or Sakzis) range from Seistan to the Arghasan valley. The Khwagani and Makus are small clans, with no distinct range or habitat. Some regard them as merely the "Hamsayahs" or clients *or adoptives* of the other three tribes.

The Alakozai tribe of the Zirak division now is to be found towards Herat, but the eponymous ancestor of this tribe—Alako—is said to have been buried at Nicharah, a valley in the Harboi mountains to the east of Kalat in Baluchistan. The tomb of Alako is said to be regarded as a Ziarat.

These tribes were known early in their history as the Abdals or Avdals. Perhaps in this name we may find a survival of the Ephthalites, called by the Persians Hiatila, the name of the dominant race in the confederacy of equestrian tribes known in history as the Huns. Durani is a later name for the Avdals or Abdals, and is popularly believed to have originated in the practice of wearing pearl earrings, but in the time of Ahmad Shah, the clansmen as a body could not have afforded such luxuries. It seems not impossible, however,that this name existed at an earlier date as it seems to appear in a 17th century chronicle, the Shahjahān-namah.

The Tarins, of whom the Abdals are supposed to have been a branch according to the fabulous genealogy of the Afghans, migrated largely to India and maintained a steady intercourse with that country through Multan, but the Duranis or Abdals for some reason do not appear to have followed this example to any appreciable extent. Probably their equestrian or nomadic way of life rendered them disinclined to settle in India.

The Tarins, on the contrary, are agricultural and commercial in their mode of life compared with the Abdalis.

NOTE.

NOTE.—The tradition preserved by the Hebrews of Bokhara (according to Dr. Joseph Wolff) gains in probability, when it is recollected that, according to classical story, Bactria was first conquered and added to Assyria by Ninus. The connection of this country with the early Persian Empire rests on a better foundation. We are told that Cyrus built the great city of Cyropolis to guard the fords of the Jaxartes (Jihun). He initiated the policy of governing Bactria, through a Prince of the Blood Royal, as the Satrap.

After the disastrous invasion of Greece, by Xerxes (about 480 B.C.), tha monarch planted a colony of Ionian Greeks beyond the Oxus. The Branchiadae, originally from Miletus ; they had been compelled to fly from this place when the Greek cities of Asia finally cast off the Persian yoke. They were obliged to escape from the wrath of their Greek neighbours because they had been guilty of betraying the treasures of Apollo of Didymi to the Persians.

Their descendants enthusiastically welcomed the soldiers of Alexander; but they were butchered by his orders presumably on account of the sacrilege committed by their forefathers. (Bactria : the Hare University Prize Essay, 1908, by H. G. Rawlinson, M. A.)

A connection between the country in the valley of the Oxus, and beyond that river—and therefore, presumably with Afghanistan—and the valley of the Euphrates and the seaboard of the Mediterranean, must have existed from times of which we have no knowledge.

CHAPTER III.

RELATIONS WITH INDIA.

THE kingdoms of the Sultans of Ghazni and of Ghor gave place to another whose capital was situated on the lower Oxus. Their territories to the west of the Indus became a part of the unwieldy kingdom of Khwarazm. On the downfall of the Ghori Sultans in the early years of the 13th century, the Mameluke of the last Sultan, who had governed his master's Indian possessions, set himself up as an independent ruler. During the predominance of the Mongols and Turks in the countries beyond the Indus, India offered an asylum to fugitives from the west, who formed a welcome addition to the military resources of the Muhammadan Rulers of Delhi. The fugitive chieftains and their followers acquired wealth and influence in India, and in course of time disputed the throne of Delhi, or established themselves as independent kings on the frontiers of Islam in India. But the vigour and resolution of the races to which they belonged deteriorated in the malarious and enervating climate of their new possessions, and the services of warlike immigrants from the west were gladly accepted and formed a valuable accession to the forces of the Muhammadan Princes, confronted as they were with coalitions of powerful Hindu adversaries. The hardy Afghans were assured of lucrative employment as mercenaries; and the Ghilzais as the nearest to India appear to have availed themselves very readily of such a state of affairs. Among these, the Lodis appear to have been pre-eminent. This tribe (which has practically disappeared from Afghanistan) belonged to the eastern section of the Ghilzais. In 978, Shekh Hamid Lodi had been appointed governor of the Lamghan district (on the Kabul river) and of Multan by the founder of the Ghaznavide dynasty, and his descendants, or members of his sept, played an important part in the history of India for about 700 years. The grandson of Hamid Lodi governed Multan (for the famous

Sultan Mahmud) till he embraced the heretical tenets of the Karmathians, numerous in Multan. Another member of this family, Malik Mahmud, accompanied the ill-fated Ghori Sultan Muiz-ud-din on his expeditions to India.

When the grandfather of Bahlol Lodi of the Shahu Khel sept quarrelled with his elder brother, it was to India that he directed his footsteps, and he appears to have prospered. The uncle of Bahlol Lodi attained to power and wealth, and is said to have given employment to 12,000 Afghan soldiers of fortune. The father of Bahlol was killed in a quarrel with the Niazīs, another Ghilzai tribe, and his son was brought up by the uncle Islam Khan, and eventually succeeded to the estates and wealth of the latter. About 1486-7 Bahlol Lodi seized the throne of Delhi, and when he died he left a fair heritage to his son (1492). The successors of Bahlol departed from the democratic mode of life and conduct of their ancestors, and a rigorous ettiquette offended their Afghan nobles. Notwithstanding his unpopularity, when he was threatened with invasion by the famous Timuride Prince, Baber, the Afghans rallied to the standards of Sultan Ibrahim, grandson of Bahlol, who took the field at the head of a vast but unwieldy force, and in the decisive action at Panipat, the Lodi Sultan fell with some 5,000 of his countrymen (26th April 1526). Among others whom the late Sultan had estranged was his kinsman, Daulat Khan Lodi, who possessed great influence in the Punjab, and who incited and aided Baber in his attempt on India.

The Afghans were, however, a power in the country, and Humayun, the unwarlike son of Baber, was driven out of India by Farid Khan Sur, who had earned the title of Sher Khan by his bravery, and who assumed the title of Sher Shah after he seized the throne in Delhi. The grandfather of Sher Shah with his son, Hasan, had come to India to seek his fortune, and Sher Shah was the son of Hasan Sur, by an Afghan lady. The Sur tribe, of which he was a member, belonged probably to that tribe of Sur, which, at an earlier period, had been independent in Ghur, but which had either become a part of the Ghilzais subsequently, or were confederated with them.

Sher Shah was killed at the siege of Kalinjar on the 24th May 1548, and the dynasty he founded endured but a few years. In the record of the troubled reigns of his successors, there appear the names of many tribes, which have practically disappeared from Afghanistan; but which at that time were powerful in India, and they prove how great must have been the influx of Afghan tribes into India, while the Lodis and Surs occupied the throne in Delhi.

The last member of this family, Mubariz Khan, was the son of Nizam Khan, own brother of Sher Shah, and he obtained the throne by the murder of his sister's son (a minor) Firuz Khan, the grandson of Sher Shah. The assassin took the style of Muhammad Shah-i-Adil. He was a worthless and dissipated person. Everywhere the Afghan nobles withdrew their allegiance from him. He raised low-caste associates to positions of trust and high rank. Chief among these was one Hemu the Dhusar, a Hindu of the trading caste, who became Vazier to the Afghan Ruler. The authority of the latter was disputed by members of his tribe, one of whom, Ahmad Khan Sur, was governor of the Punjab, and he was raised to the throne in Delhi by a number of influential Afghan Chiefs. The invasion of India by Humayun was aided by the disunion that prevailed among the Afghans. Ahmad Sur advanced to Naushahr, beyond Sirhind, and took up a position to await the invaders. For some days the armies lay inactive in sight of each other, till at last the Afghans, numbering some 80,000 men, moved out of their lines in order of battle on the 2nd May 1555. The result was fatal to their cause, and the defeated Ruler of Delhi fled into the Siwalik hills and made his way into Bengal. There remained the unprincipled Adil, who lurked behind the defences of Chunār, which he feared to leave on account of the hatred borne him by the revengeful Afghan Chieftains. To Hemu, the Hindu, was intrusted the task of maintaining his master's cause.

In the meantime Humayun had died from the effects of an accident. The young Prince Akbar and his tutor Bairam Khan—the Turkoman—had been called to the Punjab to disperse the Afghan followers of the defeated Sultan Sikandar (Ahmad Khan Sur). The Afghans of the tribes of Lodi, Sur, and the Niazis were in arms in the east, and only the country to the north of Delhi was effectively held, when Hemu took the northern road from Chunār at the head of a vast array of armed men, leaving his unworthy master safe in that fortress. Agra and Delhi were evacuated by the Moghuls, and Hemu advanced northwards at the head of an army said to have numbered 100,000 horse with 500 elephants: once more in the vicinity of Panipat the sovereignty of Hindustan depended on the issue of a decisive battle. On the 5th November 1556, Hemu, defeated and made a prisoner, was put to death in cold blood. His followers dispersed, and the sovereignty over Hindustan passed for ever from the hands of the Afghans.

Sher Khan, son of Muhammad Shah-i-Adil, was at the head of 30,000 men in 1561; but he was defeated and his followers scattered.

For a time, Afghan adventurers attempted to establish themselves in Bengal and Orissa, but they were overthrown and compelled to acknowledge the supremacy of the Moghuls. In a very short time the powerful tribes, which had emigrated from Afghanistan, lost their distinctive organisation and were absorbed into the mass of the population. A part of them appear to have returned to their original seats, preferring the unrestricted freedom among their native hills to loss of prestige in India. Those, who were unable or unwilling to follow this course, directed their steps southwards towards the Peninsula of India; and a very large influx of Afghans took place, encouraged by the existence of independent Muhammadan Principalities, which afforded an outlet to their restless natures. A part of the Carnatic was so largely occupied by these emigrants, that in the 17th century it was still known as the Carnatic of the Afghans. In Rajputana, Central India, and in the fertile lands on the left bank of the Ganges, there was a very strong Afghan element in the population. In the last-named tract the earlier colonists were reinforced from time to time by immigrants from the hills to the west and north of Peshawar, and the country in which they settled became known as Rohilkand, the country of the Rohillas. There the Afghans and their descendants became the dominant race, the original Hindu population being reduced to the condition of their serfs.[1]

The first Emperors of Delhi maintained a firm grip on their possessions beyond the Indus ; but while Kandahar was a bone of contention between Indian and Persian Monarchs, being alternately won and lost by each, the right of the former to Kabul and its Province was never seriously challenged for 200 years. With all the advantages they possessed, the Moghul Emperors of Delhi had continual trouble with their unruly subjects. The religious sect of the Roshanis afforded constant occupation for the Imperial troops even in the reign of the famous Akbar. In about 1583, an Imperial General Zain Khan built a fort at Chakdarah and defeated the Yusufzais in twenty-three engagements. Owing to the insubordination of the leaders of the reinforcements he had received, Zain Khan fell back on Peshawar. He was caught in

[1] Rohilla seems to be an Indian term. An "Afghan" must be able to prove or at least to state clearly his lineage. Members of the servile or less regarded tribes, provided they adopted a sufficiently martial air, disguised their less honourable origin under the name Rohilla or Rohela, a hillman, and were accepted at their own valuation. Among the Rohillas, the distinction between the descendants of long domiciled colonists and new arrivals was carefully maintained. The term Dési, country-born, was applied to the former implying and probably correctly a taint of indigenous blood. The term Vilayati was applied to later immigrants of approved Afghan descent on both sides of the family. Both however were called generally, Rohilla Pathan.

the Balandri Pass or defile[1] and overwhelmed by the mountaineers—about 8,000 men and 500 officers, are said to have perished; but Zain Khan, who commanded the van-guard, extricated the remains of his master's troops and retired on Attock. The next year he was back in the Yusufzai country. He built a large fort on the Panjkora river, and the lost supremacy was restored. In 1586-87, the Momands and Ghoris, under Jalaluddin, the Roshani (son of the founder of the sect), committed great depredations in the Peshawar district. Two years later, the Roshanis in Tirah had to be subdued. In 1593-94, the Governor of Kabul was killed by the Roshanis. His successor invaded Tīrah, but was compelled to retire hastily owing to a failure of supplies.

Towards the close of Akbar's reign, a Roshani leader named Ihdād (grandson of the founder of the sect), kept the Province of Kabul in a ferment. In the reign of the next Emperor, Jahangir, the chieftain dared to attack Kabul itself, and on the 5th April 1611, he took advantage of the absence of the Governor to plunder the city. Nād Ali, the Chief of Maidān, hurried reinforcements to the city, and co-operating with the garrison of the Citadel and townsmen, Ihdād was driven off with loss. The Viceroy of Kabul blockaded him for a long time in a fastness in Jarkhai, in the Kohistan of Kabul, and Ihdād fled towards Kandahar (1615). Many years afterwards he was in Tīrah, where he possessed a retreat in the Āwagarh mountain. Here he was attacked, the sangars which he had built to defend the narrow defile were stormed, 26th January 1625, and he was shot dead.[2]

After the loss of Kandahar (1622), Kabul remained in the hands of the Indian Government, and was the only city of the first rank beyond the Indus. A garrison in Ghazni controlled the country up to the limits of the Kandahar Province. Charbagh (or Karabagh) near the pools in which the Tarnak stream takes its rise, was the frontier post in this direction, to the south of which the country was held by the Persians.

In the reign of the Emperor Shah Jahan, the revenue of Kabul was stated at 40 lakhs, but it was probably insufficient for all purposes of the government of that Province as the revenue from four good

---

[1] Probably the Malandari Pass, at the head of the Barkua Stream, about 30 miles N. E. of Hoti Mardan.

[2] This stronghold was undoubtedly in the valley in which the villages of Zawo, Yasta, Kotkika, are situated to the south of the Zawagarh Peak, in the Zaimukht country, about 8 miles north of Chinarak and about 18 miles north of Thal in the Kuram. The Zawagarh Peak rises to over 9,400 feet above sea level, on the water shed between the Khanki valley and that of the Kuram.

In December 1879 (during the second Afghan war), an expedition repeated the performances of the Moghul troops. Marching from Thal, Zawo was burnt after two days' desultory fighting.

districts in the Punjab was bespoken for the expenses of the Kabul Province. The tribes probably were left alone to manage their domestic affairs by means of their tribal jirgahs ; the Viceroy of Kabul exercising a paternal and general supervision so long as the rights of the Emperor of Delhi were not infringed, and the peace of this Province depended very greatly on the character of the Viceroy. Service under the Royal Standard in India, or under the banner of tribal chieftains, who had settled on valuable estates in India, as nobles of the Court of Delhi, provided ample and congenial employment for the wilder spirits of the tribes, and afforded avenues whereby they might attain to wealth and rank. Among those who had exchanged their mountainous and unproductive patrimony for estates in India, the more distinguished were the chiefs of the Lodis, the Parni and Bangash clans, but preeminent among them was the chief of the Lodis.

The fickle and turbulent nature of the Afghans rendered them bad subjects, whether in their own country or in India ; and it was a well understood regulation that no fortresses were to be intrusted to their care. The most serious rebellion of Afghans against the supremacy of the Emperor Shah Jahan took place not in Afghanistan but in India ; and apparently was aimed at the subversion of the Moghul dynasty. The chief of the Lodis at this time was Pir Khan, a descendant of that Daulat Khan, who had urged Baber to essay the conquest of Hindustan, or of a younger branch of the same family. In the reign of the Emperor Jahangir, Pir Khan Lodi had attained to the rank of a commander of 7,000 horse with the title of Khan Jahan Khan. Among other offices he had enjoyed, were the governments of the Provinces of Multan and Malwa. Such was his influence among the Afghan tribes, that while at Multan, the trans-frontier Afghans had offered to put him in possession of the country up to Isfahan, if he would take them into his pay. But, while he was governor of Malwa, he had sold some districts belonging to the Moghul Emperors, to Murteza Nizam Shah, an independent Ruler in Southern India. The closing years of the life and reign of Jahangir had been embittered by the rebellion of his son, afterwards the Emperor Shah Jahan. In the second year, after the latter had ascended the throne, Khan Jahan Khan was summoned to Agra.

The attitude of the new monarch and his courtiers roused the suspicions of the Afghan chieftain. Deeming his honour and life in danger, he broke out of Agra on the night of the 14th October 1629 at the head of 2,000, or 3,000 Afghan retainers and fled southwards, where he hoped to find an asylum with one or other of the independent Rulers, and adherents among their Afghan subjects and troops. He is said to have despatched letters inciting the Afghan tribes round Peshawar and Jalālābād to rise and create a diverson in his favour. Escape in that direction was impossible, and the only prospect of making good his retreat lay towards the south. He succeeded in reaching the district of Baghlana belonging to Murteza Nizam Shah, with the royal troops at his heels. The Deshmuks or zamindars, of Baghlana took up arms in his defence. They beat off the Imperial forces, and neither threats nor bribes could induce them to surrender the fugitives. So important was the matter that the Emperor Shah Jahan took the field in person. Three divisions of Imperial troops under selected Commanders were detailed to suppress the movement. One division broke down the resistance of Murteza Nizam Shah, and penetrating by the western route, Khan Jahan Khan was forced to retreat further south. Muhammad Adil Shah, King of Bijapur, refused to countenance the Lodi Chief, but the Afghans had begun to join him.

The season was unfavourable, no rain had fallen, a dreadful famine was raging, and, in addition, a pestilence had broken out. Asalat Khan, eldest son of Khan Jahan Khan, died at Daulatabad. The resolution of the Lodi Chief broke down, and he began to talk publicly of retiring to Mecca. His adherents became discouraged, and recruits ceased to join. Khan Jahan Khan then formed the desperate resolution of attempting to reach the Ganges, in hopes of being able to find supporters among the Afghan settlers, and of making his way to the north to join the tribes whom he had incited to rebellion. Followed by the Imperial troops, he made his way across the Central Provinces into Bandelkand. Jagraj Bikramajit, son of Jhujhar Singh, the Ruler of that country, defeated the fugitive's rearguard killing one of his sons and Darya Khan; the Lodi Chief's best officers (11th January 1631). An attempt on Kalinjar failed, and here another son of Khan Jahan Khan was killed. He continued his flight to Sehonda[1] where he turned to bay on the bank of a tank. He allowed all his retainers, who desired to abandon him to depart. He also sent off the families and wounded or wearied followers, and with 500 or 600 of his staunchest followers covered their retreat. Here the pursuers closed with their quarry who had given them such a long chase. After a desperate conflict, in which Pir Khan Lodi displayed the utmost bravery, he was run through by the lance of Madhu Singh, a Rajput cavalier, and was cut to pieces with his son Aziz Khan (24th January 1631). Several of

[1] At that time the head of a district, now a mere village in the Banda district of the United Provinces of Agra and Oudh. Sehonda is situated among the ravines on the bank of the Ken River, which joins the Jumna forty miles further to the north. Sehonda lies about 25 miles from Kalinjar to the north.

his sons survived, and made their peace with the Emperor; but no member of this great family ever again rose to distinction.

Whether in response to Khan Jahan Khan's appeal or not, a great rising of the Afghan tribes in the Peshawar district did take place; but the movement failed to benefit the rebel chieftain. The ruling spirit of the movement was one Kamal-ud-din, a Roshani leader, and he was joined by tribal chiefs and other Roshani leaders. The glens of Tirah poured forth their warriors. The levies of the tribes of Dawar, Natu, Naghar, the Bangash, Khataks, Imāk Hajis, and even the Turis from Kuram, attended the rendezvous at Ilm Gudar, on the Bara river (about 3 miles above fort Bara). The tribes of Peshawar, and Ashghar-Khalils, Momands, and Yusufzais, threw in their lot with the other malcontents. Said Khan, the governor of Peshawar, was at Kohat when warning was conveyed to him, and he had barely time to hurry back to Peshawar to concert measures for the defence of the town before the storm burst. The assembled tribesmen surrounded the place on the 12th July 1630, but Said Khan was a brave and competent man. In a sortie in force, the ringleaders of the enemy were killed and the multitudes of armed men lost heart, and broke up. Peshawar was saved.

There seems to have been no especial trouble with the Afghans during the rest of Shah Jahan's reign. On the 22nd March 1638, Ali Mardān Khan, Chief of the Zik Kurds of Kirman, in revenge for the treatment meted out to his family by Shah Sefi of Persia, delivered up Kandahar to the Indian Government, and Southern Afghanistan once more and for the last time, became a part of the territory of the Emperor Shah Jahan. Ali Mardān rose to high positions under this Emperor, and more than once governed the Province of Kabul[1] and the immunity enjoyed by his master from troubles with the Afghans was probably due to the genius of Ali Mardān Khan. An unprovoked attack on Kabul by the Ruler of Balkh led to an expedition to the north of the Hindu-Kush and Balkh was occupied on the 5th July 1641, and there was some talk of pushing on to the conquest of Bokhara and of Samarkand, the capital of Tamerlane from whom the Indian Emperors were descended. The operations to the north of the Hindu-Kush resulted in a collision with the Ruler of Bokhara, and a two years' campaign was the result, in which the Princes Murad Baksh, and (after him), Aurangzebe, commanded the Indian forces. Shah Jahan, like his father, paid many

[1] He built the Bazar in Kabul, destroyed by General Pollock in 1843; and the principal Bazar in Peshawar.

visits to Kabul. Gradually, however, unbridled sensual enjoyments sapped his vigour, and monarch and nobles alike lost their martial ardour. Kandahar was snapped up by the youthful Shah Abbas II, who surprised it in the depth of winter, suffering terrible losses himself, owing to the severity of that season (25th of February 1648).

Three efforts were made to recapture the place, each of these failed ignominiously, and no further attempts were made to restore Indian influence in Southern Afghanistan: the country as far north as Char Bagh remained in the hands of the Persians.

In the reign of Aurangzebe, a feeling of antipathy towards that Emperor began to spread, and at last culminated in a general rising of the Afghan tribes, from Kandahar to Peshawar, which lasted four years. Imal Khan, an Afghan Chief, proclaimed his independence in the hills near Peshawar, and coined money in his own name. The Viceroy of Kabul, Muhammad Amin Khan, was surrounded at Gharib Khana on his way from Peshawar to Kabul (May 6th, 1672); and though he cut his way through the enemy, his women, artillery, elephants, treasure, and baggage, fell into the hands of the Afghans; 6,000 men also were lost on this occasion. The aspect of affairs was so threatening that the Emperor took the field in person. He placed his head-quarters at Hasan Abdāl to direct operations. He was absent from Delhi from the 6th April 1674 to the 5th April 1676. The Afghan rising was quelled, but the Imperial troops on more than one occasion were very roughly handled by their adversaries.

After peace was restored, the affairs of Kabul were increasingly subordinated to the schemes for the subjugation of the Mahrattas, to which the Emperor was compelled to devote his personal attention and the whole of his resources—and in vain. So long as there was no overt rebellion, the Afghans were allowed to do as they pleased. A succession of able governors kept the country quiet, and subsidies rewarded the good behaviour of the tribesmen, and kept open the road to Attock, where the merchants and caravans of Central Asia met those of India.

Careful arrangements were made with the tribesmen, who were heavily bribed to allow Royal Princes to visit the City of Kabul, without accidents on the way. These visits gradually became less frequent and shorter as time wore on, until in 1701-2, the last visit was paid by Shāh Alam, the eldest son of the Emperor. On this occasion the opportunity was seized to despatch an expedition into the Khost Valley, by a route not usually adopted. The tribesmen along the route resented the intrusion; the Imperial Commander was slain, and his command is said to have been annihilated. Prince Ṣhah Alam had to bribe the Afghans heavily before he could leave Kabul for Peshawar, or the road was safe for merchants.[1]

In India, the Parnis possessed a record only less brilliant than that of the Lodis. A portion of this tribe, the Borizī Parnis, are still to be found near Sibi, in the Baluchistan Agency. They attained to notoriety in the 17th century, in the person of their headman, who betrayed Prince Dara Shekoh into the hands of his brother Aurangzebe.

Malik Jiand, son of Malik Ayub, the headman of this tribe, had been a very notorious robber. He was caught at last and sent to Delhi to receive sentence from the Emperor, before whom he was produced in full durbar. Not one person in that splendid assembly had any pity for the wretched Afghan, who was sentenced to be trodden to death by an elephant—save the Heir-Apparent, Prince Dara Shekoh. He begged the life of Jiand, and when the boon was granted, the prisoner was set free and allowed to go home to Dādur.

Years passed and fortune's wheel had made a revolution, and he, who once had been like Darius of old in his splendour, was now a fugitive with a prince on his head. The unfortunate Prince, defeated and deserted, was making his way to Kandahar, where he hoped to find (with the Persians) an asylum and a respite from his pressing troubles. In an evil moment, the Prince relied on the gratitude of Malik Jiand and refused the aid of the chivalrous Sardar of the Magasi Baluchis, who had offered to escort the fugitives to Persian territory. To crown the Prince's misfortunes, his wife fell ill and died, and he sent her remains to be buried at the shrine of the famous saint near Lahore, escorted by 200 veteran men at arms, the staunchest and last of his adherents. Malik Jiand had given the Prince an ostensibly cordial welcome to Dādur, but secretly he was in correspondence with his enemy. The capture of the Prince and his small party, left only with personal attendants, had become an easy task. When the march up the Bolan Pass had been commenced towards Kandahar, they fell into an ambush planned by Malik Jiand, but carried out by his younger brother—the arch traitor did not care to appear in the matter, and had returned to Dādur, on an excuse, promising to join the party further on.[2] This deed was accomplished on the 17th October 1658.

The traitor accompanied the captives to Delhi, and when they were paraded through the city the treachery of Malik Jiand was

---

[1] Storia do Mogor, W. Irvine, Vol. III, p. 492 and note.

[2] This seizure took place near Bibi Nạni in the Bolan Pass.

execrated by the populace, for the Prince Dara was beloved by all men, and a few days later an excited mob fell on Malik Jiand's followers and evilly treated them. But the traitor received from the Emperor the rank of a commander of 1,000 horse, and the title of Bakhtiar Khan (the fortunate chief), which was borne by his descendants. After a short stay he was allowed to go home. But fortune turned away her countenance from the ingrate, and almost on the boundary of his own district, the sons of Mubārak, the Daudpotra, waylaid Bakhtiar Khan in the Lakhi Jangal, to the north of Shikārpur, and slew him in pursuit of a vendetta.[1]

The most famous of the Indian branch of this tribe was the celebrated Daud Khan, who was killed in battle on the 6th September 1715. His power and accessibility were such as to give rise to a popular saying—"if you can do it, well and good, if not, try Daud Khan Pani." He was famous among his contemporaries as a valiant soldier and as a good ruler—not an usual circumstance in those days. The Madras Records of 1709 preserve a picture of an Indo-Afghan grandee of the early 18th Century, in these words:—"Very precarious in his temper when sober, free and generous when supplied with the liquors he asks, which we always take care to supply him with; a great favorite with late and present king as a soldier fit for rough work."[2] And the lavish and barbarous mode of life of an Afghan is exemplified in the following account of this celebrated person:—"He left only a small amount of money, a hundred elephants, seven hundred horses, some Persian grey-hounds, tigers, leopards, and a number of birds. Neither tents nor equipage had he; he lived like a trooper or a mendicant."[3]

As Daud Khan had no issue by an Afghan wife, his brother after his death became faujdar of Kurnool; and the Afghans there raised him up as their chief: the family became established as Nawābs of Kurnool. They apparently became involved in the war between the French and English, but appear to have escaped the fate of the earthen pot—at the cost of most of their estates. In 1838 the Parni Nawāb rebelled and was deported, and was stabbed by a servant soon after in Trichinopoly. A pension was granted to his son which lapsed on his death in 1848.[4]

---

[1] Nicolas Manucci gives a different account of the end of Malik Jiand. Storia do Mogor, W. Irvine, Vol. I., p. 363, and IV., p. 125.

[2] *Ibid.*

[3] *Ibid.*

[4] There was a Colony of Parni Afghans at Biānah to the S. W. of Agra. This tribe were the principal adherents of the Mahdavi sect founded in 1553 by Saiad Muhammad of Jaunpur. Storia do Mogor, Vol. IV., p. 263.

A member of the Bangash tribe migrated in the 16th century from the lower end of the Kuram Valley, their ancient patrimony, and obtained valuable estates on the banks of the Ganges with the title of Nawāb. Their capital was the city of Farrukhābād. The last Nawāb was implicated in the events of 1857 and exiled to Mecca. The late Major Raverty saw him at Nasik, on his way to Bombay; and describes this exile as a womanish effeminate young man. He had probably been a tool in the hands of those around him; or he may have been eager to seize any chance, however desperate, to retrieve the decayed fortunes of his house. He chose the wrong side, and was exiled for his mistake. He died in 1882 at Mecca.

The ruling family of Bhopal in Central India is descended from an Orakzai immigrant of the 17th century, belonging to the Roshani Sect, who at first was given estates near Panipat. In the next generation, fresh estates were given to his descendants in Central India, where they appear to have become fixed. The Nawābs of Maler Kotla claim to represent the Lodis, and they retain their possession and honours; as also do the Khweshgi Afghans of Kasur.

By the casual observer the Afghan element in the population of India no longer can be recognised. Owing to climatic influences, they have lost those striking attributes of physique which at once attract attention to the Afghan newly arrived from the west of the Indus, but the Indo-Afghans preserved the traditions of their ancestry and gloried in them.

NOTE.

NOTE.—Forwards the end of the 17th century there seems to have been some Englishmen in Kabul, who were either in the service of the Emperor of Delhi, or who had visited Kabul for purposes of trade. One of them was buried there; and in 1839, Major Hough saw his tomb which bore the following inscription p. 287 :—

"Here lyeth the body of John Hicks, son of Thomas and Edith Hicks, who departed this life, the eleventh of October 1666."

The tomb was in the Muhammadan burying ground near and to the S. E. of the city. This raises a suspicion that the deceased had embraced Islam. The inscription must have been the handiwork of another Englishman (and not an illiterate person), who must have been also a resident in Kabul at the time when Hicks died there.

For Kandahar and its relations with the Indian Government of the Moghul Emperors of Delhi, see Appendix II.

CHAPTER IV.

Relations with Persia.

UNTIL the successful revolt of the Ghilzais against the Persians had brought the Afghans prominently before the world, they were regarded as barbarians, whose affairs were beneath the notice of writers of chronicles both in Persia and in India. Such works cast no light on the history and affairs of even very important tribes such as the Abdalis and Ghilzais, and these tribes themselves were too barbarous and illiterate as a body to produce any authors, who could have preserved their early history and whose record would have carried weight. The mullas, the only literate persons were given over to vain disputes and to mystical expositions of doctrine, and were ambitious only to leave behind them collections of such works, to be able to devote attention to tribal histories. Among the tribesmen, traditions are handed down orally; and these are grouped round the names of chieftains whose deeds are still the theme of story round the camp fires of the nomadic tribes. As these traditions approach the 18th century, they, however, assume a connected form and are probably correct, in a very general way, as a narrative of events. At all events they provide all the information that exists.

After the rise of the Sadozais to power as the sovereigns of Afghanistan, and in the reigns of the first and second kings of this dynasty, efforts were made to collect these traditions; and to make out of these materials a connected story of the doings of the earlier chieftains of this family, and their transactions with the Persian Governors of Kandahar. The accounts compiled by native Afghan authors of this period (18th-19th century), are therefore, of too recent a date to be regarded as being in any way authoritative. With regard to the early history of the Afghans, these authors repeat the standard genealogy of all the Afghan tribes from Kais, or Abdur Rashid, and assign arbitrary dates to various persons in the tables of descent, in order to fit these into the histories of the Arab Conquest of Khurassan, and of those dynasties which have included Afghanistan within their possessions. The later native chronicles were compiled with a view to exalt the Sadozai sept of the Abdalis,[1] and to invest the chiefs with a kind of divine right to impose their authority on their more (numerically) powerful tribesmen.

Sado (a corruption of Asadullah) was the eponymous ancestor of this branch. He is said by the author of the Tazkirat-ul-Mulk to have been born on the night of the 30th September 1558.

His father Umar had grown up in straitened circumstances, for his father had squandered the resources of the family. Umar's mother, a lady of family belonging to the Ishakzai tribe, had besought the holy men (Pirs) of her own tribe, and of the Alizais, to bless her son Umar. After that the latter had grown up and become a householder ; it is said that one day he was visited by the holy Shekh, Ako, belonging to the Alizai tribe. The Pir and his disciple were cordially welcomed, and the resources of the family were strained to do them honour. Food was placed before the reverend guest, and Umar was assiduous in his attentions. When the meal was concluded, the latter ventured to ask the Shekh for his blessing. The latter consented, but put off doing so till the time of his departure. The next morning he drew his host aside and informed him that he had seen two visions during the night. First he had seen a lion enter Umar's dwelling, and it meant that a son would be born to him, whom he should name Asad-ullah (the Lion of God). He would be greatly favoured by Providence. The other vision was that the skin of a hog was spread in Umar's dwelling, but this was to be regarded not at all as an unfavourable omen.[2] In due course Asadullah was born, and his father's affairs took a favourable turn for the tribe elected him as their Chieftain, to manage their affairs and to deal with the governor of Kandahar.

Asadullah was succeeded by his eldest son Khizr Khan, and the latter by his eldest son, Sultan Khudadād, or Khudkai Sultan as his tribesmen call him.

At this time the chieftainship of the Ghilzai tribes had become fixed in the Tokhi Division ; and Malakhe, son of Muhammad, was

---

[1] Kais, or Abdur Rashid, had a son Ibrahim. The latter had a son named Sharkhbun. The last, a son named Tarin, who had four sons. Spin (white), Tor (black), Zhar, and Bor Tarin. The name Abdal, however, gradually superseded that of Bor Tarin, and eventually became predominant when Ahmad Shah became King. The Tarins are to be found, principally in the Pishin district, near Quetta. The Spin (or white Tarins), the superior branch numbered only about 200 souls. The Tor, or black Tarins about 6,172 ; while some 20,345 souls returned themselves as Abdals in the census of 1901. Baluchistan District Gazetteer Series. Vol. V, Quetta- Pishin, 1907, p. 67 et seq.

[2] The First Afghan War, 1839-43, is believed to have been the fulfilment of this vision.

head of the famous tribes. He and Khudkai Sultan were friends and they met at Pul-i-Sangi to the south of Kalat-i-Ghilzai and fixed the boundary between certain disputed tribal lands, on the Garmāb stream. The country to the north and east of that stream was to be regarded as belonging to the Ghilzais, and all that lay to the south and west, fell to the share of the Abdalis. In 1839-40, during the Afghan War, Major Leech, C. B., Political Agent in the Ghilzai country, was shown a document, purporting to be a commission issued by an Emperor of Delhi, to Sultan Malakhe, making him responsible for the safety of the road from Kalat-i-Ghilzai to Karatu in the valley of the Arghandāb. The date of this firman corresponds to the 17th June 1613.[1]

The Ghilzai traditions represented the action of this famous chieftain to have been so effective, that in four days the Hazara marauders were driven out of this valley. The author of the Tarikh-i-Sultani states that Malakhe was alive in 1624 (this work was written in the last quarter of the last century, in Afghanistan). Both of these chiefs would appear to have been contemporaries of the Indian Emperor Jahangir. The method they adopted in settling their disputes regarding the two districts of Umakai and Gwaharai was far in advance of those usually pursued at the time. Sultan Malakhe obtained the former and Khudkai Sultan the latter as the result of the delimitation they carried out.

Khudkai Sultan resigned the chieftainship over the Abdalis to his younger brother Sher Khan. The Persians had taken possession of Kandahar in 1622 and the chief maintained friendly relations with the Governor of the Province. During Sher Khan's period of life the friendly relations between the Abdalis and the Governor were interrupted, Sher Khan is said to have accompanied an expedition composed of Persian troops, at the head of his tribal levies, into Pishin. On the return march the Persians were attacked in the Khojak Pass, lost heavily; and the governor asked Sher Khan to arrest the leaders concerned in this attack and send them to Kandahar. Sher Khan evaded the demands and cast the blame for the occurrence on the Baluchis, Kakars and other migratory tribes of Pishin. The Persian governor enraged at his attitude retaliated on the Abdalis within reach of Kandahar, and Sher Khan collected his tribesmen, took possession of Shahr-i-Safa, and cut off communications with Kandahar on the north and east.

---

[1] By some mistake however Leech has stated that the Emperor Ālamgir (Aurangzebe) issued this firman. Jehangir was ruling in 1613.

The Persian Government determined to find a rival whom they might play off against the chief. A cousin of Sher Khan's, Shah Husen, was found and was given the title of Mirza by the government. On the other hand the officials of the Emperors of Delhi (at Kabul and Ghazni) obtained for Sher Khan the title of Shahzada (Prince) and the Subehdar of Kabul and the governor of Ghazni were enjoined to aid him, whenever he invoked their aid.[1]

The Afghans also were better disposed towards Sher Khan than towards his rival.

The latter provoked by an insolent remark made by his Agent Jallil, the Alizai, stabbed the latter in the presence of the Persian governor in Kandahar. For this disrespectful act he was put into confinement, and a report was sent to Isfahan. Orders were received, however, ordering Shah Husen Mirza to be set free and fresh presents were sent to him. It was too late. During his detention the Abdalis had gone over to Sher Khan. No sooner had Shah Husen been released than he too visited Sher Khan, renounced his rivalry, and set out for India, where the descendants of Kāmrān and Bahādur Khan, sons of Sado, had already found a home, the former in Multan and the latter in Dera Ismail Khan and Tonk.

Sher Khan died from the effects of a fall from his horse. Sarmast Khan, his son, was a minor and Bakhtiar, son of Saleh Khan, was appointed his guardian. When Sarmast Khan died, his son Daulat Khan, being a minor, Hayāt Sultan, a cousin of the late chief succeeded to the chieftainship. He remained in good terms with the Persian governor (appointed in 1692). One day, however, while under the influence of wine in the company of the governor, he was induced to consent to matrimonial alliances between his tribe and the Persians. Reminded of his promise after he had recovered his wits, and aware of the temper of his tribesmen, he saw his mistake and fled to Shahr-i-Safa, where he called together the elders of the tribe and made known to them what he had done. At his heels came the emissaries of the governor demanding the instant fulfilment of the compact. Hayāt Sultan had resigned his authority to his young kinsman Daulat Khan, and the latter, with the consent of the elders of his tribes, cut the debate short by massacring the Persian agents. Persian troops despatched from Kandahar to avenge their death were met in the open field by the Abdalis, who defeated them at Band-i-Mukak, the Persian

[1] Leech.—These transactions with the Indian Government cannot be traced. The traditions may refer to a condition of things following on the final recapture of Kandahar by Shah Abbas II, February 25th, 1648, and the unsuccessful attempts to retake it made by the Indian Government.

Commander being slain. A second expedition fared no better, and after this the Persians abandoned the attempt to coerce the Abdalis by force and endeavoured to compass Daulat Khan's downfall by treachery. Hayāt Sultan, the cause of this trouble, migrated to India and settled in Multan.

Matters were in this state when Mir Weis, the Ghilzai appeared on the scene. The Persian Governor had been removed and Gurgin Khan, Wali of Georgia, had been appointed as governor of Kandahar.[1]

The new governor won over Mir Weis and two Sadozais named Izat and Atal, and by means of these persons he managed to secure both Daulat Khan, and his son Nazar Muhammad. They were put to death without delay in Kandahar. After some time spent in reprisals, the Persian Governor agreed to recognise as chief, Rustam Khan, another son of Daulat Khan, if the latter would consent to surrender his brother, Zamān Khan, to the Persians as a hostage. These terms were agreed to, and Zamān Khan was sent to Kirman. Rustam Khan remained on very good terms with Gurgin Khan, until a body of Persian troops sent against the Baluchis (which was accompanied by Rustam Khan) met with a serious reverse. Atal, the Sadozai, and Izat, with Mir Weis, took advantage of this occurrence to poison the mind of Gurgin Khan against Rustam Khan. The Abdali Chief was inveigled into Kandahar where he was put to death by Atal in revenge, it is said, for the murder of his own uncle, Jafir Sultan. The late chief had held the chieftainship for four years, and he left no issue. His grave and that of Daulat Khan are in the Rezabagh, at Kohak near Kandahar. Deprived of a leader, and exposed to the vengeance of the Georgian chief, the Abdalis took refuge in Shorawak.

It will be useful at this point to devote some attention to Mir Weis, the Ghilzai, who was the founder of the independence of Afghanistan. Sultan Malakhe, the Tokhi chieftan (to whom allusion has been made), was a wealthy man. He had wide possessions, and was the owner, probably, of innumerable flocks. One of his many shepherds was a youth, Husen, belonging to the Hotaki section of the Ghilzais. Nazo, Sultan Malakhe's daughter, and her father's herdsman, Husen, fell in love with each other, and the pair eloped. The Hotakis, fearing the resentment of the powerful chief, refused the lovers a shelter in their territory, and the pair had to take to the hills where for a season they lived on game, and dwelt in the shelter of rocks and in caves. At last Nazo, persuaded Husen to accompany her to her

[1] He was appointed to Kandahar in 1702. Storia do Mogor, Vol. IV. See note at end of this Chapter

father's presence, and to put into practice the Afghan custom of Nanawat (suing for pardon). Sultan Malakhe, notwithstanding his reputation as a warrior, appears to have been of an amiable and forgiving nature, and he not only forgave his daughter and Husen, but he bestowed on her, as a dower, the right to ten days' uninterrupted flow of water from the Ajur-ghak Karez and a piece of land below the Tabaksir hill opposite Kalat-i-Ghilzai. To the groom, who led the pony on which Nazo rode, the generous chief gave the right to two days' flow of water from the same source. This was a happy ending to the romance. It illustrates the freedom enjoyed by women among the Ghilzais, and affords a glimpse of the patriarchal system that prevails among them, and among the Afghans in general, away from the towns. In course of time, Nazo gave birth to a son, who is said to have been the grandfather of Mir Weis. This story also disproves the claim advanced by Mir Weis' son (after he had conquered Persia), of descent from Saiad ancestors. Mir Weis belonged to the Hotaki division of the Ghilzais.

Sultan Malakhe's claim to the Chieftainship over both the divisions of these tribes was challenged during his life-time, and he fell in battle with the Hotakis, at Darwazgai between Inzargai and Surkhsang, and was buried at Ab-i-Tāzi about thirty-six miles to the north-west of Kalat-i-Ghilzai on the road to Ghazni.

The grandfather and father of Mir Weis appears to have suffered many vicissitudes of fortune, and Daulat Khan, the Abdali Chief, appears to have contributed largely to their troubles. He made prisoners of Husen, son of Malik Yār, the Hotaki, with all his family, and carried them away to Shahr-i-Safa, as hostages. Husen's son was Mir Weis, and this explains the attitude of the latter towards the descendants of the Abdali chieftain. Upon the death of Jafir Sultan, Sadozai, of the Kāmrān Khel subdivision (for whose death Rustam Khan appears to have been in some degree responsible), his widow chose Mir Weis to be the husband of her orphaned daughter, Khanzād, and to manage the property and affairs of the family of her murdered husband. This brought the astute Ghilzai into relationship with the Sadozais, and at the same time provided another cause for his enmity with the latter. Land, money or a woman are the most fruitful causes of quarrels, in which vendettas originate, that last for generations and not infrequently extinguish whole families. The kinsmen of an Afghan are too often his most inveterate enemies, and this has passed into a proverb among that people. Khanzād was the mother of Mahmud, the conqueror of Persia.

Mir Weis attached himself to the Georgian Prince, governor of Kandahar, and made himself very useful to the latter. The astute Georgian was well pleased, there can be no doubt, to have at his disposal such an efficient auxiliary, and the relations that existed between them became widely known. According to an Indian Chronicle, Gurgin Khan used Mir Weis as his agent in all revenue matters, and never undertook any project without first consulting the Ghilzai; and the custody of one of the gates of Kandahar is said to have been made over to the latter.

The desire of Mir Weis' heart is said to have been to obtain formal recognition of himself as the chief of all the Ghilzais, and of his brother-in-law, son of Jafir Sultan, as the head of the Abdalis. The death of Rustam Khan without issue had left this office vacant. The two Sadozais Izat and Atal, who had compassed Rustam Khan's death and carried out the sentence, appear not to have benefited. The Georgian Prince was unable to obtain for Mir Weis the rewards desired by the latter from the government in Isfahan, and is said to have advised Mir Weis to visit the Court of Shah Husen to push his cause in person.

In the meantime, the Persians in Kandahar were becoming very unpopular. Gurgin Khan himself was licentious in his habits and his devotion to wine and sensual pleasures was a bad example to his Georgian followers. According to some authorities, he is said to have been a Christian, and there were probably very many Christians in his retinue. Gurgin Khan may have professed Muhammadanism to secure political advancement, and the same laxity of principle doubtless prevailed among his followers, who were probably as bad Christians as he was a bad Muhammadan. In addition, therefore, to their being actually foreigners, they were infidels also in the sight of their Afghan subjects, whose feelings they outraged.

Mir Weis' visit to Court did not secure the rewards he desired; but he was able to understand the condition into which Persia and the Shah's Government had sunk; and he must have been able to see clearly how weak was the hold which the Persians maintained on Seistan, Kandahar and Herat. From Isfahan he performed the Pilgrimage to Mecca and Medina. There he is said to have obtained a formal decree from the theologians and lawyers in favour of throwing off the yoke of the Persians, and as a last resource even of handing over the country to the Indian Government. Such an authority in his hands was enough to silence all opposition on the part of timid or restive supporters. Armed with this document, and with the prestige derived from fulfilling the Pilgrimage, Mir Weis returned to Kandahar. After a time he withdrew to Kalat-i-Ghilzai, where he commenced to collect adherents from the neighbouring Ghilzai tribes and waited for an opportunity to carry the designs of independence (with which he is credited) into effect.

NOTE.

The family of the Bagratians, of which Gurgin Khan was a member (p. 36), traced their descent from Shumbat, a Jew belonging to the Royal House of David, who had been taken away captive by Haikan, king of Armenia, who had joined Nebuchadnezzar, in his campaign against Jerusalem. This family occupied the throne of Georgia from the 6th century A. D. to 1800. Under both the Turkish and Persian governments, to which the Bagratians had been in turn subservient, the Princes of this House had been permitted to profess Christianity. At last dissensions arose between two brothers, each of whom claimed the throne. The younger forestalled the other at the court of the Shah, and was promised the throne of Georgia, conditionally on embracing Islam. Thenceforward, a Prince of this House, who professed Islam, was Viceroy or Wali of the Shah. The Heir Apparent was retained as a hostage in Ispahan, but was given the honorable office of governor of the capital. Tiflis was the capital of the Bagratians. Their title was Czar.

In the confusion following on the death of Nādir Shah, Czar Heraclius of Georgia, renounced his allegiance to Persia, and in 1783 a treaty was signed by which he declared himself to be the vassal of the Empress Catherine of Russia. On the 28th of September 1800 the last Czar, George the XIII. of Georgia, in his own name and in the names of his successors, renounced his crown in favor of the Czar of Russia.

(History of Armenia by Father Chamich. History of Persia by R. G. Watson.)

CHAPTER V.

Revolt of the Afghans against the Persians.

THE period had arrived (the commencement of the 18th century) when very important events in the histories of Persia and of India were about to take place, which caused the downfall of the famous line of Sovereigns of the Safavis in one country, and the decline of the Moghul in the other. Both families had become rotten to the core, and both possessed merely the outward semblance of strength, and only the reflection of their ancestors' glory, gilded the corruption which had eaten up the manhood of Sovereign and nobles alike. The Indian Government held the Province of Kabul on sufferance and diplomacy found an ample field for exercise in the disunion which prevailed among the tribes who still acknowledged the Moghul Emperor as their Suzerain. A common belief in the dogmas of the Suni school of Islam formed a bond of union between the Indian officials in Kabul and their master's nominal subjects. A knowledge of their weakness prevented the former from rousing active hostility by embarking on a vigorous policy which the enfeebled resources of the government would have been unequal to carrry out successfully. India offered solid advantages in the matter of rank and wealth, and self-interest prompted the Afghans to maintain a connection which was profitable to them.

The Persian officials in Kandahar, on the contrary, were aliens in religion and blood, and oppression on their part at once assumed a religious aspect, in addition to its political significance and provoked a correspondingly bitter feeling. The Persian hold on Southern Afghanistan was of the nature of a military occupation, and trials of strength between the Persians and Afghans were rendered inevitable. The weakness of the central government in Isfahan was unequal to the task of holding down this distant Province, and of restoring its supremacy, when the revolt of the Afghans was crowned with success.

In the long and peaceful reign of Shah Husen Safavi, the military organisation of the Persian government, in which the influence of the intrepid brothers, Sir Anthony and Sir Robert Shirley, can be traced, had completely disappeared. There was no army in existence when one was needed to save the monarch and his State from the insults of foreign enemies. The condition of Persia was no secret, but the collapse of the Safavi dynasty was ignoble. Although powerful antagonists were afoot on the western frontiers threatening to rend the kingdom of Shah Husen from his nerveless grasp, his ruin was due to the audacity of a handful of brigands. The Ghilzais forestalled both the Russians and the Ottoman Turks.

Gurgin Khan had been rewarded by the Shah, and the title of Shahnawaz Khan had been conferred on him. Secure in the approbation of his master, both he and his soldiers gave free rein to their licentious appetites, and offending the Afghans in matters affecting the honour of their families drove them to despair. Mir Weis in his retreat at Kalat-i-Ghilzai had been secretly collecting armed men to put his ambitious projects into effect, and the national feelings having been aroused by the conduct of the foreigners in Kandahar, he was able to count on the support of his countrymen. The governor had proceeded to Deh Shekh in the Arghassan Valley in order to despatch an expedition towards Maruf, across the Band-i-Gil Pass. His best troops had been detailed for this purpose, and Mir Weis and the infuriated Afghans found an opportunity at last for effecting the object they had at heart. Gurgin Khan was treacherously captured and put to death, his companions shared his fate, and Mir Weis set off to Kandahar at full speed. Outstripping the report of the tragedy at Deh Shekh, he entered Kandahar at night, with a strong body of his followers, disguised in the dress of the murdered Persians, and seized both the citadel and town before the garrison were aware of what had happened. This occurred some time in 1708-9.[1]

Kai Khasrau Khan, brother of the murdered Gurgin Khan, was despatched from Isfahan to retake Kandahar. The Duranis, who were at enmity with Mir Weis, joined the Persians and the exiled Zamān

[1] This is the date assigned to the occurrence by the author of the Jahān-Kushā-i-Nādiri, who wrote not long after it had taken place. The Indian Chronicler Khafi Khan states that it was one of the latest occurrences in the last year of the reign of the Moghul Emperor Aurangzeb, who died on the 3rd March 1707. He asserts it on the authority of the official diarists, or news-writers, of Multan and Kabul. The author of the Majma-ut-Tawarikh, writing at Murshidabad in Bengal, in 1792-3, gives the date 1710-11. He was a member of the Safavi family, a refugee from Persia. (Irvine). The Tarikh-i-Muhammadi an Indian Chronicle assigns the date 1707-08 (Irvine). LaMamye Clairac "Histoire de Perse," I. 72, assumes that it took place in 1709. This work, written in 1730, was not published until 1750—*Ibid.*

Khan, son of the late Daulat Khan, was in their camp. The invading army forced the passage of the Helmand in spite of Mir Weis' resistance and invested Kandahar, but the leader was shot dead in a skirmish or assault on the place and his troops retired to Persia (1712-13). A second expedition despatched against Kandahar, never reached it ; the leader died on the way and his forces dissolved. No other attempt was made to restore the supremacy of Persia in Southern Afghanistan.

Mir Weis took possession of Seistan ; and in 1714-15 he also invested Herat. In order to strengthen his position he despatched an Embassy to the Court of the Emperor Farukhsiyar, under his brother Hāji Anka. This Embassy was formally received on the 26th February 1715, and the Indian Government bestowed on Mir Weis the title of Ḥāji Amir Khan and 5 lakhs of rupees,[1] dresses of honour, weapons and an elephant.

The old feud between the Tokhi and Hotaki divisions of the Ghilzais broke out during his life-time. Mir Weis had called on the former to pay revenue. Shah Alam, Chief of the Tokhis, and his son disputed this claim, and the quarrel which arose was never healed, and it contributed to the downfall of Mir Weis' son, Shah Husen.

Mir Weis fell ill in 1715-16 and died in the year following.[2] He was buried at Kokaran and the Ghilzais regard his tomb as a shrine. His son Mahmud Khan was a minor, and the headmen of the clan elected Mir Weis' brother Abdul Aziz to act as the guardian of the young chief till he attained years of discretion. Abdul Aziz held this office for about a year, when he was murdered by Mahmud, who established himself in his father's place, adopting the style and state of a king, contrary to the example of his father (1718).

After the Abdalis had been expelled from Kandahar by Gurgin Khan, the tribesmen for a time had dwelt in Shorāwak. From that place they had removed westwards and the majority of the tribe concentrated in the district of Bakwa where they found pasture for their flocks in abundance. At this time the Abdalis are said to have numbered no less than 60,000 families. A part of these, however, remained in Shorāwak.

When the Persians under Kai Khasrau Khan marched against Mir Weis, the Abdalis had called in Abdullah Khan (son of that Hayāt

---

[1] Kamwar Khan, and Majma-ut-Tawarikh (Irvine.)

[2] The Tarikh-i-Jahan Kushā-i-Nādiri states that Mir Weis reigned for 8 years. The Majma-ut-Tawarikh states 6 years. LaMamye Clairac, I. 97, places the death of Mir Weis in 1715 (Irvine).

Sultan, Sadozai, who, in the time of Daulat Khan, had migrated to Multan). He with his son Asadullah came from Multan and joined Kai Khasrau Khan, and received the office of chieftain of the Abdalis. After the failure of the Persians to regain Kandahar, the Abdalis frequented the country round Herat ; and Abdullah Khan and his son went to Herat itself. They attracted the unfavourable notice of Abbas Kuli Khan, Shāmlu, the Persian governor of the city and district. The Persian element in the population of the city, at that time broke out in rebellion against the governor whom they put on one side. Jafar Khan Istājlu had been sent by the Shah to put down this sedition and to chastise the promoters. Abdullah Khan recognised the opportunity and aided by his son he went to the Koh-i-Dushak and collected his tribesmen who were in the neighbouring pastures. He seized the fort of Isfizar before Jāfar Khan arrived, and while yet Abbas Kuli was powerless to prevent the design. The Abdali levies streamed in from Bakwa and Farah, and made up their minds to essay the capture of Herat itself. Jāfar Khan, who attempted to disperse the clansmen, was made prisoner and Herat was surrounded. The Persian Government could not send the townsmen any assistance, and a party favourable to the Afghans admitted the latter into the Fīlkhana Bastion on the night of the 25th July 1717. They took possession of Herat, Ghurian, Kuhsān, Bālā-Murghāb, and Badghis ; and Obah, a strong place to the east of Herat, also fell into their hands.

Asadullah Khan thereupon took possession of Farah,[1] but returned to Herat to meet the expedition under Fateh Ali Khan, the Turkoman whom the Shah at last had despatched against the Abdalis, to attempt the recovery of that City. The Persians and Afghans met at Koh-Suieh, and the latter being undisciplined levies were defeated and put to flight. In the moment of victory, the Persian Commander ventured too far in pursuit and outstripped his men ; the Afghans turned on him and slew him and the few men of his troops who had kept up with him. The Persians took to flight and the Afghans having plundered their camp returned victorious to Herat.

Some time in the year 1718, the Abdalis became embroiled with the Ghilzais of Kandahar and Mahmud advanced to capture Farah. Asadullah marched to prevent this attempt, and in an action fought at Dilārām, on the right bank of the Khāsh Rud, the Heratis were defeated and Asadullah was killed. Mahmud, however, gave up his design against Farah and retired to Kandahar, and the Abdalis

[1] From the Ghilzais ; who appear to have taken Farah during the life-time of Mir Wois

retreated to Herat. The death of his son completely prostrated the aged man Abdullah Khan, and he became incapable of carrying on the government. He was set aside and Abdul Ghani, the Alakozai chieftain, induced the elders of the clan to raise Zamān Khan, the brother of Rustam Khan, to the chieftainship.

The first act of the new chieftain was to put to death Jafar Khan and other Persian leaders who were in prison, and these persons were publicly executed in the Avenue (Khiabān) of the Bagh-i-Nau. The aged Abdullah Khan, who was also an object of suspicion, was placed in confinement. This revolution decided Shah Husen, of Persia, to make another attempt to retake Herat. Zamān Khan took the field against Sufi-Kuli Khan, Turkestan Oghlu, and on the plains of Kāfir Kala, the Persians were defeated in a pitched battle (1720), and they were compelled to leave their camp to the Afghans. Zamān Khan returned to the city loaded with booty. He died shortly after from natural causes, having ruled his clan for two years and five months. The elders of the latter with one accord now summoned from his retreat in Shorāwak, another son of the late Abdullah Khan (who had died in prison), named Muhammad Khan, and made him ruler over themselves.

CHAPTER VI.

THE GHILZAI CONQUEST OF PERSIA—NĀDIR SHAH.

IN the year 1718, after he had overthrown and slain the Chief of the Abdalis, in battle at Dilārām, and had returned to Kandahar, Shah Mahmud, the Ghilzai, forwarded to the Persian Court a report of what he had done, making out that he had been actuated solely by a sense of duty, and that, if the Shah would attack the Abdalis, he (Mahmud) at the head of the Ghilzais would operate against those rebels from Kandahar. The simpletons, who acted as the Ministers of the Shah, were completely deceived by these professions, and bestowed on Mahmud the title of Husen Kuli Khan, with valuable presents, and a formal commission was issued by which he was confirmed in the government of Kandahar. The agents by whom the Ghilzai chief had sent his report to the Court of the Shah had also in all probability brought back a true account of the state of the country, and the imbecility of the Government.

The same year, on the pretext of acting against the Abdalis, Mahmud entered Seistan. There he found a certain Baluch chief, named Shāhdād, organising a raid, in strength, on Kirman; and the inhabitants of that place, having obtained news of the advent of the Ghilzai chief, implored him to act as their protector against the contemplated attack of the Baluch chief. Mahmud appointed Bejan Khan, a Legzi of Farah, to act as deputy in Kandahar, and advanced to Kirman. On arrival he found that the people, in the meantime, had repented of their action in calling him in, and they shut the gates of the town in his face. He immediately blockaded Kirman city, but at the end of nine months he learned that the Persian-speaking section of the inhabitants of Kandahar had revolted, and he abandoned his plans with regard to Kirman and set out for his capital.

After Bejan Khan had taken up his duties, he came to the conclusion that it was a favourable opportunity for him to seize the city and Province of Kandahar while Mahmud was far away. Malik Jafar Khan, a member of the ancient family which had ruled over Seistan for centuries, was in detention in Kandahar, and he is said to have incited Bejan Khan to revolt. The Afghan element was gradually weakened, till with the help of the Persian-speaking section of the population, he was able to expel the Afghans from the city and in this tumult numbers of them were put to death. It was a short-lived success, for as soon as he arrived, Mahmud was able to put down the movement with very little trouble, and he passed the winter in Kandahar.

The next year at the head of a composite and wretchedly armed force of Baluch and Afghan adventurers, numbering 8,000 men, he set out to capture Kirman. He again could only blockade the city and ravage the surrounding country. The Shah's Government sent no aid to the distressed townsmen, and they bought off Mahmud with presents, but refused to give up the city of Kirman, till the result of his operations against Isfahan was known. The Ghilzai having the utmost faith in his good fortune, and the ascendancy of his star, agreed to these terms. He accepted the bribe offered by the townsmen and directed his march towards Isfahan.

At the Capital, the news of the advance of the Ghilzais produced the greatest confusion and alarm. Rustics and people of the bazars, unaccustomed to arms, were hurriedly pressed into service. Armed with weapons and accoutred with armour from the Royal Arsenals, this rabble was marched to Gulunabad, some twelve miles from Isfahan, to oppose the invaders. On the 28th of January 1722, Mahmud boldly attacked the Persians ; defeated them with the loss of all their artillery and stores, and drove them into the city. He then occupied the strong suburb of Farahabad. Surprised at his success, the Ghilzai chief at first kept his men together, as he was afraid that troops from the outlying provinces would be assembled, and hurried to the rescue of the capital, the person of the Monarch and the Royal Family. But no help came.

There are several authorities for the blockade of Isfahan by the Afghans, and all agree that at first Mahmud contented himself with sending patrols of horsemen round the outskirts of the capital. Nothing can demonstrate more clearly the utter demoralization of the Persians than the fact that no serious attempt was made to relieve the capital. At first Mahmud could not have had more than 10,000 men under his orders, but once the news of his success spread abroad, he must have been joined by troops of needy Afghan adventurers, eager to share his good fortune, and hungering for plunder. The Wali of Luristan, indeed, made a half-hearted attempt to throw supplies and reinforcements into Isfahan. His troops were dispersed, and the convoy was captured by the Afghans. In the Palace, a weak sovereign and wrangling ministers were unable to devise any remedies, or to arrive at a plan of concerted action. The city was full of refugees, and with an enormous population unprepared for an investment, food very soon began to diminish. The Afghans drew together for their own use the supplies in the open country. They collected a great store, and burnt all they did not require. They were able to establish garrisons at points round the city and to patrol more effectually the intervening ground. On the 9th of May Prince Tahmāsp made his escape and went off towards Kāshān in hopes that in the country round Kazvin and in Azarbaijān he would be able to raise an army for the relief of Isfahan. Up to this it would have been possible for the Shah to have escaped, but after the flight of the Prince, Mahmud tightened his hold on the city. The sufferings of the populace increased daily, and at last it was decided to surrender.

On the 12th of October 1722[1] the city was rendered up, after a blockade of a little over eight months. The same night Mahmud sent his officers to take possession of the Treasury, the Arsenal and the Palace, and Shah Husen, the Safavi Monarch, was placed in confinement in the Palace. Two days later Mahmud entered the city, and his name was inserted in the Public Prayers in the Musjids, and money was coined bearing his name and superscription. Mahmud owed his success in a great measure to the presence of a Turkish Army on the Western Frontier of Persia, which threatened an invasion, and also to the movements of the Russians who had seized Ghilān on the Persian shore of the Caspian Sea. The general effete condition of the Shah's Government must have been notorious, but Mahmud could hardly be expected to have known the true state of affairs on the Western Frontier of Persia, so that it was merely a piece of good luck that he timed his invasion at a moment when other events contributed towards his success.

But other causes had also helped. There had not been wanting portents that were regarded by the superstitious as foreshadowing the destruction of Isfahan. In the summer of 1721, an unusual denseness of the atmosphere, and a red or bloody appearance of the sun,

---

[1] From the Tarikh-i-Jahan Kushā-i-Nādiri. The Agent of the East India Company under date the 21st October 1722 fixes the date on the 12th October—Malcolm's History of Persia: I., 436, note—Ali Hazin dates it two days later, which agrees with the date in the text of the formal entry of Mahmud.

which had lasted nearly for two months, had been regarded as symbols of Divine wrath. The astrologers had agreed that these signs were of evil import, and these wiseacres had predicted the destruction of the capital by fire or by an earthquake. Shah Husen and the Royal family, attended by all the ministers, had left the city and had encamped in tents beyond the walls. Every means that superstition or fanaticism could suggest were adopted to avert the threatened disaster. Priests went about among the people exhorting them to repent of their sins. The minds of all were depressed, and when the news arrived of the advance of Mahmud, it seemed as if the destruction that had been foretold was at hand.

Mahmud had reached the height of his prosperity. He made over to his younger brother Husen the government of Kandahar, while he himself ruled Persia from Isfahan. He gave audience to an embassy from Peter the Great of Russia, which had been despatched to Shah Husen, but which arrived at the capital after it had been invested by Mahmud. This embassy had been despatched to demand of the Shah that he should redress the wrongs supposed to have been inflicted on Russian subjects by the Lezghis and the Khan of Khiva. Mahmud was no better able to do this than Shah Husen had been.[1]

After a serious outbreak in Kazvin in which the Afghan Governor and garrison were expelled by the citizens with great loss, Mahmud gave vent to his blood-thirsty nature. He ordered a general massacre in Isfahan, which is said to have lasted for fifteen days. The capital was depopulated. The fall of Shirāz, which had held out for eight months, was also signalized by a slaughter of its inhabitants.

Towards the end of two years, Mahmud's mind seems to have become unhinged. On learning of the escape of one of the Royal Princes, he put to death all the males of the blood Royal, except the aged Shah. After this, as time went on, Mahmud's condition became rapidly worse, and at last he became hopelessly insane. His officers trembled for their lives. It is said that Mahmud's mother, who had joined her son in Isfahan, at last recognised his hopeless condition, and agreed that he should be put out of the world. His cousin Ashraf, son of that Abdul Aziz Khan, whom Mahmud himself had put to death in Kandahar, some years previously, was brought out of prison by the Afghan Sardars, and with their concurrence Ashraf ordered an end to be made of the maniac on the night of the 16th April 1725.

[1] In consequence of his inability a Russian Army, landed on the Coast of Daghestan on 4th August 1722, while Shah Husen reigned. The town of Derbend was occupied.—Malcolm's History of Persia, I. 442.

Ashraf was raised to the throne ; but his tenure was most insecure. In the east a Turkoman freebooter had collected a band of the turbulent spirits of his tribe at the head of whom he waged a successful war with Mahmud, the Seistani Prince, who had seized Meshed and had set himself up as an independent ruler in Khurassan. Nādir Kuli, the Afshār,[1] afterwards famous as Nādir Shah, in this struggle had given proofs of the military qualities which later on enabled him to drive the Russians, Afghans, and Turks from Persian soil. In the third year of Ashraf's reign, the Ottoman Turks invaded Persia in great force, and demanded the release of Shah Husen and his restoration to the throne. An express was sent by the Afghan Ruler from his camp at Gulpaigān to the capital, with orders that the Shah was to be forthwith put to death. The head of the unfortunate monarch was sent to the Turkish general as the Afghan reply to his demands. The operations against the Turks ended not unfavourably to Ashraf, and he made peace with them, but ceded some territory to the Porte (probably as the price of his recognition). A boundary was also demarcated between Turkish and Persian territories. In the 4th year of his reign Ashraf received an ambassador from Constantinople, and on the return of this mission, an agent on the Ghilzai's behalf accompanied it. This person was one Muhammad Ali Khan, a Baluch, but a man of great ability, and famed as the possessor of an oily tongue.

After he had escaped from Isfahan, Prince Tahmāsp had been able to collect a few adherents enough to protect his person, but not sufficiently numerous to effect anything against an antagonist such as Ashraf was. The character and abilities of the Prince were not those which inspire confidence. After lurking in various districts towards the west, he had taken up his residence temporarily in Teheran ; but the extension of the power of Mahmud over that place had rendered the Prince again without a fixed place of abode. Unable to cope with the Afghans, he, by a happy inspiration, joined himself to Nādir Kuli. The wily Turkoman, whose authority was by no means acknowledged by all of his own kinsmen, saw the advantage he would gain as the acknowledged Generalissimo of the Titular Shah ; and he professed himself the devoted slave of Shah Tahmāsp and took the cognomen of Tahmāsp Kuli (slave of Tahmāsp) to show his appreciation of his new position. With the Prince in his camp, Nādir had captured Meshed

[1] Born 10th November 1688. Tarikh-i-Jahān Kushā-i-Nadiri.

and had overthrown Mahmud, the Seistani, whom he had put to death.

Shah Tahmāsp was for ever urging his general to attempt the capture of Isfahan; but Nādir clearly saw the difficulties attending such a task, and the necessity of first restoring the confidence of the Persians by operations against those Afghans who were near at hand. The successes and ruthless ferocity of the Ghilzais had rendered them a terror to the Persians, and this feeling of inferiority had to be obliterated as far as possible. It was also necessary to prevent the Abdalis of Herat from joining the Ghilzais and making a diversion in their favour. Thus by beating his enemies in detail, Nādir laid the foundations of his later successes. By operations which were most carefully planned and carried out against the Abdalis of Herat, Nādir proved to his troops that the Afghans were not invincible, and that both Persian and Turkoman could hope to prevail over these dreaded antagonists. The Abdalis recognised the supremacy of Shah Tahmāsp.

This confidence was soon to be submitted to a practical test; for Ashraf having obtained intelligence of the expedition against the Abdalis of Herat, put his troops in motion to take possession of Khurassan, and marched out of Isfahan, with this object in view, on the 29th July 1729. Nādir, who had returned from Herat, was at Meshed, resting his men after their recent exertions; but on hearing of Ashraf's movement, he at once mobilized his forces, recalled his men from leave, and accompanied by Shah Tahmāsp, he took the western road from Meshed on the 2nd of September. Nādir marched by way of Nishapur and Sabzawār; but he had sent his artillery with an escort round by Sultan Maidan, joining it near Bostan.

Ashraf was operating against one of the forts in the Semnan District, the defenders of which had been exhorted by Nādir to hold out to the last extremity. On hearing of the advance of the two columns, Ashraf sent the Nāsar Chieftain, Saidal Khan, to surprise, and if possible capture the artillery. Nādir was too quick for Saidal, and this design failed as the former had united his forces just before the Afghans appeared. Saidal Khan having put to death his guides in revenge for his disappointment, fell back on Ashraf's army which had abandoned the siege operations and was in position at Mehmandost. At this place the first of a series of well-contested battles, was fought on the 19th of September. Nādir had arrayed his troops in masses, with the front and flanks protected by artillery. Ashraf, on the other hand, divided his army into three divisions, one of which he led in person against the front of Nādir's position, while the others assailed both flanks. Notwithstanding the gallantry of the Afghans, and the desperate valour of Ashraf himself, victory declared for the Persians, and late in the afternoon the Afghans began to retire, after having lost their bravest men in the effort to pierce the ranks of their enemies. They abandoned their artillery, their tents and their baggage, which the Persians seized; but Nādir would not be drawn into a pursuit, and allowed the enemy to retreat unmolested.

Teheran was at once evacuated, but before he withdrew, Islam Khan, Tokhi Ghilzai, who was the Military Governor at that place, called together the leading men of the town, and put them all to death. He then joined Ashraf at Viramin. The Afghans attempted to defend the Sar Darreh Pass (Pilœ Caspiœ) leading to that place. They took up a strong position, blocked the road with artillery supported by the flower of their army, arrayed in full armour, and on the hills to the right and left, sangars had been erected which were held in strength. Nādir sent his infantry to clear the heights and turn the Afghan position, and Islam Khan who commanded on this occasion fled to Viramin, and joined Ashraf. The latter burst his heavy artillery and fell back on Isfahan. The savage temper of the Afghans had been thoroughly roused by these reverses, and Ashraf having been obliged to reinforce his army by withdrawing the garrison of Isfahan, ordered a general massacre, in which, it is said, 3,000 citizens perished. Ashraf also demanded aid from the Turks, with whom he was on terms of friendship; and the Seraskier of Baghdad had sent an army led by several Pashas to his assistance. The Ghilzai took up a strong position in front of Isfahan, at Murcha Khurt, and waited there for his allies to join him.

On receiving intelligence of these events, Nādir and Shah Tahmāsp marched towards Isfahan, and attacked Ashraf, who had been joined by the Turks, on the 3rd of October. Fortune again turned her face from the blood-stained Afghans, and the Ghilzais and their allies were routed after a well-contested struggle. The Turks were allowed by Nādir to retire unmolested after the defeat. The Afghans passed through Isfahan, staying only one night to collect their families and effects. In the meantime Kazvin had fallen, and the Afghan garrison and the families of their compatriots had been made prisoners. Nādir and his titular sovereign halted some time in Isfahan.

Ashraf rallied his followers in Shiraz and placed his head-quarters in that city. He had collected another army and had enlisted the Arab tribes of the coast under his standard. The winter had set in with unusual severity by the time that Nādir was ready to move. Undeterred by the severe weather, he set out on his advance on Shiraz, and directed his march by way of Abar Kuh and Meshed-i-Mādar-i-Sulemān. About the middle of November, his camp was at Zārghun, fifteen miles or so from Shiraz. On a bitterly cold night Ashraf led his men out of their quarters and assaulted the Persian camp with the greatest fury. On this occasion he was very nearly victorious, and the Persians had begun to give way before the repeated and desperate attacks of the Afghans, when Nādir restored the battle with large reserves of infantry: he repulsed the Afghans with great loss, and Ashraf retreated to Shiraz.

A truce was arranged and all Afghan prisoners taken in Kazvin were exchanged for the female members of the Safavi Family, who were still in the hands and harems of the Afghan Chiefs. Saidal Khan and Mulla Zāfrān conducted these negotiations, but no sooner had the former learned that the members of his family (who had been captured in Kazvin) were safe in Ashraf's camp, than he returned to his master and persuaded him to take to flight.

Having arranged his plans and with Kandahar as his objective, Ashraf stole out of Shiraz, accompanied by a crowd of his fellow countrymen who were also endeavouring to make their way to their native land. They were pursued, and the greater part of the fugitives had not crossed the bridge at Fasah, twelve miles from Shiraz, when the advanced troops of the Persian Army came up with the rearmost of the escaping Afghans. The defence of the bridge had been intrusted to Pir Muhammad and a body of troops had been placed under his command to cover the retirement. This person had been the preceptor of both Mahmud and Ashraf, and was revered by the Afghans generally. Under the protection of the rearguard, the fugitives were filing over the bridge at their ease, when a random shot fired by some one of the Persian Scouts, killed Pir Muhammad. Instantly a panic occurred. The fugitives threw themselves into the swollen waters, and were drowned in large numbers in the attempt to ford the stream. Many were taken prisoners by the Persians, among whom were fifteen persons of rank, including Mian Sidik and Mulla Zāfrān. They were despatched to Isfahan. On the way thither, Mulla Zāfrān threw himself off the bridge over the Shin river and was drowned. The rest were publicly executed in Isfahan.

It was at this time that Muhammad Ali Khan returned from Constantinople with despatches from the Porte. These were presented to Nādir, and the Baluch entered his service, and received the government of the district of Kuh-i-Keiluyeh.

After Ashraf had fled, stray bands of Afghans infested some of the outlying districts of Persia. Numbers made their way to the Coast Ports and to Maskat, where men of good family were glad to make a bare living by serving as water-carriers. The roving Afghans in Persia gradually took service under Nādir, and at first the Afghan Contingent in his pay was commanded by Ishāk Sultan Ghilzai, who in Ashraf's time had been Governor of Yazd. He had been distinguished for his humane disposition and reluctance to shed blood. He was subsequently permitted to retire to Kandahar.

Shah Husen Ghilzai, who ruled in Kandahar, was brother to the late Mahmud, whom Ashraf had caused to be put to death. Although the removal of the insane tyrant had been a necessary and a merciful act, yet it gave his brother a very useful pretext to prevent Ashraf entering his territory. Nādir had issued strict orders to intercept the fugitive ex-monarch of Persia. Even Abdullah Khan, the Ruler of Kalat in Baluchistan, had received these orders and had enrolled himself among the friends of Nādir. When, therefore, Ashraf had reached Mala Khan on the Helmand within a comparatively short distance of Kandahar, he heard that Husen was waiting for him at the Laki Ford some thirty miles higher up the river to intercept his retreat. The fugitives struck off to the south, to make for the faint desert trail that led to Baluchistan, hoping to slip through into India. Shah Husen Ghilzai returned to Kandahar, and detailed his feudatory chief, Ibrahim Khan, the Naushirwāni of Khārān, to pursue Ashraf through the desert. One night as the wearied fugitives were resting near a well, at the foot of the Zard Koh, Ibrahim Khan and his party surprised them. A brief but desperate struggle took place, in which Ashraf was shot dead by Ibrahim Khan. The party were made prisoners and were taken to Kandahar. Among them were two ladies of the Blood Royal of the Safavis, who were in Ashraf's Harem. These events took place in 1730.[1]

Mahmud had reigned about two years, and Ashraf about six. The latter deserved a better fate than that which befell him at last.

---

[1] The celebrated diamonds Koh-i-Nur and Darya-i-Nur are said to have been found on Ashraf's corpse by the Naushirwāni Chief and to have been sold by him in Sind! Ali Hazin records a rumour that two diamonds of very great price were taken from Ashraf's body. The rumour must have got about and have spread far. Also see Malcom's Hist. of Persia I. 471.

The crimes and mistakes of the former and of the Afghans generally, entailed consequences that proved too strong for the latter, and brought about his downfall. Measured by time, the dominion of the Ghilzais over Persia appears to be of small importance ; but it gave the first impulse to the demoralization of that country, which has progressed uninterruptedly ever since and of which the end perhaps has not yet been reached.

NOTE.

During the progress of the Indo-Afghan Boundary Commission in 1896, some details regarding the death of Ashraf Ghilzai were learnt in the country where it had taken place. It seems that, in order to move rapidly through the desert and owing to some of his mules having broken down, he cachéd a part of his treasures among the ravines not far from the Mamu well. A part of this buried treasure, we were told, had been discovered by a Baluch shepherd, accidentally. He became rich ; and in order to escape the observation of his neighbbours this fortunate shepherd abandoned his inhospitable native desert.

The connection between the family of the Sardar of Khārān and Shah Husen Ghilzai, Ruler of Kandahar, is clearly established by the family records given in the Baluchistan District Gazetteer Series, Vol. VII and VIIA—Makran and Khārān. Purdil Khan was the eldest of three brothers, and next to him came Ibrahim. The latter was in close touch with the Ruler of Kandahar, and held in honour by the Ghilzai. The fame of Ibrahim eclipsed that of his eldest brother who was chief of Khārān.

The lands of Hazār Suft on the Helmand, above Landi Muhammad Amin Khan, were bestowed on the family of the Khārān Chief by Husen Ghilzai of Kandahar (so the story goes). The income from these lands is said to be still enjoyed by the Chief of Khārān.

CHAPTER VII.

The Abdalis in Herat—Nādir Shah.

AT about the time when Mahmud the Ghilzai had made his attempt on Persia, Muhammad Khan, the Sadozai (son of that Abdullah Khan who had died in prison), who ruled over the Abdalis in Herat, also dreamed of effecting the conquest of Khurassan; and he went and blockaded Meshed for four months. After ravaging the open country, he was compelled to return home, as he made no impression on the city. On his return journey, however, he took possession of the fort of Sinakan in the district of Khāf.

A revolution took place in Herat after his return, and he was deposed, and Zulfikār Khan, who had fled to Shorāwak on Muhammad's election, was recalled and made their chief by the Abdalis. The new ruler was the son of the late Zamān Khan Sadozai. The deceased chief had caused Abdullah Khan to be placed in bonds and was even suspected of having caused his death. In 1725-6, Rahmān, son of the late Abdullah and brother to the deposed Muhammad, in retaliation for his father's death, sought to kill Zulfikār Khan, and matters came to such a pass in the city that the Abdalis turned the leaders of the two factions out of Herat. Zulfikār was sent away to the district of Bakharz, and Rahmān to Farah, and the elders of the clan sent for another son of the late Abdullah Khan, named Allahyār, from Multan, and raised him to the chiefship in the year 1726.

The Alakozai headman, Abdul Ghani, however, was a staunch supporter of Zulfikār Khan; and owing to his influence and tribal following, he kept Herat in a ferment for six months trying to reinstate his friend. The Abdalis again expelled both Allahyār and Zulfikār: the former to Maruchāk and the latter this time to Farah. The Abdalis continued to manage their affairs without a supreme chief over them, till they heard that Nādir and Shah Tahmāsp had planned an expedition against Herat, and were on the point of starting. They brought Allahyār back to Herat as their chief, while his rival was ordered to hold Farah.

Nādir, with the Shah in his camp, took the field with 8,000 men in 1727-28, and by a series of carefully planned movements, the district of Khaf was cleared of the Afghans. The latter were gradually pushed back on Herat, and were cautiously followed by Nādir to the city. On this occasion, however, he was content with the nominal submission of Allahyār Khan, and retired to Meshed after a campaign of two months.

In the year 1729 Nādir again took the field against the Abdalis, who had been encroaching on the territory they had lost, and on the 24th of March, at the head of many divisions, he left Meshed, and commenced operations by the capture of the fort of Farmand ; and he fought a general engagement later on the plains of Kāfir Kala, in which the Afghans were defeated late in the afternoon, but not before they had nearly succeeded in overthrowing the Persians. Nādir himself was wounded on this occasion. The next battle was fought on the banks of the Heri-Rud near Kuhsan ; and again late in the day, by the personal efforts of their leader, the Persians signally defeated the Abdalis. The latter abandoned the fort at Ghurian, and concentrated in Herat.

An indecisive action at Rabat-i-Pariyān was followed by negotiations, but the advance of Zulfikār Khan put an end to these. Herat was invested. The fortifications protecting this city were very massive. The walls were constructed very largely of wet earth, thoroughly worked up before use, and after it had been placed in position, again thoroughly well rammed and consolidated. The *Pisé* work of Khurassan is celebrated for its durability.

Against massive walls of this material, solid round shot and shells had very little effect. In more recent times the mud walls of Bhartpur (in India) foiled troops far superior, and artillery far more effective than those of Nādir, and this failure has dimmed the lustre of the achievements of that gallant soldier Lord Lake. It is not to be wondered at that, with the Ghilzais still predominant in Persia, Nādir was not unwilling that the puppet Shah should patch up a truce with the Abdalis in Herat, so as to set him free to deal with the Ghilzais. The courage and confidence of the troops under Nādir's command had also been restored ; and he returned to Meshed on the 22nd May 1729.

The Abdalis after this withdrawal of the Persians continued to exhibit the same levity in the conduct of their affairs, which they had hitherto displayed. While Nādir was away in the West, Zulfikār Khan persuaded the tribesmen to invade the district round Meshed. Allahyār, who demurred, was again thrust out, and he joined the

Persians in Meshed. An army from Herat again appeared before the holy city, where Nādir's brother commanded. The latter had none of his famous brother's talents for war, and against express orders to the contrary, he fought Zulfikār Khan in the open field and was defeated on the 19th July 1730. The city of Meshed again baffled the attempts of the Afghans, who retired to Herat after laying waste the open country.

Nādir determined to subdue the Abdalis finally, having driven the Ghilzais from Persia. On the 13th February 1731, he moved out of Meshed. His advance was unopposed, and the Afghans again concentrated in Herat. On the 3rd March he took up a position at Ju-i-Nukrah, about twelve miles west of that city, and on the 6th was vehemently attacked by the Abdalis led by their chief in person. The Afghans were defeated, and in the teeth of their strenuous endeavours the city was finally invested; and Nādir placed his head-quarters at Urdu Khan, some four miles from Herat. On the 12th July, Zulfikār Khan made a determined assault on the Persian lines at Urdu-Khan, but was defeated. On his way back to Herat, while crossing the swollen river, the Abdali chief's horse lost its footing and fell. It was swept away by the current and was recovered with all its trappings by the Persian soldiers, while Zulfikār was rescued by some of his own troopers.

Shah Husen had been trying to keep in with the Abdalis and also with Nādir. He had sent Saidal Khan, the Nāsar, with 4,000 picked men to aid in the defence of Herat, and he also had sent representatives to the Persian camp. As time went on, famine made its appearance in the beleagured town, and the sufferings of the garrison and townsfolk rapidly increased, and were aggravated by the failure of salt. Most of the Ghilzai contingent had perished in the strife, and at last Saidal decided to escape. On the night of the 25th July, he crept along the bed of an old irrigation cutting, passed the lines of the enemy, and fled towards the south. His defection still further demoralized the defenders. Their disunion and lack of discipline also daily grew more pronounced till concerted action had become impossible. Zulfikār Khan thereupon resigned the chieftainship in favour of Allahyār, and negotiations were set on foot with Nādir.

On the 11th of August 1731, Allahyār Khan was sent from the Persian camp with the leaders of the tribes to take possession of the city. No sooner had he entered the place than he became so impressed with its capabilities for holding out and with the good condition of its defences, that he abandoned his allegiance to the Persians, shut the gates, and declared he would carry on the war. The siege was resumed, and Nādir tightened his hold on the city. Famine was his ally. In vain did the Afghans sally forth to procure supplies; the enemy was vigilant and drove them back. In vain did the famous Musa Khan, chief of the Ishakzai clan, still remembered under his sobriquet of Dungi—"the freebooter"—exert himself to pass the enemy's lines and to collect supplies of salt and grain for his starving countrymen in Herat. It was in vain that Allahyār Khan in person attempted to collect these necessary articles in the township of Kozarān. Every attempt was frustrated, and the privations had increased beyond endurance. On the 21st of November, Allahyār Khan despatched the Shekh-ul-Islam of Herat to Nādir to sue for peace, promising that if his family and the prisoners taken on the surrender of Obah were given up to him, he would yield the city. The captives were set free, but as soon as Allahyār Khan's wife arrived in the city, she was put to death by her jealous husband.

Having obtained his desires, the fickle Afghan, perhaps overruled by his followers, again broke his word. Hostilities were resumed and continued till the 19th January when Herat surrendered. This time the Afghans were ordered to march out of the place. The five great clans of the Duranis, each of which held one of the gates of the city streamed out in troops, defiling through the suburbs till they reached the place at which they were to await orders for their disposal. On the 19th, Allahyār Khan also departed for Multan, and on the 25th Nādir's governor was installed in Herat.

The Durani tribes were deported in a body to districts between Meshed and Semnan which had been assigned to them. A number of the tribesmen took service with Nādir, under the leadership of Abdul Ghani, the Alakozai, who was also made chieftain of the Duranis. This Afghan contingent was afterwards increased, and Abdul Ghani served Nadir for six years with zeal and fidelity, and in the campaigns against the Turks he distinguished himself very greatly. In requital for his services he obtained the release of all Afghan captives in the hands of the Persians, and Nādir's promise that, whenever the Ghilzais in Afghanistan, should be subjugated, the town of Kandahar should be placed in his hands.

After the death of Abdul Ghani, Nādir appointed Nur Muhammad to the command of the contingent, and to the chieftainship of the tribes as well.

We will return now to the affairs of the Ghilzais. Those persons, whom Ashraf had left to the tender mercies of his black slaves, were rescued before more than three persons had perished at the hands of their keepers. Two were killed, and the mother of Muhammad received a wound, from the effects of which she died a short time after the rescue was effected. On Nādir's arrival in Isfahan these persons were made prisoners, but later on they were exchanged for the two ladies of the Safavi family whom Ashraf had carried off with him. Shah Husen Ghilzai knew, that, although Nādir had been obliged to put off his intentions with regard to Kandahar, yet a reckoning was inevitable, and he appears to have made spasmodic efforts to enter into communication with his dreaded foeman. On the east he had no enemies whom he feared, and he pursued an active policy in this direction, and is said even to have despatched a force into India which ravaged the country round Multan.[1]

Saidal Khan, when he escaped from Herat, made his way to Isfizar, a district to the south of that city, where he lingered for a month and a half. Zulfikār Khan, with his younger brother, Ahmad Khan, joined the Nāsar at that place, after he had abandoned Herat; and in company with Saidal Khan, the Sadozai chiefs made their way to Kandahar. On arrival at this place, the two Sadozais were seized by Shah Husein, and placed in confinement, until on the fall of this city, they were set free by Nādir.

During the final operations against Herat, Nādir had despatched troops to take possession of the forts in the country to the south, and others in the direction of Kandahar, and this expedition had succeeded in capturing the forts at Girishk and Kala-i-Bist, places almost on the outskirts of Shah Husen's capital. The latter despatched troops under the leadership of Bābo Jān, the Bābi Afghan, who had been governor of Lār in Persia, under Mahmud and Ashraf, and who, on the downfall of the latter, had made his way to Kandahar and had joined Husen. Bābo Jān recovered both Girishk and Kala-i-Bist and drove the Persians back to Farah.

Affairs of greater importance claimed Nādir's attention and his presence on the Western Frontier. He also had deposed the nominal sovereign Shah Tahmāsp, and had assumed the royal dignity himself. At length, however, he had arranged matters with both the Ottoman Turks and the Russians, and was free to turn his attention to Kandahar, and give effect to his long-deferred intentions with regard to the Ghilzais.

When news reached Kandahar, that Nādir Shah was about to march towards that place, the Hotakis thought it would be as well to

[1] Seir-i-Mutakherin, Litho Text.

thoroughly crush the Tokhis, their hereditary enemies, whom they had driven from the Tarnak into the valley of the Arghandāb river. The whole of the fighting men of the Hotakis were, therefore, mobilised for this purpose ; and 4,000 horsemen were borrowed from the garrison of Kandahar. The combined force fell up on the Pirak Khel (Tokhis) at Umakai, practically destroying that tribe, not even sparing women with child. The chiefs of the massacred tribe were away collecting troops, and upon hearing of the destruction that had befallen their people they took to flight, and joined Nādir Shah's army, vowing a bitter revenge on the perpetrators of the slaughter of their people.

On the 13th of October 1736, Nādir Shah marched out of Isfahan and took the route through Kirman and Seistan. In this country he left his own Harem and the families of his officers under an adequate guard, and leaving Seistan on the 25th December, he arrived at Girishk on the 10th of January 1737, having marched by way of Dalkhak and Dilārām. From Girishk he despatched expeditions into the Zamindāwar, and also against Kala-i-Bist, and then he continued his march and crossed the Helmand on the 13th of January.

Ordinarily in the winter, forage and other supplies are scanty, but Husen removed all the supplies he could lift, and what he was unable to take into Kandahar he had burnt on the spot. Nādir Shah was, therefore, compelled to halt at Shāh Maksud for twelve days, to allow of supplies being collected in Tizin and Derawat and brought into his camp. Shah Husen took advantage of this respite to put the finishing touches to his scheme of defence. He hurried reinforcements to Kala-i-Bist, and levelled buildings that were near the walls of his capital ; strengthening the works. His son Muhammad Khan was detailed to hold Kalat (the stronghold of the Ghilzais), about 50 miles to the north-west of Kandahar.

From Shāh Maksud, Nādir Shah marched to the banks of the Arghandāb and placed his camp abreast of the shrine of Bābāvali. The same evening Shah Husen saddled his horses and rode out of Kandahar to attack the Persian camp. Under cover of the darkness he entered their lines with the impetuosity of a flood in spring time. Although they inflicted heavy losses on their antagonists, the Persian troops became panic stricken, and it was only with the greatest personal exertions that Nādir was able to rally his men on the high ground of Ashukah, and lead them back to the camp they had abandoned. Owing to the darkness Shah Husen himself was unaware of the measure of success he had obtained and retired to Kandahar.

In order to conceal the reverse he had sustained, Nādir crossed the river next morning by a ford which had been discovered opposite the village of Kokaran, and skirting the Pir Pamān hills he marched past the city under fire from the heavy guns, mounted on the Chahilzina Bastion (to which he paid no attention), to a position on the east of Kandahar (end of January or early in February 1737).

Abdul Ghafur, the Hotaki, was in Kalat at this time and his brother Abdur Rasul had gone to raise the Kharoti levies against Nādir Shah. The latter obtained news of the gathering and despatched a column to disperse the tribesmen, under the guidance of Musa Khan, "Dungi," the famous Sakzi (Ishạkzai) chief, and this column fell on the assembled Kharotis at Shibar and scattered them with great loss. The day after the Nauroz festival, which had been celebrated with great pomp, a detachment of Nādir's troops was sent out to act against Kalat (11th March 1737). A deserter, who had escaped out of Kandahar, on the second night after the march of the column, gave news to the effect that Husen Ghilzai had heard of the movement and had despatched Saidal Khan, with 4,000 picked men, to follow up and surprise the Persians. Such was Saidal's reputation, that Nādir decided to march in person to the rescue of his men, and joined them—all unsuspicious of danger, as the Afghans were on the point of surprising the negligent commander. Foiled in their purpose by the arrival of Nādir Shah, the Afghans scattered over the hills at the onslaught of the Persians, and made their way to Kalat, where Saidal joined Muhammad Khan and the other chiefs.

A large gathering of Ghilzais was dispersed on the banks of the Arghandāb; and in order to prevent sorties from the beleagured city being made, it was decided to build redoubts and block houses round the city. On a perimeter of from twenty-four to twenty-eight miles, redoubts, each of which was capable of sheltering 1,000 men, were constructed at intervals of a mile. Between each of these again at intervals of 100 paces, towers were constructed in which 10 musketeers were placed. As the Afghans were even then able to steal past the towers in the darkness singly and on foot between each of these last two other towers were erected, by means of which egress from the city was rendered impossible.

On the 3rd May 1737 news arrived of the fall of Kala-i-Bist, and the next day brought tidings of the capture of Shahr-i-Safa. At the end of the same month, the families that had been left in Seistan reached Nādirābād. In the meantime, however, the expedition into the country of Zamindāwār had failed to effect the conquest of the principal fort in that district ; and the luckless commander was recalled, and was condemned to receive the bastinado in Nādir Shah's presence. Thus encouraged, his successor proved a more energetic officer, and the place was soon after made over to the Persians.

The Afghans for several years had been preparing the town of Kandahar for a siege, and the place contained great stores of provisions and also a very large garrison, who stood manfully on their defence. As ten months had passed by, Nādir decided to capture it by assault ; and on the 21st of December the outer defences were attacked and one by one these were gained. The principal work was the Azimi Bastion, on which there were several guns mounted. It was situated on a lofty mound and was equal in height to the Chahilzina work. The garrison of Azimi were taken prisoners. The Sangin fort was next assailed. This was on the summit of a very high spur and commanded the citadel. It was situated on the north-west side in the direction of the Chahilzina work. The attack on Sangin was successful, and the garrison of 300 men were either taken or killed. Fourteen other works had also been taken and the defenders had fallen by the sword. Large bored mortars, and guns firing shot which weighed from 35 to 40 lbs., were dragged up by a very difficult and crooked path and placed in position on the crest of the hill, to bear on the Dahdar work (on the west of the citadel), in the fort Sangin. After battering Dahdar till its foundations trembled, 300 men of each of the contingents of the Bakhtiāris, Kurds and Afghans were told off to assault the position on the night of the 3rd March 1738. The garrison of Dahdar, however, were on the alert, and they beat off the storming party with a loss of 200 men.

After the Nauroz Festival had been celebrated, the Bakhtiāris were ordered to make a second attack on Dahdar, supported by 4,000 other troops. They moved up under cover towards the Dahdar fort and passed the night concealed from the view of the defenders in the ravines and chasms of that furrowed hillside. Next morning when the attention of the garrison was drawn to the assault on the other side, the Bakhtiāris scaled the rocks and swarmed over the walls into the place (13th March 1738).

The Chahar Burj was next attacked and carried on the third assault, the Persians having suffered greatly in the two attacks which failed. A general assault put them in possession of several other parts of the defences, and also of a gateway. Shah Husen fled into the Kaitul Fort accompanied by a few of his leading men, and with several of his women folk, while a great slaughter was made in the city. He perceived that his only chance of safety lay in surrendering. He, therefore, sent his own sister, Zināb by name, in company with some of his chiefs, to Nādir Shah to obtain terms. Having received assurances of safety, he made his submission to Nādir outside the Bābāvali Gate. Shah Husen with his relations and dependants, with such of their personal possessions as had remained in their hands, were exiled to Mazenderan.

Nādir Shah had fully made up his mind that Kandahar should be destroyed and rendered uninhabitable, and on the 29th of March 1737 a site had been selected in the vicinity of the shrine of Sher Surkh Bābā, and a complete city was laid out here, all the details as to public buildings, bath houses, and residential quarters, were definitely settled, work was commenced at once, and by the middle of December the place was pronounced to be ready for occupation. This city was declared to be the future capital of the province, and it was named Nādirābād.

While Nādir Shah's military chiefs were battering the fortifications of Old Kandahar, his civil officers were planning the settlement and assessment of the land immediately round the newly built city.[1]

After that Kalat-i-Ghilzai had been taken by the Persians, it was handed over to the care of the famous Ghilzai Chief, Jān, the Taraki, who exercised such power over his tribe, that even during his lifetime his influence had become proverbial :—"It rests with God and Jān the Taraki," was a saying which was current in the mouths of his

[1] Nādir divided these lands into 300 separate holdings of about 74½ acres. The holders of these allotments were obliged severally to furnish two horsemen for service, and in addition to pay as revenue $\frac{1}{10}$th of the produce of their fields. This assessment was realized in kind and half was taken in grain and the other half was taken in chaff. In order to arrive at some figures on which to base his estimates for this settlement, he had made experiments. He had ordered a plot of land of (about) the area of 74½ acres to be ploughed seven times, and when the soil had been prepared grain sown. The yield proved to be twenty-fold. On this return he based his calculation as to the revenue that was to be realized from each of the 300 holdings. This experiment was unfair, and the result was greatly in favour of the government, because land on which he had experimented had lain fallow for three years, owing to the disturbed state of the country, whereas the land that was to be assessed according to the results obtained by the experimental sowings, and which lay around Nadirabad was such that it could not be cultivated two years consecutively, so that not more than 38 acres in each holding could be put under crops in any one year.

The tenure of the holdings was that known as "Arbābi." Each individual was to be always ready to help the officials in anyway in which their services were required, and to aid also in providing a garrison for the town on occasions of emergency. These holdings were permanently occupied, and the persons who enjoyed them were of Persian descent (Farsiwān, or Farsi). They belonged to the tribes of this section of the population of the Kandahar district, such as the Ruzbehāni, Zangānah, Burbur, and Siah Mansur. These people were good agriculturists and could be trusted to make the most of their land. LEECH.

people. Nādir made Ashraf Sultan chief over the Tokhi and other Ghilzai tribes, and avenged them on the Hotakis, who were deported to the lands held by the Abdalis, to the west of Meshed in the Sabzawār district, and on the 4th April 1738 the exiled tribesmen crossed the Arghandāb on their journey to their new habitations.

Thus passed away the sceptre of authority from the Ghilzais. Theirs is a proud record. Shah Husen died soon after arriving in Mazenderan. The dissensions among the Ghilzais was the cause of his downfall. Popular belief, however, attributed his ruin to the curse pronounced on him by a celebrated Mulla of that period who dwelt in the city of Old Kandahar. The latter, named Abdul Hakim Sahib, who belonged to the tribe of Kakar Afghans, was a most influential person, and was regarded with the utmost veneration as a saint, on account of his austere life and devotion to religion. So great was this holy man's following and such was his influence in the city and country, that Shah Husen regarded him as a source of danger, and expelled him from his territory. The orders were carried out without regard to this venerated person's feelings, and as he left Kandahar he prophesied that, even as he had been driven forth, so would God remove Shah Husen from his native land and cause him to die in exile, and his descendants for ever should languish in subjection to others! When Old Kandahar was demolished, the abode of the holy person was spared at the intercession of the Abdalis, and it has ever since been maintained by the Durani Sovereigns as a shrine. The holy person himself settled in Thal-Chotiali, a district of the present Baluchistan Agency (one of the two Frontier Provinces of British India), and there in course of time he passed away.

For his faithful service Abdul Ghani, the Alakozai, was rewarded with the Government of Nādirabad, and the Abdalis were permitted to vacate their seats in exile (which the Hotakis were to occupy), and to return to Kandahar, where the outlying lands round the capital and in the districts were allotted afresh to the tribesmen. Abdul Ghani obtained the rich lands in the Arghandāb valley for the Alakozais. Nur Muhammad, the equally fertile lands of the Zamīndāwar for his tribe the Alizais. The Barakzais, who complained that they had been ill-represented in Nādir's Court at the time of the distribution of land, received those districts where the soil is light, and is not commanded by water, which have since formed their patrimony. They were obliged to acquire by purchase afterwards other properties in the fertile tracts towards the Helmand River.

Zamān Khan and his brother Ahmad Khan, the Sadozai chiefs, were released from prison, when Old Kandahar fell. The former received the government of a district in Mazenderan, and has been lost sight of. Ahmad Khan was appointed one of Nādir Shah's Yessāwals, or Heralds, and attached to his personal retinue. Under an exacting master like Nādir, the proper discharge of the duties of this appointment made great demands on the tact and discretion of the person who filled it, and the future sovereign of Afghanistan received a training that stood him in good stead afterwards.

From Kandahar, Nādir Shah marched to Ghazni, held by an Indian governor, which was surrendered to him on the 2nd of May. From this place troops were despatched to subdue the Hazara tribes of Dai Kandi and Dai Zangi and the march was resumed towards Kabul. Nādir Shah placed his camp on the meadow at Siāh Sang, about two miles from the city, and after a futile resistance of a week, the Bālā Hissar was surrendered on the 22nd of May, with the treasury, arsenal, and elephants that were in it. Twelve days after this the troops which had been detailed to reduce the districts of Ghorband and Bamiān rejoined their sovereign's camp. The affairs of the Province of Kabul had fallen into the greatest confusion. The Afghans had long been doing as they pleased, withholding revenue and slighting the orders of the Indian governor. In Nādir Shah they found a master whom it was by no means safe to ignore. He sent expeditions into the districts of the Kohistan and Charikār, into Nijrāo and Sāfi, all of which were (and are) fertile districts well watered and abounding in supplies—things which at that time happened to be scarce in the immediate vicinity of Kabul, and insufficient for his large army. The tribesmen inhabiting those valleys were speedily brought to their senses. The chief men in those districts accompanied Sadullah and Mulla Muhammad, son of Mian Ji, to the royal presence. The passes on the road to Gandamak were disputed by the Afghans, but their efforts were unavailing. Jallālābād was occupied (3rd October 1738), and an expedition was detailed against the son of Mir Abbas (an Afghan chief of note and who had put to death Nādir Shah's Yesawal on his way to Delhi), who had collected a large number of Afghans in the hills. They were dispersed with great loss and their women, including the wife and sisters of the son of Mir Abbas, were made prisoners. Nāsir Khan, the Indian Viceroy of Kabul, retreated to Peshawar after the fall of Ghazni, and there he had collected a large body of armed men, including 20,000 Afghans of the Khyber, and Peshawar, and had taken up a position in the vicinity of Jamrud to close the

Pass against the invaders. Nādir Shah left his heavy baggage at Barikāb and set out at the head of a mobile force, by the Tsatsobai Pass[1] and down the Bazaar valley. He surprised Nāsir Khan near Jamrud and defeated him. Peshawar was occupied and Nādir waited there for Prince Nasrullah, who was marching leisurely with the main body of the army and all the impedimenta which had been placed under his command. With the fall of Peshawar, the waning influence of the Timuride Sovereigns of Delhi passed away for ever from the country to the West of the Indus.

Ahmad Khan, the Sadozai, rode as an officer in his master's train, and the experience he acquired under that distinguished professor of the science of warfare, as it was understood in his day in the east, stood him in good stead in after-years, when by a stroke of good fortune he attained to the sovereignty of the country which had been subdued by Nādir Shah for the benefit of the Sadozai, as it proved in the end. The Indian campaign showed the Afghan chief the state of the country, and revealed the degeneracy of the sovereign and his nobles, and the knowledge gained by him on this occasion was put to good use by him not very long afterwards.

1. In the Tarikh-i-Jahan Kushā-i-Nādirī, from which this account has been taken, the name of the pass is written Seh-chobeh evidently a Persianized form of the Pashtu name of the Pass at the head of the Bazaar Valley.

NOTE.

The anecdote of the influence of the Pir Abdul Hakim Sahib (p.64), related by the author of the Tarikh-i- Sultani, is corroborated by the following notice in the Gazetteer of Quetta-Pishin, 1907, p. 88:—

Abdul Hakim, son of Sikandar Shah, a Shamozai Kākar of Yusuf Kach in the Pishin Tahsil, a contemporary of Shah Husen Ghilzai, and Nadir Shah * * * is credited with many miracles, including the stopping of the pistachio trees which were following him in the Khojak Pass, and the rendering of all snakes in Toba innocuous. At Khanozai he induced the people to treat his father, Sikandar Shah, as a saint and contribute to the upkeep of his shrine, and then passed on to the Duki Tahsil where he died and was buried at Chotiāli.

CHAPTER VIII.

Ahmad Shah Durani ; Founder of the Kingdom.

THERE are many stories which are firmly believed and now accepted as facts, of the favour with which Nādir Shah regarded the Sadozai Ahmad Khan, and of the prediction of his rise to sovereign power over his native land. These stories probably obtained currency after his accession to power, but they indicate the very general attention which he had attracted by his character and strong personal magnetism. The able manner in which he handled the unruly subjects whom destiny called him to govern, and the influence he exercised over the powerful chiefs of the Abdalis, who elected him as their sovereign, proves the fact most clearly. One story is to the effect that in the year 1747, Ahmad Khan, who had visited the shrine of Imam Reza in Meshed, there attracted the attention of a wandering Indian Fakir, named Sābir Shah, who made his acquaintance, and is said to have revealed to the Sadozai not only his own future greatness, but also the impending and violent death of his master. Another is, that it was revealed in a dream to Nādir Shah that the Abdali would in time become a king, and the former was so impressed with the revelation that he bespoke Ahmad Khan's favour on behalf of his descendants, in return for the favour he had always shown the Abdali. In order to impress the fact on the memory of the latter, Nādir Shah, it is firmly believed, made a slight incision in the ear of the future sovereign.

The story of Nādir Shah is well known. In course of time he became a suspicious and morose tyrant, unable even to trust his first born son, who had served him with courage and distinction. After the prince had been blinded by his father's orders, the lust for blood that took possession of the latter increased by indulgence ; and at last no one was safe. The lives of his highest officers, and of all those about his person rested on a very precarious tenure—the whim of a remorse haunted and homicidal despot.

At the instigation of his nephew, Nādir Shah's most trusted officers including the captains of his personal guards (men of the same Afshār tribe as their master), entered his pavilion at midnight following the 19th June 1747, as he lay asleep on his couch, and after a brief struggle struck his head from his body. The scene of this act was close to Fatehabad, eight miles from Kabushan (the modern Kuchan).

The next morning the whole camp was in an uproar. The Afghan and Uzbeg contingents held together, and under the leadership of Nur Mahammad, well seconded by Ahmad Khan, they took up arms, loyal to the memory of their late master, and endeavoured to prevent the pillage of the Royal tents. They were outnumbered; and Nur Muhammad drew his men out of the camp, and the Afghans made for Kandahar.

Sābir Shah who had followed Ahmad to the camp, rejoined him on the way eastwards. This person was one of those wandering and semi-insane fakirs (very common even in the present day), whose incoherent utterances, and irresponsible actions are regarded still with awe by superstitious persons, as inspired by the Almighty.

Nur Muhammad was an eccentric and irritable person who owed his promotion to Nādir Shah, but he was unpopular with the Abdalis whom he commanded. As long as they were on the march the authority of their commander was regarded, but when Kandahar was reached in safety, Nur Muhammad was set on one side.

The leaders of the tribes, such as Hāji Jamāl Khan, the Barakzai, Muhabat Khan Popalzai, Musa Dungi the famous Ishakzai chief, Nur Muhammad, Alizai, Nasr-Ullah Khan, the Nurzai Sardar and others, met in solemn conclave at the Shrine of Surkh Sher Bābā. They were quite unanimous that it was very expedient that they should have a king to manage their affairs, for the times were troublous and there were persons on all sides asserting their claims to independence. The question to be decided was who should be king. Not one of these powerful chiefs would acknowledge the superiority or the claims of his peers. Ahmad Khan by virtue of his rank and family was present at the debates, and Sābir Shah's calling also made him welcome. He cut short the discussion by producing a tiny sheaf of wheat, and placing it in Ahmad Khan's turban, declared that no one in that assembly was so fit for the kingship as Ahmad Khan, the flower of the Duranis. The words and act of the eccentric fakir were regarded by all as a happy solution of the difficulty. Probably, also, they were regarded as a manifestation of the Divine will revealed through the holy man to the assembled chiefs. The scene was the shrine of a well-known saint, who might be regarded therefore as being interested in the debate. The choice of the Dervesh was acclaimed, the Sadozai obtained the suffrages of his peers—it is said, because the tribe to which he belonged was numerically weak, and he would be in a great measure dependent on his nobles, all of them the head chiefs of powerful clans, who hoped to be able to coerce the sovereign—and if he proved not amenable, to depose him if necessary.

As may be imagined Sābir Shah the Dervesh had great influence with Ahmad Shah. The latter used to allow the holy man to sit by his side when holding his court; and the sovereign bowed to the spiritual authority of the mad fakir.[1]

Having been elected to be king over them, Ahmad Shah forthwith set about attaching the chiefs to him; and as he had learned at the court of Nādir Shah, he bestowed titles and offices on each. Shah Nawāz Khan Bāmizai was appointed Vazier with the title of Shah Wali Khan. Sardar Jahān Khan Popalzai was appointed general-in-chief with the honorific appellation of Mir Bizan, and Khan-i-Khānān (first of all the nobles). Shah Pasand Khan, the Ishakzai Chieftain was raised to the dignity of Amir Lashkari. These were the most powerful among the electors, and they received prompt acknowledgment of their sagacity. The sovereign himself assumed the title of Ahmad Shah by which he is mentioned in history.

He was a sovereign, but with an empty treasury; and possessed none of the insignia of Royalty. Both however were soon after acquired by the seizure of treasure destined for Nādir Shah. Taki Khan, Akhta Begi[2] the Shirāzi, had been despatched while his master was alive, to collect and bring away the tribute imposed on Kabul and Peshawar. In company with Nāsir Khan (the former governor of Kabul, an Indian Noble), he arrived at Kandahar with the treasure —amounting to two crores (£2,000,000) of rupees which was seized by Ahmad Shah, who appropriated the money and provided himself with

---

[1] The latter was a native of Lahore, and after a time a restless fit seized him and he wandered away to his native place. There he used to shape pieces of cotton cloth and make little tents and arrange them on the ground. He used to make little figures of wet clay, resembling horses, and arrange these in front of the miniature tents. In reply to questions as to the reason for so employing his time, he used to say that he was preparing Ahmad Shah's dominion in Lahore. These sayings disturbed the minds of men. The old order of things was changing, there was trouble in the air. The Viceroy of Lahore Shah Nawaz Khan, son of Zakariah Khan, meditated setting up himself as an independent ruler over the Punjab and Multan, which he governed on behalf of the Emperor of Delhi. These sayings of the Dervesh irritated the Ruler and seemed to forbode illsuccess, to his own plans. He therefore seized the fakir and placed him in bonds, and some time after had him put to death.

[2] He is said to have been mutilated by Nādir Shah's order.

the insignia of his exalted rank. In addition Nāsir Khan promised to furnish five lakhs of rupees (£50,000) from Kabul and was released from confinement. The Afghans of Kabul refused, however, to recognise Nāsir Khan any longer, and as the latter was unable to fulfil his engagements he fled to Peshawar.

Kabul was occupied soon after, and there is a letter in existence addressed by Ahmad Shah to Muhammad Hashim Khan, an Afridi chieftain, dated the 15th July 1747, in which the latter was ordered to acknowledge the Durani Monarch as his Suzerain. This was evidently intended by the latter as a prelude to his first campaign in India, for which an uninterrupted passage through the defiles leading to Peshawar was an important matter. The occupation of Peshawar in 1747 brought the Afghan sovereign to the threshold of Hindustan, and a campaign in that country would be popular among his subjects and distract their attention from domestic affairs, for at this period there was some trouble experienced in obtaining their acquiescence in the exercise of the rights of a sovereign. An Indian campaign was probably determined at an early date after his accession, as likely to be profitable in more ways than one. An Indian author goes on to say—knowing as he did the disorganization of the government of the Moghuls of Delhi, the disunion that prevailed among the self-seeking and degenerate nobles, and the imbecility of the womanish Emperor, Ahmad Shah pushed boldly forward to Lahore. The Viceroy Shahnawāz Khan, son of the late Nawāb Zakariah Khan Bahadur, sauntered out of Lahore at the head of a large array of armed men and artillery, and took up a strong position on the banks of the Rāvi. The Afghans camped at first on the opposite bank, but Ahmad Shah, calling to mind the tactics of Nādir Ṣhah, (when he crossed the Dijleh in front of the Turks,) on the 20th January 1748, stole out of his camp at the head of 10,000 horse, and forded the river at a considerable distance below his camp and hurried towards Lahore. Shahnawāz Khan abandoned his position and the city as well, and fled towards Delhi. The Afghans captured the camp, and all the stores of the Indian troops in Lahore, when they entered that city on the 22nd January.

Muhammad Shah sent a strong force led by his eldest son and the Vazier to repel the invasion. The latter met his nephew the late governor of Lahore, from whom he was able to learn authentic details of the forces of the enemy. The Royal Army marched towards the ford of Machiwāra on the Sutlej river, and the families of the commanders were sent off to Sirhind, where the Vazier had established a depôt. Ahmad Shah slipped past the Vazier's right, forded the Sutlej river on the 11th March, and captured and sacked Sirhind, and advanced to meet the Indian troops, for the Vazier had broken up his camp and was advancing towards that place, 13th March 1748.

As soon as the Indian troops came into touch with the enemy about eight miles from Sirhind they halted and their camp was strongly fortified with field works. So formidable were these that Ahmad Shah declined to assault them. From the 13th to the 21st March 1748, the two armies lay facing each other and the outposts only were engaged, till at last the Indian leaders determined to risk a general engagement in front of his lines. Before the battle had fairly commenced a round shot killed the Vazier as he knelt at his devotions in his tent. The Indian Nobles and their troops, however, were faithful and brave, and the issue of the battle had not been declared, when a great wagon-load of war rockets exploded in the Afghan ranks. The missiles ploughed their way through the troops, causing a general panic. Ahmad Shah withdrew his forces and commenced to treat with his opponents. The death of the Vazier having depressed the Indian troops, their leaders also were not at all ill-disposed to come to terms with the invaders.

As in the days of Nãdir Shah, the Indus was again fixed as a tentative boundary between Indian and Afghan possessions. After this settlement had been concluded Ahmad Shah set out on his return journey to Kandahar, placing as he went along, in his newly-acquired territory, responsible persons who should conduct the administration.

The retirement of the invaders elated the Indian officials, and it was decided that Prince Ahmad, who was the nominal leader of the Army, should cross the Sutlej and proceed towards Lahore, and a report was sent to the capital announcing the fact of the Vazier's death and the retreat of the Afghan forces. The forces, however, came to a halt some miles from Ludhiana; and it was decided that the Muin-ul-Mulk, the late Vazier's son, should be appointed Governor of Lahore, and on the evening of the 2nd April 1748 he was formally invested with the government; and the next day the prince at the head of the forces began his return march towards Delhi.

After the battle near Sirhind, Ahmad Shah retired towards Kandahar by Multan, and proceeded from that place into Sind and reached Rohri on the Indus about the 11th of April; from that place he continued his march towards Kandahar, and reached his capital on the 22nd of May 1748.[1]

From the spoils he had acquired on his return to Kandahar, the Durani sovereign rewarded his followers, but the jealousy of certain of his nobles was excited who considered they had been insufficiently recompensed. They conspired together to take the life of their sovereign. This plot was revealed to Ahmad Shah, who himself had previously regarded their attitude as suspicious. Nur Muhammad Khan, Alizai Mir Afghan, Muhabat Khan, Popalzai, Kado Khan, and Uthmān Khan, the Commander of the Artillery, and several other leading Afghans were the moving spirits of this plot. These men, as they were riding away to their homes from the capital, were intercepted at a township to the north of the City, named Maksud-i-Shah, and they were there put to death.

Some time after his return to his own country, Ahmad Shah summoned Ashraf Sultan Ghilzai (whom Nādir Shah had appointed Chief of the Tokhis), with his son Halim Khan, to the capital. Both of these had accompanied their sovereign on his Indian campaign, but both were nevertheless thrown into prison. Allahyār, the Ghilzai, was enticed from Isfahan, and was also put into confinement on his arrival in Kandahar. All three chiefs perished. Amin Khan, another son of Ashraf, and Rahmat-ullah, son of Allahyār Khan, fled to the Sulemān Khel country to Zurmat and Katawaz. Azam, a third son of Ashraf Sultan, with some young children, eventually escaped to Persia, where Azam was given the government of Khabis and Narmashir. Ahmad Shah made Surkai Khan, Babakarzai, chief of the Tokhi tribe. This chief had two sons, Rahmat Khan and Lashkar Khan. The former accompanied his sovereign on his campaigns, the latter was stationed at Kalat-i-Ghilzai.[2]

On the 24th June 1748, Ahmad Shah put into effect his design for the conquest of Khurassan, which had been under the nominal sway of Shah Rukh Mirza, a grandson of Nādir Shah. Herat was governed by Amir Khan, a chief belonging to an Arab family, and after a siege of four months, as no aid arrived, and a famine raged within the walls, the city was rendered up to the Durani sovereign by the treachery of some of the inhabitants who admitted his men by the Khakistar

[1] The death of the Vazier in the action near Sirhind had been kept secret. The Afghans were unaware of the fact until some time after, and Ahmad Shah was greatly annoyed, as he would not have retired without making further efforts, had he obtained intelligence of the occurrence, while he was in the presence of the Indian troops.

[2] Leech.

Bastion into the city. After settling the affairs of Herat, Ahmad Shah marched against Meshed.

This was evidently a bad year everywhere, the defenders of Meshed were harrassed by famine, and Shah Rukh was glad to agree to the terms of the Abdalis, and to ransom the city for a large sum of money. One of the objects of the expedition was the recovery of Prince Timur (the eldest son of Ahmad Shah), who had been born in Meshed, and was there when his father retired to Kandahar on the murder of Nādir Shah.

The Durani Sovereign directed his steps to Nishapur from Meshed. The ruler of Nishapur, Abbas Kuli Khan, found himself unprepared to make a successful resistance, and he was advised to protract the negotiations until the winter (which was at hand) should have set in. Abbas Kuli kept the Afghans waiting before the walls for two months, until the cold had attained to a very considerable degree of severity and the blizzards also to their full strength. Ahmad Shah, having at last discovered that he was being deceived, broke up his camp and withdrew his troops from Nishapur, and hastened to get back to Herat. It so happened that both the cold and the blizzards were more severe than usual, and had set in early; and men say, that during the night in which Ahmad Shah's troops were encamped on the plains near Kāfir Kala, human beings and animals, owing to the cold, lost the power of movement. Those individuals who were able to do so, cut open the bellies of their camels which they killed, and having removed the intestines, found a refuge from the cold inside the bleeding cavity. Others who desired to take refuge in villages in the vicinity of the camp, and who attempted to cross the River of Herat to reach shelter, were frozen to death in the water. In short, 800 soldiers in the army died from the effects of cold. The guns had to be left behind, owing to the loss of horses, and Ahmad Shah and his army entered Herat in a miserable plight.

He remained some time in Herat, but at last having placed his eldest son Prince Timur in charge of the City, he went on to Kandahar. Next year the Abdali Sovereign again took the western road intending to capture Nishapur. As, however, he possessed no siege guns, or was unable to transport them so far, when he reached that place and found himself paralysed for want of heavy ordnance, he resolved to cast a gun of great calibre on the spot, which, when made, by a single discharge, terrified the inhabitants into surrendering.

A part of the Turks of the Bayāt tribe, who inhabit the Nishapur district, were taken into service by Ahmad Shah, and they with their families settled about Kabul and Ghazni, where their descendants still are to be found. Abbas Kuli was re-appointed governor, and the Durani sovereign marched on Meshed.

After the death of Nādir Shah, his nephew had made himself King and transferred the vast treasures that had been collected in Kalat-i-Nādiri to Meshed. After a short time, he was deposed by his own brother who, in his turn, was handed over to Shah Rukh (the grandson of Nādir and the son of the unfortunate Prince Reza Kuli), whom some of his grandfather's nobles had placed on the throne in Meshed. Alam Khan, an Arab chief of Kain, seized Meshed and the person of the Prince, whose sight he destroyed. Ahmad Shah, the Abdali, recovered Meshed, 10th March 1750, took Kain and put Alam Khan to death, and placed Shah Rukh on the throne again, promising to aid him whenever necessary. The districts of Jam, Bakharz, Turbat, Khaf and Turshiz were attached to the kingdom of Afghanistan. Seistan also became a part of that kingdom, and with Bam in Eastern Persia as an outpost, the influence of the Abdali was felt at Kirman.[1]

While the Durani Monarch was absent in the West, a force of Afghans appear to have raided the Punjab (1748) and to have got as far as Lahore. But four years later he again in person took the field and proceeded to Lahore ; and in the neighbourhood of that city he defeated the Governor Muin-ul-Mulk, on the 5th April 1752. The Rajah Kauri Mal, a Khattri, and the Governor's right hand man, was killed on this occasion, and the latter was made prisoner but afterwards released. It was then that the sub-divisions of Sialkot, Gujrat, Aurangabad, and Pursaror[2] were annexed to the Kingdom of Afghanistan. On this occasion the Afghans did not advance beyond Lahore, and only the Shah's envoys were despatched to Delhi, where they were kept waiting for an audience, while preparations were being made for the Emperor to lead in person an army towards Lahore.

---

[1] The chronology of Ahmad Shah's Western campaigns is very confusing. The events to which it relates at and round Meshed, during the life-time of Nādir Shah's grandson, Shah Rukh, had little effect beyond a comparatively short radius of that city. Nor were these conquests of the Durani Sovereign at all of a permanent nature. The successors of the latter continued to exercise a nominal suzerainty over the districts annexed by him, but these were gradually absorbed in to the Persian Empire, as the fortunes of the Sadozais waned, and as the Kajar Dynasty in Persia rose to power. The conflict of dates given by various authors of the events of Ahmad Shah's Western campaigns is, therefore, of not very great importance from a practical point of view ; and there is no need to do more in this place than to draw attention to the fact that the dates given in the foregoing paragraphs are in no way to be regarded as being conclusive.

[2] The revenue from these districts ha always been set apart towards defraying the cost of the Administration of the Kabul Province by the Indian Government of the Moghul Emperors.

Ahmad Shah was gradually tightening his hold over the country of Sind and also of Baluchistan (Kalat). With regard to the latter he seems to have assumed that the allegiance paid by the Khans of that State to Nādir Shah had descended to him after the death of that famous sovereign. In November 1753, the news spread abroad in Sind that Ahmad Shah was about to enter Hindustan by way of that country, and the 17th of January saw the Afghan camp pitched at the town of Rohri on the banks of the Indus. On this occasion he did not proceed further than Multan. In the meantime Muin-ul-Mulk had died near Lahore on the 8th November of the preceding year, and from his camp at Multan, the Abdali Sovereign issued a Commission to the infant son of the late Governor conferring on him the Government held by his father. The stay of the Afghan army in Multan could not have been for any length of time, for the news of this Commission having been issued reached Delhi on the 11th February and the Durani forces reached Kandahar on the 29th of March 1754.

For two years Ahmad Shah does not appear to have undertaken any warlike operations, and he was probably engaged in consolidating his authority in his native land. Oriental chroniclers very rarely condescend to record any but high political matters, expeditions, and the coming and going of armies and of ambassadors. Domestic affairs of a peaceful nature usually do not interest these writers.

Affairs in Hindustan had in this time been going from bad to worse. The House of Timur was degenerating fast, and the Emperor of the day was powerless to arrest the development of the intrigues that divided the Muhammadan Nobility, led by the Vazier, and the Viceroy of Oude, into different parties, whose quarrels ended in encounters between their partisans. The roads leading to the north from Central India and the Deccan, were also becoming yearly more infested with squadrons of southern horsemen drawn northwards by the lust for plunder, and on the alert to profit by the general disorganization that prevailed in Northern India. Ever ready to sell their services to whosoever paid them most, it did not matter to the Mahrattas who it was that won, or who lost, for the substantial fruits of success were gathered in by the wily leaders of these free lances. In addition, there was the satisfaction of revenging the insults suffered by them in the past at the hands of the sovereigns of Delhi and the nobles of Hindustan.

In the midst of this wild turmoil, the effeminate descendants of Baber vegetated in the recesses of the great Fortress Palace in Delhi, where a semblance of regal state barely could be maintained; and that under the tutelage of some powerful noble who acted as Vazier. Within the apartments of the Royal Harem there were pale, shadowy, womanish things, bearing the form of men, from whom a puppet could always be selected to serve the ends of the predominating faction.

Notwithstanding the inroad of Nādir Shah, there were still some pickings to reward the diligent efforts of those who gleaned the remains of the harvest reaped by that illustrious freebooter. The prospect of a winter campaign in India filled with joy the hearts of the needy Afghan tribesmen. Enough still remained to fill their saddle bags and their religious fanaticism was glutted with the pillage and massacre of Hindus. 'A man may count as his own, that which he has eaten, everything else is Ahmad Shah's' was a proverb long current in the Punjab. The massacres at Ballamgarh and again at Muttra (28th February 1757), gave the Sovereign the title of Ghazi, and his men the means of satiating their cupidity and lust.[1]

The stay of the Abdali monarch was cut short by an outbreak of cholera. His unruly followers also were impatient to be off with their booty to the temperate climate of their native land, and on the 27th March he began his retirement from Delhi. Prince Timur his eldest son, who had been married to a Princess of the Royal House of Delhi, was left to govern the Punjab. The Popalzai Chief, Jahān Khan, was deputed to remain with the Prince, to aid him in the task of administering the Province, and if the necessity arose in warlike operations as well.

---

[1] An eye witness has left on record a terrible tale of these atrocities. To every man a damsel or two, and the night made dreadful with the lamentations of the wretched captives who were compelled to submit to their captor's desires. Corpses festering in the sun of the early Indian summer poisoned the air, and myriads of flies combined to make existence in the camp well nigh intolerable. The river Jumna that passed by the town of Muttra was reddened with the blood of the victims of the butchery that had made the place a shambles. Seven days afterwards the waters of the river still were stained yellow, the deeper hue of the polluted river having by that time faded. One lakh of rupees, about £10,000 was all that reached the Sovereign's Military Chest.

Not only did the Hindus feel the rigors of the Afghan methods. The same author has left on record an equally graphic account of the methodical and thorough manner in which the Palaces in Delhi of the nobility were searched for treasure, by the Nasaqchis (military police) of the Abdali Monarch. The son of the late Vazier Kamar-ud-din Khan (killed in action) had bid £2,000,000 for the office of Vazier to the puppet monarch of Delhi, and had hoped to have been allowed time to collect the money. The Afghan Sovereign however wished it paid down on the spot, and when it was not forthcoming, orders were issued to make a thorough search for the buried hoards reputed at £20,000,000 left by the late Vazier. Only about a quarter of a million rewarded the zeal of the search parties. Not only did they search this Palace, but the residences of other nobles were entered and ransacked. The city of Delhi echoed with cries of "bring gold! bring gold!" and an exceeding great fear fell upon the inhabitants.—Indian Antiquary; January—March 1907.—W. Irvine.

CHAPTER IX.

AHMAD SHAH ABDALI—*continued.*

PRINCE Timur had not an easy task assigned to him when he was appointed to govern the Punjab after his father had set out for his own country. The inroad of the preceding winter had reduced the affairs of India to a condition of the most complete disorganisation. In the Punjab itself the Sikhs had revolted, and the Prince and Jahān Khan had their hands full with these turbulent sectaries, when a discontented local Muhammadan chief invited the Mahrattas to enter the Province. The latter had been hovering round the capital of Hindustan, on the watch to take advantage of any chances that might offer, and they were not slow to avail themselves of this invitation. The Sikhs either expelled or killed most of the Afghan officials in charge of outlying districts, and the Afghan Governor of Sirhind, who had hitherto held his own against the Sikhs, was slain by the Mahrattas on their advance towards Lahore. The Prince and Jahān Khan, unable to hold the Province with any prospect of success, in the month of March 1758, took the road towards Peshawar, and were pursued as far as the Jhelum River by the Mahratta Cavalry. The whole of the Punjab as far as the Indus was overrun by the latter.

In 1759, Jahān Khan Popalzai entered the Punjab and advanced unopposed to Wazirabad; the Mahratta leader, Sahibji Patel, falling back first to Batāla, and then continuing his retreat to Jullundur. The Vazier who had identified himself with the Jats and the Mahrattas, was called on to take the field with them, and declare himself openly. In Lahore the prayers were read in the name of Prince Timur and money was also coined in the name of the Prince.

While order had been restored to some extent in the Punjab, Hindustan was in a condition of anarchy, Mulhar Rao Holkar was at the head of a large force near Jeypore, where Raja Madhu Singh kept him engaged. In Delhi an attempt had been made to remove the

Royal Family to Agra, but the disorders culminated in the assassination of the puppet Emperor Alamgir II. This imbecile Ruler had been induced to place himself in the power of his faithless Vazier, Imād-ul-Mulk, and at the instigation of the latter, a Moghal Rasaldar, Bālābāsh Khan, murdered the wretched Sovereign, and his corpse, stripped of all its cheap finery, was cast naked on the sands of the Jumna. This event took place on November 28th, 1759. Another member of the Royal Family named Muhi-ul-Millat was raised to the throne under the title of Shahjahan II.

In the meantime the Durani Sovereign had other matters to attend to. It is believed that in the summer of 1758 he was obliged to march into Baluchistan, where his feudatory, Nasir Khan of Kalat, is known to have become restive under the ever increasing demands for tribute which he paid in return for the government of his country, and personal service at the head of the armed forces of the tribesmen. According to a local chronicle the small fortress of Kalat detained the Shah for forty days, and then only the diplomacy of Shah Wali Khan induced the refractory Khan to submit to his suzerain.

It was not till the end of 1759 that Ahmad Shah was able to enter the Punjab in response to an appeal made by Najib-ud-Daulah, the Rohilla chief, to defend Islam from the assaults of the Hindu infidels, who were in great force and threatened to over-power the followers of the Prophet. In November the Durani Sovereign invaded Jammu and received the submission of the Rajah. As the country along the direct route from Lahore to Delhi had been ravaged by the Mahrattas, Ahmad Shah marched to the Jumna by Ludhiana keeping towards the hills, and crossed into the district between that river and the Ganges, after a skirmish with the Mahrattas on 9th January 1760. The Rohillas held this tract. Supplies were forthcoming, and having been joined by the Bangash Nawāb of Farukhābād, the Afghan Sovereign took the offensive and sent forward a force of cavalry to locate the enemy, whom they found near Sirhind. A running fight was kept up to within a short distance of Delhi, where the Mahrattas concentrated their forces, and Ahmad Shah with his main army having crossed the Jumna, also joined his advance guard. A battle was fought in February 1760, the Mahrattas were put to flight, their leader Dataji Sindhia was killed, and the Afghans pursued the fugitives as far as Narnol to the south of Delhi. In the meantime Holkar, who was at the head of a considerable force of southern horsemen, tried to intercept a large convoy of supplies and treasure from Afghanistan destined for the army of Ahmad Shah. The greater part of the convoy escaped across the Jumna, and Ahmad Shah despatched

15,000 horse to deal with Holkar. These troops are said to have traversed the distance between Narnol and Delhi in a day and a night,[1] rested the next day in the city and riding out again at midnight, they surprised Holkar's camp at Sikandra. The Mahratta chieftain, with 300 companions fled away on barebacked horses, leaving the remainder of his men to take care of themselves. His camp fell into the hands of the Afghans. Ahmad Shah returned to Delhi. The country in the vicinity of that city had been devastated, and the monsoon was setting in, so he decided to cross the Jumna, and form a cantonment for his troops between that river and the Ganges. At Anupshahr, about thirty miles from Delhi, he passed the season of the rains. In July 1760, Shujā-ud-Daulah, Viceroy of Oude, arrived in the Afghan Camp.

Jankoji, nephew of Data, had carried to Poona the news of the defeat of the Mahrattas, and great preparations were made to collect an army and to equip it for service against the Afghans. Every effort possible was made to insure success. The Mahratta regular cavalry was stiffened by the presence of nine battalions of Indian infantry each 1,000 strong, armed with flintlock muskets and provided with a train of artillery, the whole disciplined and instructed on the European system. These were led by Ibrahim Khan, Gāradi, an Indian soldier of fortune, who is believed to have been trained under French officers and to have risen in the French service from an ordinary messenger or mace-bearer, to be the commander of their Sepoy battalions, with which he is said to have deserted to the Mahrattas. A cloud of irregular horsemen, Pindaris, also joined the main army which had collected round the Bhagwa Jhanda, or national standard, and which was set in motion to the north to restore the prestige of the nation, and to assert their claim to the sovereignty of India.

A junction with Holkar at Muttra was effected without opposition and as the Jumna was impassable (owing to the heavy and long continued rains), the Mahrattas turned aside to Delhi and entered the city on the 22nd July 1760. Yakub Ali, Bāmizai, a kinsman of Ahmad Shah's Vazier [2], held the fortress palace with a small garrison, and inside the walls were the families of the Durani Chiefs. An attempt to escalade the Asad Burj failed, but Ibrahim Khan placed three guns in position and shelled the Palace. The Afghan Governor surrendered, and was allowed to depart with his troops and the families in his care, and

---

[1] About 75 miles by road.

[2] Nawāb, Mohsin ul-Mulk, Yakub Ali Khan, was the descendant of a Bāmizai, who had settled in Shahjahanpur, Rohilkand, some generations earlier. Yakub Ali had been sent by Najib-ud-Daulah on a mission to Ahmad Shah and the Vazier Shah Wali had recognized his Indian kinsman's relationship.

on the 3rd of August he crossed the river, and joined his Master at Anupshahr. The Mahrattas stripped the Palaces of the remains of their ancient splendour and obtained, it is said, 17 lakhs of rupees (£ 170,000). Soon after they were compelled to evacuate the city, for they had exhausted the supplies round the walls. On the 10th October 1760 they marched out of Delhi.

Two Afghan officers held the fort of Kunjpurah on the right bank of the Jumna above Delhi, keeping open communications with the Punjab. Ahmad Shah moved to the aid of his outpost, but though the rains had ceased, the river was impassable, and the Mahrattas who had reached Kunjpurah, reduced the fort by means of Ibrahim Khan's artillery, unmolested by the Afghan main army. The ruler of Oude advised Ahmad Shah to try the ford at Bāgpat, lower down the river, and about 20 miles north of Delhi, and on the 28th October the Duranis reached the ford. It was even then barely practicable, but Ahmad Shah determined to make the attempt: the leading division of his guards showed the way. Some waded and others swam their horses across, and each horseman carried a foot soldier behind him. No one was drowned, but as the crossing was effected under the fire of the Mahratta videttes, a good many were killed before the opposite bank was gained.

The Mahrattas who were marching towards Sirhind were astonished to learn that the Afghans had crossed the river. Divided counsels prevailed in their host. Holkar and other influential chiefs advised the usual tactics of their nation, and stood out for the predatory system of carrying on hostilities. Ibrahim Khan was all for taking up a position and fortifying it with field works on which his guns could be mounted. The predilections of Sada Sheo Bhao, who had witnessed the successes of infantry in the French wars in Southern India, favoured this plan and it was decided to adopt it. The army retraced its march to Pasinah to the south of the town of Panipat, and finally fell back to that place, and raised strong fieldworks to protect their camp, and also placed the town in a defensible condition. The nature of their entrenchments can be judged from the fact that as recently as 1872, the late Sir Denzil (then Mr.) Ibbetson was able to trace a part of the works in the plain to the south of Panipat.[1]

The baggage of the Afghan army and the artillery was carried over by elephants, and after halting his troops to allow them to dry

[1] Mr. Ibbetson's Settlement Report of the Karnal district.

Another account says that 25,000 Mahratta cavalry had occupied Sarai Sambālka and were driven out by the Afghans.

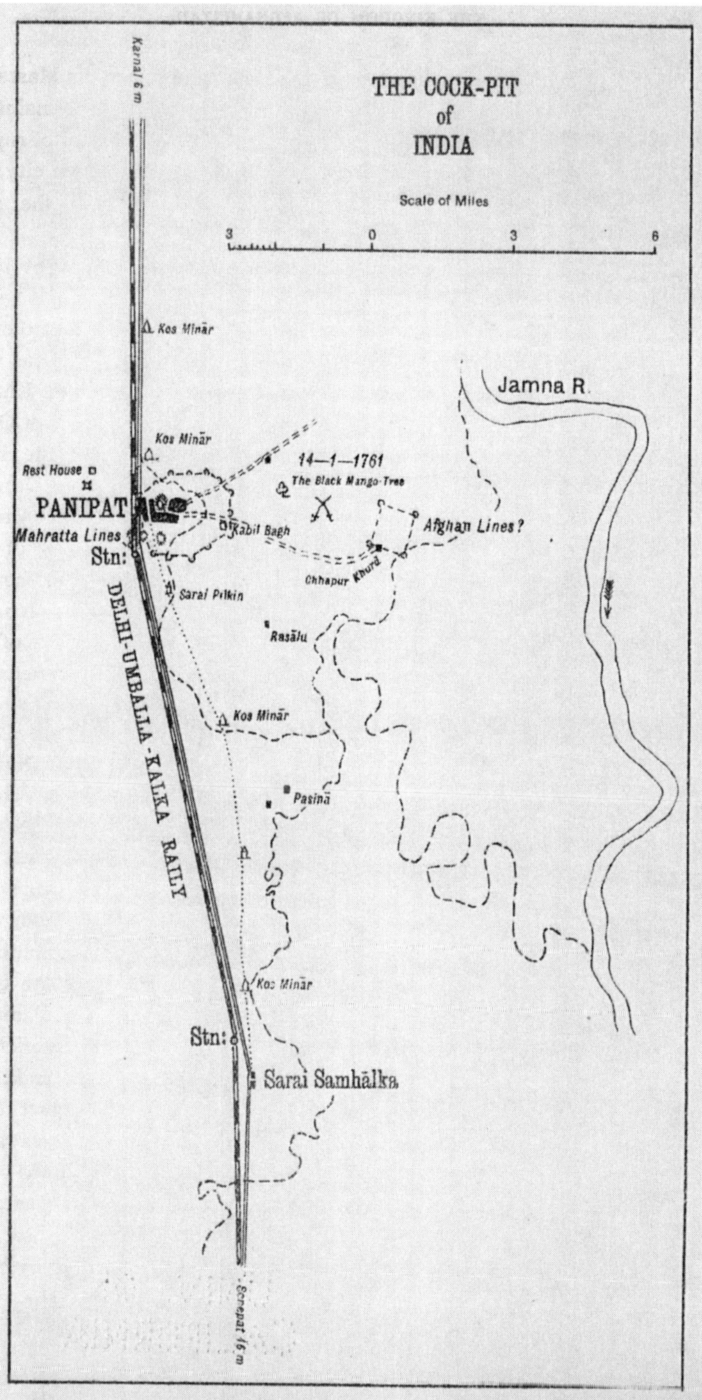

THE COCK-PIT
of
INDIA
Scale of Miles
3
0
3
6
Karnal 6 m
Kos Minār
Jamna R.
Kos Minār
14—1—1761
Rest House
The Black Mango-Tree
PANIPAT
Kabil Bagh
Afghan Lines?
Mahratta Lines
Stn:
Chhapur Khurd
Sarai Pilkin
DELHI-UMBALLA-KALKA RAILY
Rasālu
Kos Minār
Pasinā
Kos Minār
Stn:
Sarai Samhālka
Sonepat 16 m

their accoutrements, Ahmad Shah advanced, on the 1st of November, by Sonepat to Sarai Samhālka, and took up a position beyond this place.

For two months the armies faced one another. The Mahrattas are said to have established a *Runkham*, a place where single combats took place,and in these encounters the individual skill of the Mahrattas as adroit men at arms enabled them to kill their Afghan antagonists who accepted their challenges. The videttes and scouting parties of both armies were also in daily contact, but the balance of success [1] in these encounters lay on the side of the Afghans ; and their good fortune reduced the enemy to great straits for supplies. The ford at Bāgpat allowed Ahmad Shah to draw his from the Antarbed, the country between the Jumna and Ganges, where his staunch ally Najib-ud Daulah was predominant. A partial but fierce engagement on the 6th December terminated in favour of the Afghans.

Gobind Punt Boondela, a Mahratta official, who was in charge of the Etawah district, attempted to make a diversion in favour of his countrymen by advancing on Meerut, the head-quarters of Najib-ud-Daulah, in order to lay waste the country round it. Five thousand horsemen were detailed by Ahmad Shah to stop the Pandit, led by the son of Abdus Samad Khan, who had been killed at Kunjpurah. He crossed the Jumna at Bāgpat, drove the Mahrattas from Shahdara, and from Ghazi-ud-din-nagar (the modern Ghaziabad), and on the same day that this action had been fought (18th December), the Afghans fell on Gobind Punt in his camp at Jalālābād. He was killed and his men dispersed. With the head of the Mahratta leader raised aloft on a spear, and with the plunder of his camp in their train, the Afghans rejoined their main army.

A detachment of Mahratta cavalry, each man carrying a bag of treasure, mistook the Afghan camp for their own, and were cut off before they found out their mistake. The successes of the Afghans had reduced the Mahrattas to great straits, for the former used to ride abroad without fear, cutting off foraging parties and stragglers, while the latter cowered behind their massive field works. The negotiations which they had commenced, soon after leaving the Deccan, in order to detach the Ruler of Oude and the Rohillas, from the Afghans, proved ineffectual. These parties were not indisposed to listen to the

[1] Fath Khan, brother of Ibrahim Khan Gāradi, is said to have been repulsed in a night attack on the Afghan lines.

An attack on the Mahratta camp was ultimately repulsed with a loss of 3,000 men—only 500 of the Rohillas, under Inayat Khan (the nephew of Hafiz-ul-Mulk Rahmat Khan), who had formed the attack, returned to their lines, wounded.

6

overtures made to them, for they had the Mahrattas ever at their doors. Najib-ud-Daulah was obdurate, and declined to listen to any proposals, and as long as he proved resolute, the others were ashamed to withdraw from their Afghan alliance. [1]

Driven to despair by imminent starvation and the unsanitary condition of their camp, the Mahrattas resolved to risk a decisive battle. Long before dawn their troops had fallen in, and a last message was sent to the agent, through whom the negotiations had been conducted, and who was in the camp of the Ruler of Oude—Kāsi Rao Pandit, who has left a graphic record of the decisive battle he witnessed. This letter was received at 3 a.m., and immediately the information was conveyed to Ahmad Shah. In the gray light of the dawn of the 14th January 1761, the scouts of both armies had come into touch, and the Durani mounted one of the chargers always ready saddled, and proceeded to draw up his line of battle in advance of his camp,[2] where a tent had always stood as his station of observation.

The Mahrattas advanced slowly, and their guns began to play as they came within range of the enemy. The discharges of firearms gradually became heavier, and the Gāradi (Ibrahim Khan), rode up to the Bhao and saluting him, told him he would now see that the regular infantry had deserved their pay, on the prompt discharge of which he had always insisted. Galloping back to his division, he ordered his men and guns to cease firing. Two battalions were detailed to protect the flank of his column from attack by the Durani horsemen of Barkhurdār Khan and Amir Beg, and with a colour in his hand he led the other seven battalions of infantry to attack the Rohillas, under Hafiz Rahmat Khan and Dhundi Khan, with the bayonet. The Rohillas were crushed after a desperate struggle, and the advance of the Durani cavalry were repulsed by the steady behaviour of the two battalions detailed for this purpose, but six of Ibrahim Khan's regiments were almost annihilated and he was severely wounded by several spear thrusts.[3]

---

[1] It is said that Ahmad Shah was approached regarding an arrangement but he refused to entertain any proposals. He had come to make war on the infidels, and he was bent on fighting. Asiatic Researches, Vol. I., 1799.

[2] According to another account, this position had been occupied by the Afghan guns, and during the day by the various divisions which were however withdrawn at night, leaving the artillery men and an escort with the guns. These were almost taken by surprise by the Mahrattas in the misty light of the early dawn. There was just time to strip off the canvas covers and to fire the loaded pieces.

[3] Damaji Gaekwar's horsemen were to support the infantry attack, but the brunt of the combat was borne by the infantry.

All the troops were engaged, and the Mahrattas under the personal leadership of the Bhao and Wiswas Rao, were almost successful. Ten thousand Afghans were driven before their onset, for the Afghans received the charge at the halt. The Persian musketers were ridden down, and it was the personal intrepidity of the Vazier Shah Wali Khan which snatched the victory from the enemy. Sheathed in full armour he dismounted from his horse to rally the broken Afghans, and at the head of his clansmen, the Popalzais, and the Baluch contingent, he showed a front, while messengers were despatched to Ahmad Shah demanding reinforcements. The latter sent 1,500 of his guards to clear the camp of fugitives with orders to slay all who refused to return to the field. Ten thousand of his guards (apparently fresh troops) were led at a gallop against the Mahrattas, while their efforts were seconded by the stout Rohilla Chieftain Najib-ud-Daulah, and by the men of Shah Pasand Khan and Amir Khan. It was noon when Ahmad Shah received intelligence of the state of affairs in his centre, and about one, the succours reached the Vazier. About 3 p.m. Wiswas Rao was wounded and unhorsed and had to be lifted on his elephant. The battle was stubbornly contested, but the Mahrattas had shot their bolt and were spent with their exertions. All of a sudden "as if by enchantment" the Mahrattas turned their backs and fled at headlong speed. The instant they broke the victors pursued them with the utmost fury. The final effort had been made at close quarters with sabres and battle axes, and the carnage was said to have been dreadful, as no quarter was given when the Mahrattas broke. The pursuit was kept up for a distance of about twenty miles, it is said. There remained the standing camp of the enemy to be plundered, and the town of Panipat which was crowded with fugitives and followers. The prisoners were arranged in lines, and a little parched grain and some water was given to each one, and then the task of butchery commenced, and was carried out in cold blood. In the Durani Camp every tent (with the exception of those of the Shāh and his principal officers), had piles of heads before the entrance. There were said to have been 500,000 souls in the Mahratta Camp, and only a fourth of their fighting men escaped. The inhabitants of the country rose against the fugitives and killed all whom they caught. Antaji Mankeser, a chieftain of high rank, was killed by the zamindars of Farukhnagar. Jankoji Sindia was made prisoner and put to death. The Ruler of Oude tried his best to save the gallant Ibrahim Khan, whom his people had captured, but Ahmad Shah demanded his surrender, and he was executed in the presence of the Afghan Monarch.[1] Damaji Gaekwār and Holkar escaped with one or two other chiefs. One of the wives of Sada Sheo escaped on horseback to Deeg where she found an asylum with Raja Suraj Mal, the Jat, who sent her on afterwards to the Deccan by way of Jhansi. The body of Wiswas Rao was found, and with the greatest difficulty it was rescued from the soldiers who wished to stuff it and carry it back to Kabul as a trophy. Owing to the strenuous efforts of the Hindustani chiefs it was cremated in due form. A headless trunk was discovered about twenty miles from the battle-field and was said to be the corpse of the Bhao.[2]

The author of the Seir-i-Mutakherin states that 20,000 women and youths, the majority of whom belonged to families of Sardars and men of note in the Deccan, were taken alive and distributed among the Afghan chiefs. The descendants of the captives, which fell to the share of the Khan of Hoti near Peshawar, it is said, are still easily recognis-able owing to their complexion and physique, which at this day differ from the Afghans of that place.

This disaster put an end to the dreams of supremacy cherished by the Mahrattas. It was long remembered in the south, for there was probably not a household in the Mahratta country that did not have to mourn the death or captivity of some member, on the field of Panipat. A Kasid (or express messenger) engaged by a firm of Hindu financiers, under covenant to reach Aurangabad (in the Deccan) in 9 days from Panipat, gave the news of the terrible misfortune that had befallen the nation, to the Peshwa, whom he met on the banks of the Nerbudda. The reports of the unfavourable course of events preceding the final disaster had led to the assembly of reinforcements which Balajee Rao was leading towards the north. He returned to Poona and died not long afterwards.

At Panipat, a ballad composed by a local poet, shortly after the battle, preserves the memory of the triumph of Islam over the Mahrattas, and the people point out the field, in which the Bhao took post, near a solitary mango tree, known as the "black mango tree."

[1] Ahmad Shah was very anxious to take Ibrahim Khan and his trained battalions and artillery into his service, doubtless in order to make him independent of his fickle subjects to a great extent, but the Gāradi had steadfastly refused to desert the Mahrattas in spite of repeated invitations to join the Durāni monarch.

[2] His fate was never accurately known. A few years afterwards a man who claimed to be the Bhao appeared in Benares, and was recognised by persons who had known the Bhao (by marks on his body), and who ought to have been able to identify the claimant. Others refused to credit the story put forth by the latter. Among them were bankers with whom the Bhao had deposited large sums of money. They refused to pay any to the claimant, who ended his days in poverty, but he never swerved from his story.

The tree has succumbed to the ravages of time, but the plot in which it stood is still called the field of the black mango.

After the battle, Ahmad Shah advanced towards Delhi which he reached in four marches. Whatever designs he may have entertained regarding the seizure of the Empire of Hindustan, were frustrated by a serious mutiny of the Duranis, who demanded an instant settlement of arrears of allowances for two years, and a rapid movement back to their own country. They refused to be mollified, and the camp was the scene of the utmost confusion. At last matters came to such a pass that the Ruler of Oude withdrew to his own territory. Ahmad Shah being unable to control his men any longer, and having received forty lakhs of rupees (£400,000) from Najib-ud-Daulah as the price of his assistance, broke up his camp at Shālimār on the 22nd of March 1761, and commenced his homeward journey.

No sooner had the Afghan army withdrawn than the Sikhs became troublesome. Among those chiefs who had built forts, was Charrat Sing, grandfather of Ranjit Singh, who had established a stronghold in his wife's village of Gujranwālā to the north of Lahore. The Afghan Governor, or his deputy Khwaja Obeid, went to attack and reduce this place. The Sikhs assembled their forces to relieve it and the Afghan was beaten off. He was compelled to abandon his baggage and fly to Lahore where he shut himself up in the fort. The Afghan Governor of Sirhind held his ground, with the aid of an active Indian Afghan Chief, Hinghan Khan, of the ancient family of Maler Kotla, and owing to the loyalty of the Sikh Chief of Jindiāla who adhered to Ahmad Shah. The "army of the Khalsa" assembled at Amritsar, the faithful performed their ablutions in the restored sacred tank, and perhaps the first "Gurumutta," or diet, or conclave, was held on this occasion. The possessions of Hinghan Khan were laid waste, and Jindiāla was invested preparatory to more ambitious attempts by the exultant Sikhs.

In the end of 1761, Ahmad Shah entered the Punjab and relieved Lahore. Marching southwards to Sirhind he inflicted a crushing defeat on the Sikhs (5th February 1762), at a place twenty miles to the south of Ludhiana. He did not advance further than Sirhind. The bigotry of the Afghans was satisfied by the destruction of the renewed temples in Amritsar, and the pollution of the Sacred Tank. A Hindu, Kabuli Mal, was appointed by Ahmad Shah as Governor of Lahore on his return to the city on the 4th March, and the Durani hastened back to Kandahar where a disturbance had broken out. The Sikhs under Jussa, the distiller, in a very short time again asserted their predominance in the Punjab (1762-63). In 1767 Ahmad Shah entered the Punjab for the last time. He avoided Lahore and only advanced as far as Amballa. He made over the Government of Sirhind to Amar Sing, the Chief of Patiala. The latter was so famed for his loyalty and devotion to the Afghan Sovereign, and the Vazier, that he had been nicknamed Amar Sing, the Bāmizai.

But Ahmad Shah had not been idle. He had conducted a campaign against the Amir of Bokhara, and wrested from the Uzbeg that precious relic, the cloak, or vestment, of the Prophet Muhammad. The Oxus was fixed as the boundary between the two States. The sacred garment was borne in triumph through Afghanistan and lodged in a shrine in Kandahar (1765).

In addition to his other conquests, Kashmir was annexed by Ahmad Shah, and remained for about fifty years a province of the kingdom. The Khatri Sikh, Jiwan Sing, originally an accountant in the office of the Vazier Shah Wali Khan, had been appointed to the charge of the revenue administration of Kashmir, when (in 1753-4), the last Governor on behalf of the Emperor of Delhi was expelled from the valley by Afghan troops under Abdullah Khan. A few years later Jiwan Sing turned out the Afghans and had obtained a Commission from the Emperor Alamgir II as Governor, and had coined money in the name of the Emperor. The first expedition against Jiwan Sing despatched by Ahmad Shah failed owing to the treachery of the Raja of Jammu, but in 1762 the Raja had been attached to the Afghan interests by the good offices of the Vazier and now he assisted an army under Nur-ud-din Khan which penetrated into the Valley. After some resistance Jiwan Sing[1] was defeated and captured and Kashmir attached to the Durani kingdom. This outlying province, however, proved a source of weakness, and the successors of Ahmad Shah were for ever occupied in putting down the revolts of ambitious Governors, who planned the conversion of their charge into an independent principality.

It is said that after Ahmad Shah returned from India crowned with the laurels won on the battlefield of Panipat, he set himself to build a capital. The city of Nadirabad had become overcrowded and was unhealthy, and he set to work to select a better site for the city he intended to build. His first selection was objected to by the descendants of Abdul Ghani Khan, the Alakozai, for the tribesmen declined to part with any land. The next site chosen by Ahmad Shah lay to the

[1] He was a benevolent and wise ruler, and deserved a better fate. He is said to have been a patron of learning and in his brief reign there was a revival of literature—Seir-i-Mutakherin.

west of the village of Mard Kala. The Barakzais to whom the district belonged also refused to give up land for the city. The Popalzais, however, came to the rescue of their Sovereign, and gave him land for the object in view.

About nine hundred acres of land were taken up and the present city of Kandahar was laid out. The services of Indian and Persian Engineers were utilized in raising the buildings and defences, the great dome which covers the intersection of the four principal thoroughfares—called the Chahar Su, in particular, was the work of an Indian architect. It is said to be 50 yards in diameter. The land round the city was divided into twelve thousand allotments and the revenue was assessed. The settlement made by Ahmad Shah remained in force till the time of the Barakzai Sardars who acquired Kandahar.

It was not only the insubordinate character of his subjects which interfered with Ahmad Shah's plans with regard to his foreign policy. His health failed. He appears to have become a victim to cancer, and his face is said to have been covered with this growth. The elevated tract of the Toba plateau was used by him as a summer resort, and he succumbed to his malady on the night of the 19th October 1772, on his return journey to Kandahar, at Margha Chaman; close to the outpost of Chaman garrisoned by our troops at the present day. He was buried in a garden inside the city and a mausoleum was built over his tomb.

Like many oriental monarchs, Ahmad Shah dabbled in literature and left behind a collection of verses, which, however, are said to be of no especial merit. His task of government was one of great difficulty, as the Afghans have always been averse from the exercise of the Royal Prerogative, and his assumption of the sovereignty was not altogether relished by them. Filibustering expeditions in foreign lands, brilliant victories, and great spoils, however, reconciled his democratic subjects to the new order of things in their country, and the tact and firmness he displayed in his dealing with the Chiefs of the tribes; and the advantages, the Duranis especially obtained, enabled Ahmad Shah to assert his authority over his stiffnecked subjects, and to bequeath a goodly heritage to his successors.

NOTE.

The Mint-Towns of Ahmad Shah, Durani, were :—Multan, Lahore, Meshed, Sahrind (Sirhind), Peshawar, Dera, Kabul, Ahmad Shāhi (Kandahar), Shah Jahānābād (Delhi), Surat, Najibabad, and Aonla.—Jour. As. Soc. Bengal, Vol. v., No. 8, Nunismàtic Supplement, August 1909.

Jussa struck coin bearing the following inscription :—Sikkah Zad dar Jahan ba Fazl-i-Akat Mulk-az-Ahmad Girift Kallāl. Coin was struck by favour of the Eternal. The country was taken from Ahmad by the Kallāl Majma-ul-Akhbar-Har Sukh Rai Irvine.

CHAPTER X.

TIMUR SHAH—A PERIOD OF CONSOLIDATION.

THE state of Ahmad Shah's health latterly had rendered it impossible for him to take an active share in the business of his kingdom. The Vazier Shah Wali Khan had induced his master to appoint his Heir to govern Herat, and to issue peremptory orders for him to stay there. On the death of the King, the Vazier placed Prince Suleman (his son-in-law) on the throne in Kandahar ; a step which seems to have been regarded by several of the Durani Chiefs with disfavour, and they retired to Herat and joined Prince Timur. The officials and chiefs round this Prince were afraid that the eloquence and diplomacy for which the Vazier was famous, would undermine their own influence with the easy natured Prince, and they made such a good use of their opportunities, that the Prince agreed to put the Vazier to death without according him an interview.

The Prince set out from Herat in order to be present at the Fateha ceremony to be performed at his father's grave. The Vazier in order to allay suspicions had started to meet Prince Timur at the head of a slender escort of his own retainers, and accompanied by two sons and two of his nephews. No sooner had he entered the Prince's camp at Siahāb, one stage to the east of Bakwa and twenty-four miles to the west of Dilārām, on the Kandahar road, than he was arrested and put to death. Prince Timur marched at his ease to Kandahar, where he ascended the throne in 1773, with the concurrence of the Durani Sardars, and assumed the title of Timur Shah.

The execution of the Vazier created ill-feeling, and though the new king confirmed all the chiefs in their dignities and offices they enjoyed, the resentment he had roused was not effaced. After Timur Shah had set out for Kabul, the malcontents set up a rival in the person of Abdul Khalik, also a Sadozai. Further executions in Kabul decided them to proclaim their nominee and to march on

Kabul with the view of establishing him on the throne. The vigorous action of Timur Shah, who took the field at the head of only 6,000 men and the desertion of waverers who abandoned the pretender's cause, resulted in his defeat and capture. His eye-sight was destroyed, so as to render him innocuous in the future.

Among those whom Timur Shah rewarded after this victory, and on his return to Kabul, was Payandah Khan, Barakzai, whom he created Sarfaraz Khan, and in addition appointed to the chieftainship of the clan. His elder brother, who held the chiefship hereditary in this family, was set aside owing to his uncouth manners and coarse language.

Timur Shah was extremely partial to Persians and those of Persian descent, whose deferential courtly manners were a great contrast, to the rough boisterous manners of even the great Durani nobles. From the former he chose his officials and confidants, and with the exception of two or three chiefs, the court of the sovereign was composed of foreigners or persons of foreign origin. Kabul also was made the seat of Government on account of its central position. This city is three hundred and eighteen miles by road from Kandahar, and the change was not calculated to render him popular, nor could he watch the Duranis closely from Kabul. The prestige enjoyed by the latter probably influenced the decision, for it had long been the capital of the Indian territory west of the Indus. The people of Kabul also were better versed in the amenities of civilized existence, and better able to minister to the desires of a pleasure-loving sovereign such as Timur Shah was, than the less civilized population of Kandahar.

It had become necessary, also, to revive or impose taxes on the people of the country which, in the ardour of foreign conquests, had been allowed to remain in abeyance, or which were not considered, to be advisable. Military service in some instances was discontinued and a yearly revenue in money was imposed. Accuracy of some kind was insisted upon; accounts of governors and officials were scrutinized. Opportunities for peculation were curtailed, and dishonest or careless officials were liable to be called to account. It was a period of consolidation, but none of these measures were calculated to increase the popularity of the sovereign in whose reign they were instituted.

Adventures in foreign countries were no longer possible—nor were they likely to prove as profitable as they had been in Ahmad Shah's reign. In Persia the Kajar Dynasty had been founded by the genius of Agha Muhammad Khan, whose attention was fixed on the territory in Khurassan, nominally controlled by the Afghans. In the

Punjab nothing could be got but hard knocks from the Sikhs. The restless disposition of the Afghans could no longer expend its force in filibustering expeditions, and domestic intrigues and quarrels alone afforded scope for its expression. Notwithstanding these unfavourable circumstances, and the estrangement that grew up between the Durani chiefs and their sovereign, the awe which the genius of Ahmad Shah had inspired, still obsessed the minds of the turbulent nobles, and Timur Shah reigned in peace.

Even the Ghilzais were quiet. That Muhammad Amin Khan (son of Ashraf Sultan), who had fled from Ahmad Shah into the Sulemān Khel country, was invited to court by Timur Shah, who reinstated him in the chieftainship of the Tokhi division of the Ghilzai tribes, and also of the Hazaras within the jurisdiction of the governorship of Kalat-i-Ghilzai, which also was bestowed on him. Amin Khan was killed in the expedition afterwards despatched to put down the rebellion of Azad Khan in Kashmir. At the same time Nurullah Khan was created chief of the Hotaki division, with the title of Ikhlās Kuli Khan, and received the revenue from Dera Ismail Khan, Dāman, Bannu and Urghun. On his death, his son Abdur Rahmān succeeded to his father's honours and emoluments. These arrangements kept the Ghilzais quiet.

With Kabul as the capital, the city of Peshawar was an obvious winter resort: it was conveniently situated with respect to the Afghan interests in the Punjab. The surroundings of Peshawar were attractive and suited the temperament of the sovereign. It was at Peshawar that his life and reign were very nearly brought to an abrupt and tragic termination. Faizullah Khan Khalil, one of the principal land holders in that district, conceived the idea of making himself king. He was joined by Asadullah, of the Momands, and they had won over Yakut, Ahmad Shah's chief eunuch. Under the pretext of taking them against the Sikhs, they had obtained permission to raise a body of armed men, and they had secured free access to the citadel wherein was the Shah's Palace. When, therefore, the conspirators, at the head of a band of retainers, appeared before the gates, the unsuspecting warders allowed them to enter. Instead of pushing on at once to the quarters occupied by Timur Shah, who was asleep after his breakfast, the conspirators attacked the guards. Some of the slave girls of the Royal household had time to rouse the king, who took refuge in a small apartment on the south wall, which was reached by a wooden ladder which he drew up after him. The garrison and troops in the vicinity of the citadel hurried to the rescue and a desperate struggle raged in the court yards. Amir Khan, of the Kazilbash tribe Juwān Shir of Kabul, was in prison in the citadel for some irregularity in his accounts, he managed to join the combatants, and loaded with irons as he is said to have been, he took a leading share in the defence of his sovereign, which earned him an unconditional pardon. The emeute was put down with an indiscriminating severity. Faizullah Khan, his son, and the eunuch Yakut were executed at once. Asadullah Khan escaped to Lalpurah, but a great many innocent persons in Peshawar city were put to death in the retaliatory measures set on foot by the enraged king (1778).[1]

In the year previous the Afghan Monarch interfered in the domestic quarrels of the Kalorah family, who still ruled over Sind, but his troops were defeated by Mian Abdun Nabi Kalorah and his commander Mir Bijjar Tālpur, before Shikarpur.

In 1778 the Sardar-i-Sardarān, Madad Khan, the Ishakzai Chief, was despatched to retake Multan, captured by the Sikhs. The rising in Peshawar caused the chief to abandon the attempt, to hurry back to his master's aid.

In 1779 Timur Shah in person took Multān from the Sikhs after operations lasting 40 days. He appointed Nawab Muzaffar Khan as governor of the town and province.

In 1780, Mian Abdun Nabi Kalorah murdered Mir Bijjar, Tālpur, and the Tālpurs expelled the Kalorahs from Sind. The Sardar-i-Sardarān marched to Sind and restored the Kalorah. The Nawab of Bahawalpore adopted a hostile attitude and sheltered the Tālpur Chief in his fort of Dirawar. Mian Abdun Nabi ruled for 6 months. He murdered several of the leading Tālpurs. They took the field and defeated him at Helani-Bhelani (1781). The Kalorah fled to Kabul and the Tālpur Chief was recognised as the Ruler of Sind.

In 1786 the Shah was induced to attempt to reinstate the Kalorah by the large promises made by the latter as to tribute. Sardar Ahmad Khan, Nurzai and Mian Abdun Nabi were defeated at Hala Kandi by the Tālpur Chief Fateh Ali Khan.

In 1788 Timur Shah in person subdued the Nawab of Bahawalpore, and the stronghold of Dirawar in the desert was taken after a siege of three months by Sardar Madad Khan, Ishakzai. The Nawab paid an indemnity and agreed to remit an yearly tribute to Kabul, and the Shah hastened to meet the inroads of the ruler of Bokhara, who

[1] It was discovered that Mian Mahdi a Pirzādā, and son of Shekh Umar, who lived in the village of Chamkanni, was accessory to this attempt on the Shah's life. Orders were given for the destruction of this place. But the Durani nobles objected to such harsh measures and the order was cancelled.

had recovered all the districts ceded to Ahmad Shah on the left bank of the Oxus, and had devastated Merve.[1] After obtaining some minor successes, Timur Shah was forced to be content with a treaty favorable to the Uzbeg, in order to return to Kabul before the passes of the Hindu Kush were closed, as it was he lost many men and horses in crossing the range on the retirement to Kabul.

In 1787 Azad Khan, son of Haji Rahim Dād Khan Bāmizai, on his father's death, turned out his brothers from Kashmir and proclaimed his independence. The rebel chief was successful at first, but was afterwards defeated by Sardar Madad Khan, Ishakzai, and he committed suicide in order to escape an ignominious death.

In the year 1790, Sarfaraz Khan, the Barakzai Chieftain, invaded Sind at the head of an army by way of Dera Ghazi Khan, to reinstate the Kalorah Abdun Nabi. The representatives of the Tālpur Rulers, at the Shah's court, obtained the recall of this expedition, and Sarfaraz Khan retired from Rohri by way of Shikarpur to Kandahar, having done nothing.

Asadullah, the Momand, after leading the life of a brigand for a few years, was betrayed to the Shah by Islam Khan, another Momand Chief; and was trodden to death by an elephant. A similar punishment was meted out to Fath Khan, Chief of the Utman Khel, Yusufzais.[2] He had charge of the road to Kashmir, and of the town of Muzaffarabad on the Jhelum, where it is necessary to cross the river; but he was continually rebelling and had become very troublesome.

As his affairs became more settled, Timur Shah gave himself over to sensuality, and owing to his intemperance, his health broke down. It was necessary at last to remove him from Peshawar to the cooler climate of Kabul. His third son, Prince Zamān, who governed Kabul, met his father at Chaharbagh, about 6 miles west of Jalalabad, and took charge of him. Instead of deriving benefit from the change, his condition grew rapidly worse, and Timur Shah died at Kabul on the 18th of May 1793, aged 47 years, and after a reign of about 20 years.

He left many sons; five of these appear in history, and with these only are we concerned.

---

[1] The famous band or weir was destroyed which ruined the cultivation dependent on it. Bairām Ali, the Kajar Chief, was killed, and his son Muhammad Husen and his Afghan Allies overpowered. The Turkish inhabitants were removed to Bokhara, and in 1790-1 the Sarik and in 1834, the notorious Tekke Turkomans took possession of Merve.

[2] In 1798-99, his son Zafar Khan ruled over the country from Muzafarabad to Hasan Abdal, but he would not visit his sovereign's court, but, though practically independent, he was not actively rebellious.

Emir Masum, of Bokhara, carefully observed his engagements with the Afghans, and Timur Shah reaped no immediate harm from his neglect of the affairs of the districts in the valley of the Oxus. Service in these remote and wild parts of the kingdom had become most unpopular, and was regarded by the Afghan officials as exile; while the profits of office were too small to compensate for the very manifest disadvantages of employment in these remote districts. On receiving news of Timur Shah's demise, the Bokhariot Ruler resumed his attempts on the districts on the left bank of the Oxus.

NOTE.

The destruction, by fire, of the scriptures of the Sikhs, the Adi Granth, at Kartarpur in 1756; their defeat at Barnāla (5th February 1762); the destruction of the Temples and pollution of the Sacred Tank in Amritsar, utterly failed to crush their fanaticism; nor did the appointment of the Patiāla Chief, as governor of Sirhind conciliate them. The Sikhs dogged the retreat of the Afghans, and hardly was Ahmad Shah across the Indus, then the Sukerchukia Confederacy, led by Charat Sing, blockaded Rohtās, aided by a part of the Bhangi Confederacy.

South of the Sutlej the Sikhs were predominant and with the Mahrattas aimed at partitioning the remains of the Moghal Empire in Hindustan. The declining years of Najib-ud-Daulah were disturbed by the inroads of the Sikhs, led across the Jumna by the Bhangi and Krora Singhia Chiefs; and he was compelled to propose an alliance against them, to his ancient enemies, the Mahrattas. Enterprising sections of the various Mists, or Confederacies, each led by an elected Sardār, crossed the Sutlej, and carved out principalities beyond that river.

Rohtās surrendered in 1768 and almost at once the Bhangis seized Rāwalpindi. Under Charat Singh, Gujranwāla from an obscure hamlet became a flourishing town. Ranjit Singh was born there. The Ramgarbia and Kanhaia Confederacies shared the Bāri Doab, and the latter also seized Kangra. After Ahmad Shah's death the Bhangi Mist overran the country up to the Jammu hills, dividing the territory among their leaders. In 1765 Gujar Singh, the Bhangi Chief, had defeated Mukarrab Khan, the Gakhar Chief, and had taken the country up to the Jhelum river. After his death his son Sahib Sing came into collision with Mahān Singh, father of Ranjit Singh, and son of Charat Singh. But in 1798 the Bhangi Chief was forced to recognise the supremacy of the latter.

Timur Shah, Durani, appears to have regarded (very wisely) the Indus as his boundary and refused to involve himself in hostilities with the Sikhs. Endowed with a great deal of political sagacity, Timur Shah recognised (apparently) the futility of attempting to re-conquer the Punjab—a task too difficult even for his father's genius: but to which his ill-fated son, Zamān, was lured by a vain glorious desire to emulate his grandfather's fame as the Champion of Islam; and encouraged to essay it by the dissensions which had broken out among the Sikh Confederacies.

CHAPTER XI.

Shah Zamān—Sikhs and Afghans.

TIMUR SHAH DURANI, at the time of his death, had twenty-one sons alive. Of these the eldest Prince Humayun, and Prince Mahmud, the next in age, were by one mother; and Zamān who had been declared the Heir, and Shuja (afterwards Shuja-ul-Mulk) were by the same mother (a Yusufzai Lady). With the exception of the above and of Prince Firuz-ud-din, who was with Mahmud in Herat, and who is said to have been a full brother of Mahmud; and Abbas, who was in Peshawar as his father's representative; the remainder of the late king's sons had been kept under surveillance in the Bala Hisar.

As soon as the funeral ceremonies of the late king had been concluded, his last testament was put into effect by the nobles and Military and Civil Officers who were in Kabul, who declared Zamān Shah King in accordance with the wishes of the deceased. Prince Abbas and the other Princes, who were opposed to this measure, were seized and despatched to Multan, where their uncles already were in durance.

On the 23rd May 1793, the public prayers were read in the name of Shah Zamān, and coin was struck bearing his superscription, and on the 23rd of May, the actual enthronement of the youthful sovereign (he was twenty-three years of age) took place.

He was at once threatened with serious dangers, and the opening of his reign was a forecast which was only too completely fulfilled. Basālat Khan Alakozai was appointed Governor of Farā Bagh, on the Frontier of the Kandahar Province, over which Prince Humayun ruled. Ahmad Khan Barakzai was deputed to be his master's representative in Peshawar and also to administer the districts of Bangash, Jhang and Attock. The infant son of the king was given the government of Kabul itself.

Prince Humayun had disregarded his father's wishes and had declared himself as Ruler of Afghanistan in Kandahar. Mahmud was quiescent in Herat, but he might be expected to favour his own brother's pretensions and support him. A revolt had taken place among the tribes in Afghan-Turkistan and the district of Balkh, but Muhammad Khan, the governor, was able to deal with this movement, and seven hundred heads despatched to Kabul proved both the efficacy of the repressive measures and the severity with which they were carried out.

On the 19th of June 1793, the advanced guard of the troops destined to operate against Kandahar marched from Kabul, and Shahāb-ud-din Tokhi was appointed to the command of Kalat-i-Ghilzai. Mauladād Khan (Musakhel) Tokhi, who held the place, had declared for Prince Humayun; but he was forced to give up Kalat to Shahāb-ud-din. Zamān Shah, who had followed with his main army, was at Ab-i-Tazi, thirty-six miles distant; and Humayun prepared for war; and as an opening move, he sent his son Sultan Ahmad and his Arzbegi, Shādi Khan, the Achakzai chief, with 8,000 men to recover Kalat. Shahāb-ud-din abandoned it and fell back on Shah Zamān. The latter advanced his brother Shuja and the Barakzai chief, Sarfarāz Khan, who retook Kalat; and at Bagh-i-Babro, about six miles to the east of that place, Humayun was defeated and fled to Baluchistan in company with Shādi Khan. Many influential chiefs had deserted to Shah Zamān, including Mir Hizbar Ali Khan, the Ishakzai Sardar and Rahmatullah Khan, Sadozai.[1]

The former was given the title of Shah Pasand Khan, and appointed Mir Akhur (Master of the Horse), and the latter became Vazier to Shah Zamān; and contributed very greatly to the ruin of his indulgent and confiding Master.

Shah Zamān hastened to Kandahar and took possession of the place. Partisans of Prince Mahmud took to flight and joined him. In order to compel Mahmud's obedience, the Shah detached Prince Shuja with nearly 30,000 men to march on Herat. Mahmud sent his brother Firuz-ud-din, with Ahmad Khan, the Nurzai Sardar, to garrison Farah, the outpost of Herat; but at the same time Mahmud wrote to his brother begging to be confirmed in the government of Herat and Khurassan, and promising obedience. Shah Zamān behaved generously and agreed to Mahmud's request. Prince Shuja was recalled to Kandahar, before he had reached the Helmand. Prince Haidar was summoned from Kabul to Kandahar, and was placed in it as his father's representative; and the King marched from Kandahar, 28th Oct. 1793, and

[1] He was the son of Fathullah-Khan, Sadozai, of the Kāmrān Khel subdivision, who had come to Court during the lifetime of Shah Timur, from Multan.

retraced his steps to Kabul encamping at Bagh-i-Zāfrān close to the city. He entered the capital on the 13th November.

As it was considered advisible that he should march in person to Dera Ghazi Khan to consolidate his authority over Sind, the Shah took the field, and on the 9th of January 1795 he arrived at the town of Dera Ghazi Khan. Having collected arrears of revenue on the 15th of the same month, he set out on his return to Peshawar, and arrived there on the 11th of February. At this place he gave audience to the Vakils of Muzafar Khan, Sadozai, Nazim of Multan, and of Bhawal Khan, ruler of Bahawalpur. An embassy also arrived from the Wazir of the "Bādshah of Farang."[1]

Shah Zamān also sent off messengers to Shah Alam, Emperor of Hindustan, from Peshawar. The rising in Afghan Turkistan had been instigated by the Amir of Bokhara, and the latter, taking advantage of the disturbances, declared himself openly and crossed the Oxus with an army. The governor, Muhammad Khan, had been ambushed by men of a rebellious tribe, who made a prisoner of him and delivered him up to the Bokhariot Amir, who thereupon invested Balkh. The Afghan garrison, however, held out bravely, and at the end of three months and having lost 300 men killed in a final assault on the defences, the Ruler of Bokhara withdrew to his own territory. Sarbuland Khan in the meantime had been despatched with reinforcements to Balkh, and the news of his safe arrival there reached Shah Zamān on the 6th February 1794.

In the reign of Shah Timur, Kashmir had been governed by Mirza Khan, son of Mir Hazar Khan, Alakozai, as his father's deputy, the latter having been employed in Dera Ghazi Khan. Mirza Khan rebelled, and when his father arrived to take over the government, he was made a prisoner by his son. Nawab Khan, Ishakzai, had been sent to bring Mirza Khan to book, and he entered into negotiations with the latter, who sent his father to Court with Nawab Khan, and also bills of exchange for a large sum of money ; at the same time praying that he might be pardoned and given the appointment of governor of Kashmir, when he would attend Court whenever his presence was desired.

[1] The king of Kabul had always been the resource of all the disaffected in India. To him Tippoo Sultan, Vizier Ally, and all other Mahomedans, who had a quarrel either with the British or with the Mahrattas, had long been in the habit of addressing their complaints—Elphinstone's Cabool Intro. I, p. 56.

The Embassy from the Vazier of the King of France or Europe may have been despatched from Mysore (Tippo Sultan) to Kabul. In Shah Timur's reign Mirza Ahsan Bakht, a prince of the Royal Family of Delhi, had fled to Kabul, and he instigated Prince Abbas to object to his brother's nomination.

Both the presents and the requests were refused, and Nawab Khan's action was repudiated. Shah Zamān on his march from Peshawar had sent Ghazi Khan and Ahmad Khan Ishakzai with 12,000 men to garrison Attock. Orders were now sent to them to march at once on Kashmir and subdue the rebellious Mirza Khan. In spite of the difficulties they had to overcome, due to the nature of the country, the inclement weather that prevailed and the resistance of the enemy, these chiefs were victorious, and the news of their success reached the Shah a fortnight after his return to Peshawar.

Shah Zamān was able to leave Peshawar, and on the 11th April 1794 he began the journey to his Capital. From Nimla he recalled Ahmad Khan Ishakzai from Kashmir and appointed Khanzād Khan to that office. At the stage of Bari Mahal, Ahmad Khan, the Nurzai Chief, who had forsaken Prince Mahmud in Herat, appeared at Court, and the Shah arrived at Kabul safely on the 30th of April 1794.

In the meantime Prince Humayun, who had found refuge in Baluchistan, had betaken himself to Shikarpore, and from there had returned to Kalat. Orders were issued to Mir Nasīr Khan, the Ruler of Kalat, to apprehend the Prince and to keep him in safe custody. Nasīr Khan died in the early spring of 1794 and was succeeded by his son Mir Mahmud who received the same instructions regarding Prince Humayun. The Khan of Kalat, a minor, inexperienced and negligent, allowed Humayun to escape and he made his way to Shikarpore. There, however, he found escape barred in every direction, owing to peremptory orders having been sent to Multan, Bhawalpore and to the Rulers of Sind, to prevent his further passage. He, therefore, returned once more to Kalat.

In the meantime, the affairs of that Khanate were in great disorder. Bāhrām Khan (grandson of Mir Muhabbat Khan, who had been a vassal of Nādir Shah, and Ruler of that State), as representing the elder branch of the family, had laid claim to the gadi of Kalat;[1] and he was at the head of a strong party of adherents. As the Shah was not satisfied with regard to Mir Mahmud's good faith, he decided to march to Kandahar, and Ahmad Khan had been sent to assemble the Durani contingents on the 25th of April 1794. The Shah himself left Kabul on the 5th of June 1794. From the halting place of Deh Mirang, Hasan Khan, the Amlah Bashi, was detached to reinforce Sarbuland Khan in Turkistan; and the Shah continuing his march, arrived at Kandaḥar on the 5th July 1794. At this place, he heard

[1] Kalat; a Memoir on the Ahmadẓai Khans of Kalat, Cal. 1896, G. P. Tate.

a rumour to the effect that Prince Mahmud was marching on Kabul from Herat, and Prince Kaisar, a son of Zamān Shah and Sarfarāz Khan, the Barakzai Sardar, with 12,000 men, were sent off to aid Prince Safdarjang, who had been left as the nominal governor of the Capital in his father's absence. They were recalled as soon as reports were found to be without truth. Mahmud, however, was marching against the Shah towards Kandahar, and had reached the boundary of the Zamindāwar district; and Shah Zamān took the field against him. After a stubbornly contested engagement, lasting several hours, Mahmud's partisans were routed. His camp and nearly four thousand prisoners were taken; and among the latter were many chiefs of rank and name among the Duranis, Khurassānis, Imaks, and Firuz kuhis. At the Vazier's intercession, all were pardoned, with the exception of one chief, who had deserted Shah Zamān, and this person was beheaded. Ahmad Khan Nurzai was sent to Herat to interview Mahmud, and Shah Zamān marched back to Kandahar, where he arrived on the 23rd of July 1794. On the 18th of August Ahmad Khan arrived and reported to Zamān Shah that Mahmud's garrison had evacuated Farah on the approach of the Royal troops. On the following day, the 9th August, the troops destined to restore order in Baluchistan and to put down the pretender Bāhrām Khan, to bring the men of Sind to obedience, and to take over the fugitive Prince Humayun, marched from Kandahar. On the 19th August, Sher Muhammad Khan, the Mukhtar-ud-Daulah (son of the famous Shah Wali Khan, Bamizai), who had been taken up and honoured by Shah Zamān, with Saiad Khudadād, left Kandahar for Baluchistan, while the Shah himself set out for Kabul. On the march, at Maidān, the son of Mir Hazar Khan, who had rebelled in Kashmir was produced before Shah Zamān, who forgave him his past offences. On the 25th September 1794 Zamān Shah entered his capital, and on the same day Ghulam Muhammad Khan, who had been sent on an embassy to India, and on other business, returned to Court, and presented an elephant and other rarities. The king having made up his mind to open a campaign in the Punjab, issued orders for bridges to be thrown across the Indus at Attock; and on the 5th of November 1794 the Royal cortege arrived at Peshawar. Khanzād Khan, Mashir-ud-Daulah, Munshi Bashi, governor of Kashmir, arrived at Court and was given an audience.

When the Mukhtar-ud-Daulah had begun his march towards Baluchistan orders had been despatched to Mir Mahmud, of Kalat, to make over Prince Humayun to the Commander of the Royal forces, who was to send him in charge of Saiad Khudadād Khan,[1] to Court. These orders having been faithfully executed, the Saiad and his charge started for Kandahar, while the Mukhtar-ud-Daulah, with Mir Mahmud and his Baluch contingent, marched against Bāhrām Khan. They succeeded in putting down the pretender and taking possession of the territory he had usurped. After the Royal dues had been realized, the lands in question were handed back to the Khan of Kalat.

But Saiad Khudadād had proved a traitor, and the Achakzais and Kakars persuaded Prince Humayun to make an attempt on Kandahar. Prince Haidar advanced to meet his uncle in the open field, and the latter narrowly escaped defeat, by personally wounding and making a prisoner of his young nephew. An attempt to rescue the lad failed, and the troops serving under the latter dispersed, a part joining Prince Humayun, who took possession of the City.

Ahmad Khan, the Nurzai Sardar, marched from Farah to attempt the recapture of Kandahar, and Prince Humayun advanced to Kokerān to intercept him. The Nurzai Chief, however, evaded the enemy, but when he arrived before the City he found the gates closed, was refused admittance, and was fired upon from the walls. His retirement towards Kalat-i-Ghilzai was intercepted by Prince Humayun, and in the action that took place Ahmad Khan was wounded and taken prisoner. Humayun at first intended to execute Ahmad Khan, but the intercession of his chief partisans, who were too powerful to be slighted, induced the Prince to forego his intention, and great inducements were offered the Nurzai Chief if he would forsake Shah Zamān.

The Mashir-ud-Daulah was ordered to return to Kashmir, on receipt of the news from Kandahar. Prince Shuja was left to govern Peshawar, and Shah Zamān marched for Kandahar. Instead of returning to Kabul, the king apparently used the Gomal route, the Gwalarai Pass, a long tortuous and difficult passage, which, however, was safely traversed and the Royal Camp at length was pitched at Deh Pir Makar. Orders had been issued to collect supplies at this place, and these were obtained with great difficulty and at fabulous expense. However, the necessary supplies were forthcoming; and Shah Zamān arrived at Maruf. At this place he was joined by persons who had previously declared for Prince Humayun, but when Shah Zamān reached the Arghassan, the outlying district of Kandahar, the forces of his brother dissolved, and the latter fled to Herat.

[1] He belonged to one of the Saiad families of Peshin.

Shah Zamān entered Kandahar on the 7th January 1795. At this place Amir Arsalan Khan, Jawān Shir, Kazilbash, was appointed governor of Kashmir, in place of the Mashir-ud-Daulah; and the Kazilbash chief nominated his uncle Muhammad Khan to act as his deputy. Here the Mukhtar-ud-Daulah, accompanied by Mir Mahmud, Khan of Kalat, and 6,000 Baluch levies, joined the King.

Humayun having persuaded his brother Mahmud to take the field, Shah Zamān marched from Kandahar on the 20th January 1795 in the direction of Herat. Prince Mahmud, however, was unwilling to proceed to extremities and he sent his mother to meet Shah Zamān, and she had an interview with the King at Dilārām, two stages from Farah. Her intercession proved effectual, and Mahmud was pardoned, and his mother was dismissed with the present of an elephant and a litter with golden appointments. Zamān Shah retraced his steps towards Kabul and entered the city on the 16th June 1795.

Prince Humayun having plundered a caravan bound for Irak, obtained a great deal of loot, and by means of this ill-gotten wealth he collected a number of needy adventurers and once more advanced upon Kandahar, after his brother had returned to Kabul. But at Bagh-i-Mariz, three or four miles to the west of Kandahar, on the 9th August 1795, he was utterly defeated by Ahmad Khan, the Nurzai Sardar, and the other Durani nobles who were stationed at Kandahar. A thousand men were detailed to pursue Prince Humayun till he was captured.

Relieved from his pressing anxieties with regard to his brother, Shah Zamān was able to obtain a little relaxation from the cares of his kingdom, and we are told that on the 1st of September he left Kabul for twelve days to hunt in the Koh-i-Dāmān or (Kohistan)[1] to the north of his capital. At the expiry of this period of rest, he returned to the capital, where his brother Shuja, then eleven years old, was married to a daughter of Wafadār Khan, the Vazier, the ceremony being celebrated with great pomp.

But Shah Zamān was dogged by his evil fortune, for barely were the nuptial rites of his brother completed than he received the news (29th September 1795) of a rebellion which had taken place in Kashmir. This time Miyān Khan, a Baluch, had created the disturbance; and had seized Muhammad Khan, the Deputy Governor. The

[1] The plains of Lombardy as seen from the Appenines do not exceed the Kohistan of Kabul in richness or brilliancy of verdure, whilst the latter far surpasses them in point of situation, being backed by an amphitheatre of enormous mountains. Vigne's Travels, 2nd Edition, London, 1843.

Mukhtār-ud-Daulah was despatched to Kashmir to put down the insurrection, and the Shah decided to pass the winter in Peshawar and Attock. On the 28th of October when he was encamped at Nimla, on the way to Peshawar, news reached him that Prince Humayun at last had been made a prisoner by the Deputy Governor of Leiah—the representative of Wafadār Khan. Prince Humayun, after his defeat near Kandahar, had retired to Baluchistan ; but after taking possession of Sibi and keeping the Kachhi in a ferment, his fortunes became so desperate that at last, accompanied by his son Ahmad and with only fourteen followers, he had made his escape across the Indus. News of his arrival having reached the Deputy Governor of Leiah (on the left bank of the Indus opposite to Dera Ismail Khan), the latter surrounded the fugitives. Not until his fourteen adherents and his son had been slain was the Prince himself made a prisoner. From Nimla the Shah despatched persons whom he could trust to take over the captive, and a red hot needle drawn across his eye-balls deprived him of sight and rendered him incapable of further mischief. Zamān Shah arrived at Peshawar on the 18th December 1795, and on the 30th of this month Prince Humayun was brought in and he was sent away to Kabul, to be kept a prisoner in the Bālā Hisār; his women and dependents were sent there also. These events had caused delays and now that the season for entering the Punjab was over, Shah Zamān decided to proceed only as far as Attock and Hasan Abdal. At Akora he was met by the Mukhtār-ud-Daulah who had brought in the rebel Miyān Khan ; the latter was pardoned. After inspecting the defences of the fort at Attock, Shah Zamān went on to Hasan Abdāl where he remained only seven days, returning once more to Peshawar.[1]

From Hasan Abdāl, Ahmad Khan, an official of his Court, in command of a force of Duranis, was sent to subdue the country up to the Jhelum river, and to take possession of the fort of Rohtas. The objects of this expedition were successfully attained, but Ahmad Khan despatched a force to take possession of Gujrat. After initial successes, the Afghans were compelled to retire, and were chased by the inhabitants as far as the Jhelum river. Dissensions broke out among the Afghan leaders, and Ahmad Khan was compelled by them to abandon his conquest and to retire to Peshawar. The Shah held an enquiry into the circumstances of the retreat, and the upshot was that Ata Muhammad Khan, Chief of all the Ghilzais, and also

[1] 3rd January 1796. Elphinstone, II., p. 314.

Governor of the Zamindāwar, was found to be at fault. He was deprived of his honours and appointments which were conferred upon Rahmat-ullah Khan Ghilzai as he was considered to be loyal, and in addition he was given the title of Hāsir Khan. Zamān Shah returned to Kabul.

Agha Muhammad Khan, Kajar, in pursuit of his design of creating a State out of the various principalities into which Persia had been divided after the death of Nadir Shah, was able at last to turn his attention to Khurassān, where Shah Rukh, the grandson of Nadir, possessed a semblance of power under the protection of the Afghans, and held his court in the holy city of Meshed. Other chiefs in that country were also independent, such as the Arab rulers of Tabas, Kain, and Turshiz. The Tajik, Ishak Khan of Turbat-i-Haidari, whose possessions extended to the gates of Meshed on the north, and included Khāf in the opposite direction. Sabzawār to the west of Meshed was the capital of Ali Yār Khan, a Turkish chief. Kabushān (Kuchan) and Chinārān to the north-west of Meshed were held respectively by the Kurd Chieftains Gunah Khan, Zaferanlu and Mamesh Khan. Nīshapur was in the possession of Jafar Khan, a son of Abbas Kuli Khan, Bayāt. Owing to the generosity of Ahmad Shah Durani, the blind Shah Rukh still occupied Meshed; safe under Afghan protection from the attacks of his neighbours, as long as Ahmed Shah lived. The Chief of Chinārān had indeed taken possession of Meshed and had retained it for five years, but he had been forced to resign it by Timur Shah. The population of Meshed was reduced at this period to about 20,000 souls. The country up to the walls was constantly raided by the Uzbegs; and a great part of the slender revenue of the principality had to be paid as black mail to neighbouring chiefs to purchase exemption from attacks which the blind Ruler's weakness invited. Meshed also had become a scene of distraction owing to the incompetence of Shah Rukh, and the disputes of his sons Nasr-ullah Mirza, and Nādir Mirza until the death of the former left the field clear to his brother.[1]

Shah Rukh, however, still possessed many of the priceless jewels which Nādir Shah had brought from India; and the existence of these had excited the cupidity of Agha Muhammad Khan, who regarded them as the property of the Crown of Persia. When, therefore, he had been victorious in his struggle with the Zends, and had subdued Georgia as well, Agha Muhammad marched into Khurassān at the head of an overpowering force; and the petty rulers of Khurassān hastened to make

[1] Malcolm's History of Persia.

their submission to him. Nādir Mirza fled to Herat on the approach of the Kajar chieftain, leaving his blind father to make his submission and deliver up the city. Nādir Mirza sent on his brothers Reza Kuli and Ali, to the court of Shah Zamān, and followed them later and they met him on his arrival from Peshawar at Kabul.

While, therefore, the shadowy rights of suzerainty which the Afghans still claimed over Khurassān had been endangered by the rise of Agha Muhammad Khan to supreme power in Persia ; in the opposite direction the Indian possessions of the Sadozais were threatened by the Sikhs who had been in virtual possession of the greater part of the Punjab even during the last years of Ahmad Shah's life. The indolent but sagacious Timur Shah apparently had never taken any steps to assert and secure his rights in the Punjab ; but Shah Zamān's mind seems always to have been filled with idle hopes of an Empire in India. In this design, however, he was encouraged by various rulers in India. The memory of Panipat had not yet been effaced ; and from Delhi to Mysore, and as far east as Oudh, the Afghan Sovereign was still regarded as the champion of Islam, whose sympathies and active intervention could always be appealed to successfully in favour of the followers of that faith when they were hard pressed by infidels, at the time, the British, whom circumstances had compelled to advance to the North-West from Bengal ; and the Mahrattas who were recovering from the catastrophe of Panipat.[1]

Shah Zamān having made up his mind to enter Hindustan, despatched the Mukhtār-ud-Daulah to Kandahar to raise the Durani clans. Ata Muhammad Ghilzai, who had been disgraced by the king, fled to Prince Mahmud to Herat. When Shah Zamān

[1] Shah Alam, Titular Emperor of Hindustan, ascended the throne in Delhi in 1771. He was, however, a nonentity and in the hands first of one and then of another of his Ministers. Madhaji Sindia was consolidating his power in Hindustan and from 1771 to 1803, the Emperor was subject in turn to the insults of the Jats, his own rebellious subjects, the Mahrattas, and in 1788 Shah Alam had his sight destroyed by the notorious Ghulam Kādir, the unworthy grandson of the gallant Rohilla chief Najib-ud-daulah. The memory of Panipat weighed heavily on the spirits of Madhaji Sindia, and in order to propitiate the Durani King, the wily Mahratta had sent the Nawab Wajih-ud-din, as his representative to the Court of Shah Timur and again another agent to Shah Zamān. (History of Bhawalpore). On the 26th October 1794, Ghulam Muhammad Khan, Rohilla (who had usurped the authority in Rohilkand), was defeated by a British force under Sir Ralph Abercrombie, and in 1795 the defeated usurper crossed the Punjab (History of Bhawalpore), to induce Shah Zāman to intervene on his behalf. Asaf-ud-daulah, Nawab Vazier of Oudh, also despatched an agent at the same time to the Court of the Sadozai (*ibid*). With the exception, perhaps, of the Sikhs, the various powers in India greatly overestimated the strength of the Afghan Ruler. (Elphinstone, Cabool, II, 308, states that Shah Zāman was induced to invade India in 1795 by a refugee Prince of Delhi and also was encouraged to do so by Tippoo Sultan).

was on the point of leaving Kabul, Husen Khan, Kārāguzlu, the envoy of Agha Muhammad Khan, arrived at court. He was accorded a gracious reception, and a money present, robes and a charger were bestowed on him ; and permission was given him to return to Meshed. Kado Khan Barakzai accompanied the Persian Ambassador as the Afghan Envoy, to the court of the Kajar Prince.[1]

Shah Zamān arrived in due course at Peshawar, and was joined by the Mukhtār-ud-Daulah with 15,000 Durani horse. A halt of a month was made in Peshawar and the time was passed in collecting more troops. On the 28th of November 1796 the Shah encamped at Chamkanni, four miles to the east of Peshawar. On the 4th of December he crossed the Indus, by a bridge, at Attock ; and from the banks of the Jhelum, the Mukhtār-ud-Daulah was despatched in command of the Vanguard.

The confederacy of Sikh chieftains offered no opposition to the advance of the Afghan forces. Among the Sikhs, Sahib Singh of Gujrat, and Ranjit Singh of Wazirabad, were most distinguished on account of the organisation of their forces ; and with Lehna Singh of Lahore, and Gulāb Sing of Amritsar, were the most powerful chiefs in the Punjab, at that time. Shah Zamān was delayed for three days at Gujrat by heavy rain, but his progress was not impeded by the Sikhs, and he entered Lahore on the 1st January 1797.[2] Although the Afghan Sovereign was at the head of 30,000 men, he strove to conciliate the Sikhs and to render his supremacy an agreeable burthen to chiefs and people alike. Expeditions were, however, despatched against the Sikhs of the Manja, and against Amān Kot in which Sahib Sing had taken up an equivocal attitude. Amān Kot was invested, and at last Sahib Sing offered to send his son and his brother to the court of Shah Zamān, and professed his willingness to come in person and make his submission. These offers were accepted and Sahib Sing's son and brother met with an honourable reception. The Afghan garrison in Sialkot, however, had been surrounded by the Sikhs, and an expedition was despatched to relieve that place, which was successfully carried out ; and minor skirmishes with the Sikhs were of frequent occurrence.

---

1 Tarikh-i-Sultani—Litho text.

2 The author of the Tarikh-i-Sultani gives the following date :—Crossing of the Indus at Attock, 12th Jamada II 1211 A. H.=13th of December 1796. Though discrepant it establishes his claim to be considered a reliable author. He could not have invented or guessed this date. Elphinstone gives the date of the entry into Lahore, 3rd January 1797. II, p. 315.

Shah Zamān had been about one month in Lahore when he received information that his brother Mahmud in Herat had revolted once more.[1] The Sadozai king was compelled to leave Lahore and on the 30th January 1797, he commenced his retrograde movement towards his own country.

Ahmad Khan (an official of his Court) was appointed to hold charge of the Rohtās Fort and was detailed to reduce Pind Dādan Khan.

---

1 An invasion of Hindustan (the country to the south of the Sutlej) would have thrown the whole country into a condition of anarchy. The Muhammadans looked to the Durani king as their deliverer and hoped for the restoration of the House of Timur through Afghan intervention in the affairs of Hindustan. The partisans of Shah Zaman had set on foot intrigues in many parts of India. The Rohillas took up arms. Every follower of Islam anxiously looked for the coming of the champion of Islam. Dissensions among the Mahrattas had drawn their forces to the south; and they were dismayed at the prospect and looked for help to the British. The attitude of the Sadozai king had compelled the authorities in Calcutta to assemble an army at Anupshahr; and to raise new regiments and the 4th Bengal Light Cavalry; and the 26th, 27th, 28th and 29th regiments of Bengal Infantry had been raised in 1796. When the news of the arrival of the Afghans in Lahore had spread abroad it caused increased alarm in India, and the 30th, 31st, 32nd, 33rd, 34th and 35th regiments of Bengal Infantry had been raised, in anticipation of the further advance of Shah Zaman to Delhi. In 1790 M. De Boigne had been commissioned to raise a brigade of regular troops by Sindiah and by 1793 his regular troops numbered 24,000 men, with 130 guns, led by European officers of different nationalities, all under M. De Boigne's command. Franklin's Life of Shah Alam. These adversaries would have proved too strong for the undisciplined Afghan hordes.

NOTE.

The following remark of Sir John Malcolm on this subject is illustrative of the position of the Sadozais in the estimation of their countrymen, and of the Afghan notion of government.

The appointment of Ramatullah Khan, commonly called Wafadar Khan, was spoken of with great disapprobation when I was in Persia in 1800. It was considered as a departure from all usage; and the grounds of objection were, "that though it was proper the King should be a Sadozai, and have his person held sacred, from belonging to that venerated tribe, his Vazier ought not to be of the same tribe, as if he also was safe from attack, no one would be responsible for the acts of cruelty and oppression that might be committed: others deemed the king impolitic in appointing a Sadozai to be his Vazier, as such an officer might aspire to the crown, on the ground of being one of that tribe." (Elphinstone's Caubool 1839, II. 251).

The arrogance and despotic character of the Vazier, secure in the unfaltering support of his king, rapidly alienated the nobles; and his oppressive measures he had to find the money for his master's ambitious designs in India—estranged the common people. The continual movements of the king; from the Punjab to Herat and back again; must also have harassed all classes of his subjects. These movements were productive of nothing but hardship for the tribal levies which formed his army.

George Thomas of Hansi estimated the military strength of the Sikhs in 1800 at 60,000 horse, 5,000 foot, and 40 field guns. The Sikhs were, therefore, too powerful to succumb to raids such as Shah Zamān only could make, with Mahmud ever ready to act against Herat in his absence and with the danger of open invasion by the Shah of Persia.

CHAPTER XII.

SHAH ZAMAN—RELATIONS WITH PERSIA AND INDIA—(*contd.*)

From Shamsābād, near Attock, an expedition was despatched to reduce a rebellious tribe in the Hazara[1] District, which was successfully accomplished. On the 23rd of February 1797, Shah Zamān entered Peshawar, where he learned that the fort of Pind Dādan Khan[2] had been surrendered after some resistance, by the Kotwal[3] of Ranjit Sing. Shah Zamān marched from Peshawar on the 1st March and reached Kabul on the 16th March 1797.

Here it was discovered that Mahmud had been instigated to rebel against his brother by Ata Muhammad the Ghilzai and other malcontents, but that he had not actually committed himself. Orders, however, were sent to him to despatch Ata Muhammad the Ghilzai to his brother's court, and as Mahmud refused to carry out these orders, Shah Zamān took the field and on the 16th of June 1797 he marched from Kabul.

At the stage of Kala-i-Kāzi on the road to Kandahar, Abdullah Khan (Alakozai ?), the governor of Kashmir, arrived at Court and presented the usual gifts. He was given leave to return to Kashmir. At the stage of Hakān, an embassy from India arrived, bearing presents and a friendly letter.[4]

Shah Zamān reached Kandahar on the 6th July 1797.

At this place news arrived of the assassination of Agha Muhammad Khan, Kajar, the Ruler of Persia.[5]

---

[1] To the north of Attock and adjoining Kashmir.

[2] Now a subdivision of the Jhelum District.

[3] Civil governor.

[4] The name of the ruler who sent this mission is said to have been Pato Shah (Pato-ji?). It was probably from one or other of the three independent Mahratta Chiefs in northern India, or it may have been despatched from Poona, the headquarters of the Mahratta Power.

[5] After compelling the wretched Shah Rukh to give up the remaining jewels and precious gems in his possession, Agha Muhammad Khan marched to Teheran, after leaving 12,000 men to garrison Meshed, and taking with him the unhappy grandson of Nadir Shah, who died on the march. At Teheran he passed the winter, having reached his capital in September 1796. Here he received M. Olivier charged with a Mission from the French Republic to the Minister of Agha Muhammad. In the spring of 1797, the Kajar Ruler led an army towards the Aras against the Russians, and had taken possession of the fortress of Shishah on the further bank, when his career was terminated by his murder, by some of his personal attendants—(Watson's History of Persia, London 1866, p. 96 *et seq.*)

Nādir Mirza, son of Shah Rukh, on hearing of this occurrence left the Afghan Court and having collected troops gained possession of Meshed where he proclaimed himself independent.[1]

At Kandahar Shah Zamān also received the news of the murder of Ata Muhammad, the irreconcileable Ghilzai Sardar, by a fellow tribesman; and at the same time the Vazier also induced Zamān Khan, the Bāmizai, to desert Mahmud and take service with Shah Zamān. Troops were raised for service against Herat, and Mir Mahmud, Khan of Kalat, arrived at the head of the levies of Baluchistan. A vanguard composed of 10,000 to 12,000 selected horse was thrown forward under the command of Prince Kaisar, with Sardar Ahmad Khan Nurzai, Shah Pasand Khan, the Ishakzai Sardar, and other leaders to advise and to exercise authority on behalf of the young prince; while a force of irregular horsemen under Jahandād Khan was despatched to lay waste the country round Herat and to harass Mahmud. Zamān Shah followed with his main army and his artillery on the 8th September 1797.[2] On arrival at Farah he learned that Jahandād Khan had captured three hundred of Mahmud's partisans left at Obah, and had occupied that district. Mahmud on hearing of Prince Kaisar's approach had taken up a position outside Herat, at the Rauzah Bāgh, and had despatched 5,000 horse to oppose the invaders at Obah. The latter drove back Mahmud's troops who retired on Herat, the Prince lost his nerve and made up his mind to stand a siege in the city. In the meantime Wafadār Khan, Shah Zamān's Minister, had been tampering with Mahmud's adherents, who forestalled the Prince by seizing the town and Citadel of Herat, and closing the gates against their master, and firing on him from the walls. The latter for a day and a night turned his artillery on the defences, and made a desperate effort to retake it by assault. Foiled in his endeavours, and alarmed at the advance of Prince Kaisar's force, which was only four leagues from Herat, Mahmud ceased his efforts to recapture Herat, and accompanied by his son Kamrān

---

1 Fath Ali Shah, nephew of Agha Muhammad Khan, ascended the Throne of Persia on the 28th July 1797. (4th Safar 1212 A.H.) He warned Nādir Mirza of the consequences of his action, and when his remonstrances were unheeded he marched against the latter.

Nishapur was taken by storm, and Turbat was also captured. After a lengthy blockade Nādir Mirza was pardoned by the Shah but some years after he was seized by the inhabitants after he had desecrated the Shrine of Imām Reza, and had slain the chief priest with his own hands, and handed over to the Shah and was put to death with atrocious cruelty in 1802—Watson's History of Persia, p. 121, *et seq*.

2 Elphinstone gives this date 8th September 1797, II, at p. 316.

and his brother Firuz-ud-din and a few devoted followers he took to flight.[1]

Shah Zamān arrived at Herat on the 14th of October 1797. He camped outside the walls and visited the famous shrines in the neighbourhood. Prince Kaisar was appointed Governor of Herat, with Zamān Khan[2] Bamizai as his adviser, and after a stay of ten days Shah Zamān began his return march to Kandahar, taking with him the principal adherents of Mahmud; and arrived there on the 11th November. He continued his retirement to the Capital and the only incident worthy of remark was the despatch of an expedition from Ab-i-Tāzi, on the road to Kabul, against some plunderers or bandits. On the 6th December[3] 1797, Zamān Shah entered Kabul.[4]

Shah Zamān in pursuit of his dreams of establishing an empire to the east of the Indus urged thereto in all likelihood by the scanty resources of his native land, decided to resume the thread of his policy in the Punjab, and on the 4th January 1798 he marched in the direction of Lahore.[5]

The Sikhs, it is said, fled into the low hills on the borders of the Punjab, and the King having confirmed Abdullah Khan Alakozai in

[1] The author of the Tarikh-i-Sultani states that owing to the murder of Ata Muhammad at the instigation of Hazar Khan, dissensions broke out among Mahmud's adherents. Kilich Khan, the powerful Taimuni Sardar, seized the citadel and another chief the town, which they held on behalf of Shah Zamān. Mahmud found a refuge with the Shah of Persia, and after a stay in Kashān for some time, he returned to Kain where he was hospitably treated by the Arab chieftain of that place.

[2] Son of Haji Karimdād Khan, Tarikh-i-Sultani. The author of the Tarikh-i-Sultani states that Shah Zamān's Ambassador to the late Agha Muhammad Khan, Kajar, returned to his master at Herat, and that Shah Zamān was at Herat four months.

[3] The author of the Tarikh-i-Sultani says in Rajab 1212. The month of Rajab was from 8th November to December 1797.

[4] Here the MS. entitled the Wakai-i-Zamān Shāhi, by Mirza Abu-l-Hasan Khan, Munshi, comes to an abrupt conclusion with a remark that Shah Zamān passed the summer in Kabul; and a few other remarks as to the devotion of this sovereign to the doctrines of the Nakshbandi Sect. The dates given towards the end of the MS. are not very clear. While carefully recording the days of the week and of the month the author omits to record the year. The latter is the case especially in the last year of which the record treats and this year has been restored by reference to the Tarikh-i-Sultani, a recent work, and for that reason not a very first rate authority. But the restoration of the year by this means, brings the dates into correct relation with those of events in Persia and the Punjab, obtained from other sources; and the details given by the recent author are in close agreement with those contained in Elphinstone's Cabool, and other authors who treat of the events that took place in Persia and the Punjab at this time.

The author of the Wakai-i-Zamān Shāhi seems to have been an official who was not an actual eye-witness of the events he has recorded. But his narrative is that of an author contemporary with those events, and as such his record is invaluable.

[5] Tarikh-i-Sultani; the date A. H. given there is 14th of the month Shaban, 1212. No notice of this raid on the Punjab appears in either Elphinstone's Cabool or in Cunningham's History of the Sikhs.

the Government of Kashmir, the Government of Lahore was made over to Ahmad Khan Barakzai as before ; after this he retraced his steps to Kabul. Here he was met by letters from Herat, despatched by Prince Kaisar, and Zamān Khan regarding the reappearance of Mahmud and his designs on Herat. The Prince had been well received by Amir Ali Khan, of the Arab tribe of Khuzaima, Ruler of the Kaināt, and he having raised four thousand foot soldiers from the Arabs of that country in company with Amir Khan, Tabati, put Mahmud in possession of Farah. From thence they went on to take possession of Isfirār. Prince Kaisar and Zamān Khan, having collected a force, advanced to meet the invaders ; and at Imārat, to the south of the fort of Isfirār, they were defeated by Mahmud, who blockaded them in Herat, where they had fled. All the Persian-speaking section of the populace were devoted to Prince Mahmud ; and Prince Kaisar and Zamān Khan were hard pressed. However, by means of forged letters, which were allowed to fall into Prince Mahmud's hands, the fears of the latter were excited, and notwithstanding the protests of the chief of Kain and his other adherents, the Prince fled on the same night to Puza of Kabutar Khan. From that place he sent his son Kāmrān and his brother Firuz-ud-din to Persia to the Court of the Shah Fath Ali Shah, while he betook himself to Bokhara. By the time Shah Zamān arrived in Herat, he found that Mahmud had fled. Mulla Abd-ul-Hak with the leading men of the priestly families were sent to Bokhara, to the Ruler Shah Murad Khan, to demand that either Mahmud should be apprehended and kept under restraint, or that he should be expelled from the territories of Bokhara. After a stay at Herat of a few months letters reached the Shah to the effect that the Sikhs had resorted to arms and had overpowered Ahmad Khan Barakzai, the Governor of Lahore, who had lost his life in battle with them ; and that they were everywhere predominant in the Punjab. Shah Zamān sent his baggage and impedimenta round by way of Kandahar towards Kabul, and made Prince Kaisar Governor of Herat, with Mir Afzal Khan, the son of Sardar Madad Khan, Ishakzai, as his Deputy Governor. Then, taking with him Zamān Khan, the son of Haji Karimdād Khan, Bamizai, Shah Zamān marched through the country of the Hazara Dai Kandi and by way of Bamiān, and reached Kabul in twelve days. There he collected material and stores and he set out for the Punjab. He left Peshāwar on the 25th of October 1798 [1] and advanced to Lahore without finding any opposition offered to his progress. The Sikhs had sent 5,000 men to watch

[1] Elphinstone's Cabool, II, p. 311.

the ford of the Jhelum, but they were brushed aside without difficulty. On his arrival in Lahore the king renewed his measures of conciliation combined with threats. "He found an able leader, but a doubtful partizan, in Nizam-ud-din Khan, a Pathan of Kasur, who had acquired a high local reputation, and he was employed to coerce such of the Sikhs, including the youthful Runjit Sing, as pertinaciously kept aloof. They distrusted the Shah's honour ; but Nizam-ud-din distrusted the permanence of his power, and he prudently forbore to proceed to extremities against neighbours to whom he might soon be left a prey." [1]

The Shah was grieved to find the signs of the ravages of the Sikhs who had attacked Lahore ; and during this invasion, he seems to have been much impressed by the character of Ranjit Sing, who was regarded in a similar light by the other Sikh chieftains. In despair of being able to maintain peace with an Afghan governor in the country, the Shah made up his mind to intrust the government to Ranjit Sing. The latter also coveted Lahore, the possession of which was associated in the minds of all men with the possession of power. Ranjit Sing was invested by the Shah with the office of Governor of Lahore ; and letters were despatched to the King of Delhi to inform him that circumstances had prevented a march to Delhi ; but that the Shah would embrace the earliest opportunity of returning, to replace him on the throne, and to place Islam in the position of the paramount power in India. On the way back to Peshawar owing to heavy rain the river Jhelum came down in flood, while the Shah's army was crossing, and his artillery and baggage was swept away ; Ranjit Sing and Sahib Sing, however, recovered the Shah's guns which were sent on after him to Peshawar, where the Shah arrived on the 30th January 1799. From that place he continued his march to Kabul, and after placing his brother Shuja as governor in the capital, he turned his steps towards Kandahar. The cause of the Shah's hasty retreat from Lahore was the presence of the Shah of Persia at the head of a large army in Khurassān, over which the Afghan Sovereign claimed the right of the Suzerain power.

A wave of unrest had passed over Khurassān and Shah Fath Ali Shah had been compelled to march against the insurgent governors of Sabzawār and Nishapur. But there were other causes which in the end brought about Shah Zamān's downfall. The Afghan menace kept the whole of India in a state of unrest, and the Shah's inroads caused a yearly alarm which was harassing the British and was the

[1] Cunningham's History of the Sikhs.

cause of extra military expenditure. In order therefore to create a diversion in their favour and to operate as a check to the Sadozai king's ambitions with respect to India, the British authorities had deputed Mahdi Ali Khan (a prominent merchant in Bombay, and one who was well known at the Court of the Shah), to Persia in order to prevail upon the Shah to attack the Afghans. For this purpose Herat was a vulnerable point and the presence of Mahmud offered special facilities. By keeping open the Herat ulcer, the plans of the Sadozai King with regard to India could always be thwarted, and his strength drained, and the pretensions of the Shah, who regarded Afghanistan as a province of the Persian Empire, rendered this course likely to succeed. Shah Zamān sent an Embassy to the Shah's Court with a request that Khurassān should be recognised by the Shah as belonging to Afghanistan. In reply, Haji Ibrahim, the Shah's minister, was ordered to say that it was his master's intention to restore the south and eastern limits of Persia to the condition in which they had been in the time of the Safavi monarchs of Persia. That he proposed to overrun and annex Herat, Merve, Balkh, Kabul, Kandahar, Ṭibet, Kāshgar and Seistan.[1] The danger from Persia was by no means imaginary with Mahmud at hand as a convenient tool, and the hasty return of Shah Zamān in 1798 was due to the anxiety caused by the attitude of the Shah who had probably instigated the abortive attempt by Mahmud on Herat. In 1799 the task which had been given Mahdi Alikhan, was to urge the Shah to move against Afghanistan. When Shah Zamān had arrived in Kandahar he despatched Tura Bāz Khan to the Shah, then in Khurassan, laden with presents, who was to request the Shah to withdraw to Teheran. This the latter agreed to do on the condition that the Princes Mahmud and Firuz-ud-din should be received back in Afghanistan in a manner suitable to their rank.[2] The success which had attended Mahdi Ali's negotiations had not been known in Calcutta when the Earl of Mornington selected Captain Malcolm for the purpose of proceeding to the Court of Teheran. The objects of this Mission were three in number. To make an arrangement with the Shah for relieving India from the recurring annual alarm of an Afghan invasion. To counteract any possible designs, the French nation might entertain with regard to Persia; and to re-open and restore trade with Persia to somewhat of its former prosperity.[3]

---

[1] Watson's History of Persia, p. 125, *et seq.*

[2] *Ibid*, p. 125, *et seq.*

[3] (*Ibid.*)

In the meantime however events took place in Afghanistàn itself which led very soon to Shah Zamān's downfall and the ruin of the Sadozai family. The minister Wafadār Khan had offended the Afghan Sardars by his arrogance; and the latter, driven to despair by the complete ascendancy he had obtained over his Royal Master, formed a plot to assassinate the minister; to remove the king, and to raise Prince Shuja to the throne. So general was the resentment against the Minister that one morning doggrel verses were found written on the Mihrāb of the Royal mosque in the Bālā Hisār in Kabul—(the limit of) the duration of the dynasty of the Duranis, consider to be the year 1217 (1802). After that every province shall have its own ruler, who will reign two or three days, two or three months, or two or three years.

The author was supposed to be a wandering fakir, but he was never arrested.

When in 1800 the Shah was in Kandahar the principal Sardars who had become privy to this plot against the minister and the king, decided to put their plans into effect. The chief conspirators were Payandah Khan (Sarfaraz Khan) Barakzai; Islam Khan, the Zabt Begi of the Popalzais; Hikmat Khan Sarkāni; Muhammad Azim Khan, son of Mir Hazār Khan, Alakozai; Mir Arsalan Khan, chief of the Juwānshir Kazzilbash; Jafir Khan, Juwānshir; Yusuf Ali, one of the Eunuchs of the palace; Sharif Khan Munshi, and Nur Muhammad Khan Bābari. They met at the hermitage of Miān Ghulām Muhammad, an Indian Fakir, and having sworn on the Koran, they proceeded to arrange the details of the execution of their designs. Payandah Khan (Sarfaraz Khan) Barakzai was to summon his clansmen to the city; while Muhammad Azim Khan, Alakozai, was to assassinate the Vazier when the latter, as was his custom, left the city on a Thursday to hawk on the lands of his Kārez about four miles to the east of the city (the place is still known as Tor Vazir). The other conspirators were to seize the king. The plot was revealed to the Vazier. The hawking expedition was postponed, on the pretence of urgent business; and the conspirators were summoned one by one, to the presence of the king. The gates of the citadel were closed and the chieftains were executed. As a rigorous search was instituted to discover those who were implicated in this plot, Fath Khan the eldest son of Payandah Khan (Sarfaraz Khan) Barakzai, his brethren and clansmen, fled from the city. They betook themselves in the first instance to their fort of Nād Ali on the Helmand, and from there Fath Khan went off to Persia and joined Mahmud at Turshiz. The Fakir Miān

Ghulām Muhammad escaped to Dādur, in Baluchistan, where he was apprehended and executed. His body was buried at Dādur; but his head, taken as a voucher to the Vazier, was afterwards interred outside the Herati gate of Kandahar near the Payāb canal.[1]

Notwithstanding the disaffection that was spreading among his subjects, Shah Zamān appears to have been lulled into a false tranquillity by the success of Tura-Bāz Khan's Embassy. Letters also, received from Shah Shuja, gave the king intelligence of the increasing turbulence of the Sikhs, and his ambition drew him towards the Punjab. In the year 1216 A. H. (begins 25th May 1801, ends 13th May 1802) he marched from Kandahar at the head of a numerous army for Peshawar and the Punjab. Mihr Ali Khan, the Ishakzai Sardar, who had been given the title of Shah Pasand Khan, was left in Kandahar as the governor. No sooner had Fath Khan, Barakzai, heard of Shah Zaman's movement towards Peshawar, than he urged Mahmud Khan to essay the capture of Kandahar.

Mahmud after his abortive attempt on Herat had fled to Bokhāra, where he was placed under surveillance. With the aid of a friendly Uzbeg chief, he made his way, first to Khiva, and then across the desert to Asterabad. From this district he made his way to the Shah's Court, where he was received with marks of respect, and lodged in the palace of the Sadr-i-Azam. He accompanied the Shah into Khurassan (1800), but when the task of reducing the turbulent chiefs was found to be not an easy matter; or in compliance with Shah Zamān's wishes; Fath Ali Shah retired to Teheran, Mahmud was dismissed to Turshiz, where provision was made for his support. Encouraged by Fath Khan Barakzai, Mahmud

---

1 The author of the Tarikh-i-Sultani, states that the A. H. date 1215, corresponding to 1800-01 (beginning on 25th of May 1800 and ending on 13th May 1801) was obtained from the chronogram on the tombstone of Payandah Khan (Sarfarāz Khan). Elphinstone places this event in 1799. The Mirat-i-Abbasi (a MS. History of Bahawalpore) places the conspiracy in the winter of 1209 A. H., *i. e.*, of 1794-5, and the execution of the sixteen persons implicated is said to have been carried out immediately before his march to India. The name of Sarfarāz Khan, who was Amir-ul-Umara, or the first noble of the realm, does not appear in the record of events after that year, which is singular, for his place was either by the side of his sovereign, or in some other responsible position; either of which would have insured mention of him.

According to this History of Bahawalpore the actual downfall of Shah Zamān followed on an insult offered to the Mukhtār-ud-daulah, Sher Muhammad Khan, the Bamizai Sardar, by Wafadār Khan, the Vazier; this is said to have occurred in 1210 A. H. (18th July 1795 to 7th July 1796). At the instigation of the insulted chief, the Duranis not only abandoned their allegiance to the Shah, but entered into communication with the Sikh Sardars and encouraged them in their resistance to Shah Zamān. In this same year the verse was scribbled on the Mihrāb of the Royal Masjid in the Bālā Hisār of Kabul.—Hist. of Bahawalpore.

set out with forty-one followers to make his attempt on Kandahar; travelling by way of Seistan.

When the party had reached Tagrīsh Fath Khan separated himself from Shah Mahmud and went off to the Helmand, to raise the Barakzai clansmen. The fort of Girishk was empty, and Mahmud and his followers seized it and made it a rendezvous for the malcontents of the country. Shahnawāz Khan Barakzai, who was in Kandahar, urged Mahmud to make his attempt on that city before the road from Kabul was free from snow, and reinforcements could be despatched by Shah Zamān to strengthen the hands of his governor and adherents in Kandahar. Mihr Ali Khan, Ishakzai, having perceived that Mahmud was gaining strength, moved out of Kandahar at the head of 5,000 horse and foot to break up the forces of the pretender, but was defeated at Bagh-i-Hurmuz, to the south of Kushk-i-Nakhud, and shut himself up in Kandahar. After a blockade of forty-two days Fath Khan effected an entrance, being aided by some of the Farsiwān inhabitants. Mihr Ali Khan put to death Imam Baksh Khan, and Hasan Khan, who were the cause of this treachery, and fled from Kandahar, carrying the news of the fall of the city to Shah Zamān in Peshawar. The Shah abandoned his projected enterprise in the Punjab and hurried back towards Kandahar. From Ghazni he sent on ahead, with 10,00c horse, Sardar Ahmad Khan Nurzai. Mahmud had levied a forced contribution of money from the merchants of Kandahar, and having enlisted men, advanced to meet his brother. A battle was fought between Mukur and Kalat-i-Ghilzai, which was decided in Mahmud's favour, by the desertion of the Nurzai Sardar who had been estranged from Shah Zamān by the outrageous conduct of his haughty Minister. Shah Zamān retreated to Kabul and endeavoured to raise a fresh army, but finding that his forces were melting away he removed his treasures and stores, and retired to Jalālābād, and summoned his brother Shuja, who was governor of Peshawar to his aid. At this place he was able to collect the tribesmen of the Khaibar and the Yusufzais, and at the head of a great gathering of armed men he prepared to dispute the advance of Mahmud and Fath Khan. The Kazilbash inhabitants of Kabul, whom the execution of Arsalān Khan had estranged from Shah Zamān; delivered Kabul into the hands of Mahmud, and joined him in arms, on his advance towards Jalālābād. At Āshpān, about thirty-six miles from Jalālābād, Shah Zamān was utterly defeated; and separated from his men, he and Wafadar Khan passed the night in a ravine, and the next morning they made their way to the fort of Ashik, the

Shinwāri who had received many benefits from Shah Zamān. This person received the fugitives with a great show of respect, but he sent word secretly to Mahmud and prevented his guests leaving the Fort. Shuja after the battle had a small band of followers at his disposal, and he sent a hundred horsemen to bring in his brother. Ashik, however, refused to give up the fugitives, and the party was obliged to return to the Prince, with the news of his brother's capture and detention by Ashik.

Shah Zamān had on his person valuable jewels set with gems of great price. One of these was the famous Koh-i-Nur diamond and another was the equally celebrated ruby, known as Fakhrāj. When he found that the treacherous Shinwāri had made him a prisoner, the Shah resolved that neither of these gems should fall into his hands, nor into his brother's keeping. The diamond he concealed in a crack in the walls of his chamber and the ruby he threw into a deep irrigation channel. Mahmud, on learning of the detention of his brother and Wafadār Khan, despatched a brother of Fath Khan, Barakzai, to take over the Shah and his Minister from Ashik, and he condemned Shah Zamān to undergo the same punishment which the latter had inflicted on his brother Humayun, and the unfortunate Shah Zamān had his sight destroyed by the application of a heated skewer to his eyes. Wafadār Khan and his brother were put to death by Fath Khan in retaliation for the death of Sarfarāz Khan (Payandah Khan) Barakzai, and Zamān Khan Bamizai, in retaliation for the death of Hāzir Khan, brother of Muhammad Akram Khan, who had been executed by the former while deputy governor of Herat.

The defeat at Āshpān took place in the summer of 1801. Shah Zamān was barely 32 years of age when his sight was destroyed. He lived to a good old age and died in Ludhiana, a pensioner on the bounty of the East India Company. He had several sons, none of whom, however, displayed any talent, or distinguished themselves in the events that took place in Afghanistan. Those that were living at the time when the Sadozais were driven from Afghanistan, swelled the number of the Afghan refugees in Ludhiana and shared the stipend allotted for their support.

Mahmud was a very different man to the brother whom he dethroned and he did not merit the good fortune to which the mistakes of his brother caused him to attain. In him animal appetites were combined with ferocity and the indulgence of his animal desires was all he lived for, after he gained the means to allow of their gratification. When a revolution of fortune's wheel had placed him at the mercy of the incensed and vengeful Shuja-ul-Mulk, it was due to the personal and vehement intercession of the blind Shah Zamān that Shuja consented to relinquish the right of retaliation, the exercise of which national customs would have justified and his religion have sanctioned: Mahmud's sight was spared through the noble generosity of the brother whom he had irreparably injured.

NOTE.

On arriving in Seistan, on his way towards Kandahar, Mahmud was received with open arms by Malik Bahram Khan, Kaiāni, the ruler of that country. The latter gave his daughter to Prince Kāmrān, and equipped Mahmud's party, but his offer to assist Mahmud with the levies of Seistan, in his enterprise against Shah Zamān, was rejected on Fath Khan's advice.

While the former was at Peshawar he despatched a force of 15,000 men under Mulla Ahmad and Mir Weis to reinstate his authority in Kashmir. The services of these troops would have been invaluable in his struggle with Mahmud. Owing to the imprudence of Mulla Ahmad, the troops dispersed before arriving in Kashmir.

Another highly imprudent act, at this time, was the severe punishment dealt to Abdullah Khan Alakozai, the Governor of Kashmir, who had visited the Court in Peshawar. On receiving news of his brother's ill-treatment, Saidal Khan, and the Alakozai clan, at once declared for Mahmud.—(Elphinstone's Cabool II., 321 *et seq.*)

The father of Wafadār Khan had come from Multan to the court of Timur Shah and had been appointed to an office near the person of the King. Wafadār Khan and the future King had been boys together, and the friendship which had grown up between them in boyhood and the compact of perpetual friendship the youths had ratified was never broken. When Shah Zamān ascended the throne his comrade's advancement was assured and the latter was supported loyally by his master who placed implicit confidence in him, and both were involved in a common destruction.

Shah Zamān died in exile and was buried in a graveyard, to which a peculiar sanctity is attached, near the town of Sirhind, now in the Patial State.

In this reign the Mint-towns were: Lahore, Bhakkar (Sind), Ahmad Shāhi Dera, Kabul, Peshawar, Derajat and Multan.

His successors (1) Shuja V, (2) Mahmud had money coined at—

(1) Ahmad Shāhi, Bahawalpur, Derajat, Multan.

(2) Bahawalpur, Ahmad Shāhi, Herat, Bhakkar (Sind), Peshawar, Multan, Derajat, and Ahmadpur (the old capital of the Bahawalpur State).

Jour. As. Soc. Bengal, Vol. V, No. 8, Numismatic Supplement, August 1909.

CHAPTER XIII.

Shah Mahmud and Shah Shuja-ul-Mulk—the Downfall of the Sadozai Dynasty and the Rise of the Muhammadzais to Power.

AFTER the overthrow of Shah Zamān at Āshpān, the defeated sovereign's camp and treasure amounting to two crores of rupees, fell into the conqueror's hands. The money was divided among his followers by Mahmud. On the 25th of July 1801, he was proclaimed King in Kabul, and assumed the title of Shah Mahmud. To Fath Khan Barakzai, was assigned the Vaziership, with the honorific title of Shah Dost Khan, but in his case the title has completely disappeared and he is famous in the history of his country as plain Fath Khan, or with the prefix of Vazier. The other Chiefs also were fittingly rewarded.

Shah Shuja marched from Peshawar on the 20th September 1801 to make an attempt to gain the throne; but again on the field of Āshpān, he was a second time defeated, and on this occasion he was deprived of Peshawar. He struck across the hills following byepaths, till he reached the Gwalarai (or Gomal) Pass and entered the country of the Ghilzais at the head of 200 horse and 300 foot soldiers.

Hāji Prince Firuzdin had separated from his brother in Persia, and had made the Pilgrimage to the Holy Cities of Islam. After his return, he had settled down in Yazd as a business man; but when Shah Mahmud had removed Shah Zamān from the throne, Prince Kaisar, whom the latter had left to govern Herat, was deposed, and Hāji Prince Firuzdin was summoned from Yazd and installed in the citadel of Herat.

Almost as soon as he had ascended the throne, Mahmud was confronted with a general rising of the Ghilzais, who considered the opportunity too good to be neglected, for attempting to assert their claims to supremacy in Afghanistan. One of their Chiefs was raised by the clan to the diginity of their King. This quarrel dragged on for some time, but the Ghilzais were reduced to subjection in the end, as with their wretched weapons, and lack of cohesion they were not a match in the open field for the Duranis, who were better armed, had the advantage of possessing artillery, and were led by experienced commanders. The Ghilzais had been loyal to Shah Zamān, and the rising may have been connected with the attempts to recover Kabul made by Shuja-ul-Mulk ; but, if so, the movement was badly timed and did not have the effect of creating a diversion in his favour. It will be as well to enter into details, in this place, as the particulars of the Ghilzai rising show the attitude of this powerful section of the people towards the Durani Sovereigns.

Muhammad Amin Khan whom Timur Shah had made Chief of the Tokhi division of the Ghilzais, and also governor of Kalat, and who was killed in the expedition to Kashmir, left three sons, named in order of seniority : Wali Muhammad Khan, Fath Khan, and Mir Alam Khan. On the accesssion of Shah Zamān, he gave to the first-named the title of Wali Niamat Khan and the chiefship of the Tokhis. Owing to his tender years, Mauladad Khan (Musa Khel) was appointed his deputy. In the account of the reign of Ahmad Shah Abdali, it has been mentioned, that Allahyār Khan Ghilzai was called from Persia and put to death ; and that his son Rahmat-ullah Khan escaped with Muhammad Amin Khan to the Suleman Khel country. Rahmat-ullah had a son who became famous. His name was Shā'budin. The Amin-ul-Mulk, a Bābi Afghan and an official of Shah Zamān, fell out with Wali Niamat Khan, and the former took up Shā'budin and brought him into notice, and a split was thus caused among the tribes, part siding with one and part with the other. Kalat was at times in the hands of one faction and at other times, in the possession of the other. In one of the many skirmishes that took place Mauladād, deputy of the young Tokhi Chief was slain. Wali Niamat Khan was killed in a skirmish with some robbers, who had plundered a caravan bound for Kabul in which there were some horses belonging to Shah Zamān. At the head of a few of his Yessāwals, the Chief attempted to arrest the robbers, who had taken to the hills. He was killed in the attack and his corpse was carried to Kalat and buried in his father's grave. Fath Khan, his next brother, soon after avenged Wali Niamat Khan's death on these very persons. Fath Khan also had taken up his brother's quarrel with Shā'budin, and they were engaged in this when war broke out between the Ghilzais and the Duranis.

The course of events at this period suggested to the Ghilzais that it was a good opportunity to declare their independence, and to make an attempt to establish a Ghilzai Kingdom. Abdur Rahmān Khan, Hotaki was declared King and Shā'budin(Shahab-ud-din) his Vazier, the hearty co-operation of the latter being secured by the former giving his daughter Sahib Jān to the latter (with whom, when in her father's house he had been in love), the wife of the defeated, and (now) blind Shah Zamān (to whom she had borne Princes Nāsar and Mansur), with all her jewels, handsome carpets, and household effects. Shā'budin was left to stop communications on the high roads, while Abdur Rahmān went off towards Kabul to raise the Suleman Khel. Troops were despatched from Kabul, and the Ghilzais were defeated; the tribe of Ibrahim Ghilzais losing 5,000 to 6,000 men. Abdur Rahmān retired on Kalat, and a force of Duranis having marched from Kandahar, the Ghilzais left their strong position on the hill to meet them (Fath Khan had already gone over to the Duranis). The battle was fought between Jaldak and Umakai, on the ridge called in Persian Tapa-i-Surkh, and in Pashtu Sur Ghār. The Ghilzais were defeated, the Tokhis losing 700 to 800 men. The Hotakis being chiefly horsemen, escaped comparatively unscathed. Winter put an end to hostilities. This year 1802 is still remembered by the Ghilzais as the "Sāl-i-Katal" or the year of the massacre. The Chiefs on the Ghilzai side were Abdur Rahmān Khan, Hotaki, and Shā'budin Tokhi; those on the Durani side were Abdul Majid Khan, Barakzai; Saidal Khan, Alakozai; Azim Khan, Popalzai; Shādi Khan, Achakzai and Samandar Khan, Bamizai.

In the ensuing spring, Ahmad Khan, Nurzai, marched with an army from Kabul. On his arrival at Hulan Rabat, the Jallālzai Tokhis under Mulla Zāfrān, a descendant of Sultan Malakhe, opposed him, but were defeated with a loss of 600 men. Ahmad Khan proceeded to Kandahar, and brought out a large force of Duranis with guns. This time the Tokhis under Shā'budin Khan and Fath Khan kept to the hill of Kalat, and every attempt of the Duranis to dislodge them failed. The latter then determined to attack the women and children of the Ghilzais in the Arghandāb Valley where they had been sent away for safety. Openly boasting of their intention, they informed Dāra Khan one of the Ghilzai Chiefs of their plan. The latter hastened by a short cut and was in time to protect the camp of the families by a Sangar. After three repulses, the Duranis carried the position, and put all the women and the children to death. The Duranis lost 100 men.

This was the last battle fought between the Ghilzais and Duranis. Abdur Rahmān and Shā'budin retired to the Mamai hills. Shuja-ul-Mulk had also taken refuge in the Kakar country, where he organised a powerful faction which Shā'budin and Fath Khan Babakarzai joined, as well as Shukru-llah Khan, son of Abdur Rahmān Khan, Hotaki, when Shujā recovered the throne, the Chiefs attended on him, but Shā'budin never did as long as he lived, for which the Shah never forgave him. Hearing that this Chief had built a fort in Nāwak, Gulistān Khan (Achakzai), governor of Peshawar, was despatched to destroy it. Fath Khan Babakarzai accompanied him. On entering the Nāwak district, so certain was the Achakzai Chief that Shā'budin would shut himself up in his fort, that he accepted Fath Khan's invitation to his place at Samiyat. Shā'budin getting intelligence of this sallied out with his cavalry and fell on the Duranis as they were carelessly straggling on to the end of the stage, routed the cavalry, killed the artillery men, burnt the gun carriages and spiked the guns, which remained there all the winter. Next spring, Sohbat Khan Popalzai was despatched from Kabul with a force, he recovered and mounted the guns and made use of them for several days without effect against the fort walls, which remained entire until they were destroyed by British Sappers in the autumn of 1839.

Shā'budin and Fath Khan for a long time were at enmity, and were played off by the tribe against each other. The quarrel was considerably increased by Shā'budin Khan's brother Mir Muhammad (long remembered as a bold warrior), being killed by Fath Khan in the district of Khakah. This enmity continued unabated until the death of Fath Khan (the rival chiefs had generally two or three fights every season of harvest). On the death of Fath Khan, Shā'budin made the usual mourning visit to his son, Samad Khan, and the long standing quarrel was made up. Samad Khan married a daughter of Shā'budin Khan, giving one of his own daughters in return to Mansur Khan, grandson of Shā'budin; and thus the blood feud was healed.

Shuja-ul-Mulk reached the Ghilzai country shortly after this movement had come to an end. He was welcomed by the clan and helped on his way towards the south; and he married the daughter of Fath Khan. He passed the winter in the district in which Quetta (now) stands, and made an abortive attempt to take Kandahar. Defeated in his designs, Shuja-ul-Mulk retired to the Bori Valley, on the confines of the Derajat; and tried to dispose of a small part of his jewels in order to raise funds. He was joined by Prince Kaisar and Madad Khan. From the Bori Valley Shuja had been sending letters to those he considered his friends in Kabul to excite them against Mahmud. He at the same time began to work his way northwards through the mountains, with proceeds of the sale of the gems. In course of time, he reached the Zurmat country, and he bestowed a few of his jewels on the leading Ghilzai chiefs in order to raise men for service with him.

Meanwhile, events had been taking place which resulted in his favour. A dissolute member of the Shiah community in Kabul had abducted a boy belonging to a Suni family. A serious riot broke out, the Sunis and Shiahs seized their weapons, and severe fighting took place in Kabul on the 4th and 5th June 1803. The ranks of the Suni faction were reinforced by the people living in the surrounding country, and Mahmud from motives of policy, and his Vazier also, had to intervene on behalf of the Shiahs who were in danger of being exterminated. The Sunis called in Shuja who marched from the Zurmat country to Altimur, where he was welcomed by a deputation [1] who brought him to Kabul (13th July 1803). The Vazier Fath Khan was absent in the Hazara country collecting revenue; and Shah Mahmud[2] shut himself up in the Bālā Hisar. An effort to relieve him made by the Vazier failed, Mahumud surrendered and was imprisoned. It was at first proposed to destroy his sight, but the pleadings of Shah Zamān induced Shuja to forego his intention. Prince Haidar, a son of Shah Zamān, with 6,000 armed men, recovered Kandahar, and Mahmud's son, Prince Kāmrān, escaped to Farah; and the Vazier to the Tobah, a tract in the hills to the north of modern Quetta.

A Persian army also laid siege to Herat, but after a forty days' ineffectual blockade, they were bought off and retired in 1807-08.

Shuja-ul-Mulk pardoned the Vazier Fath Khan who was induced to make his submission, but he took to flight not long after.

Shuja assumed the title of Shah Shuja. One of his first acts was the punishment of Ashik, the Shirāni, who was blown from a gun in Kabul. The Koh-i-Nur and the ruby, Fakhraj were also recovered.

Prince Kaisar, son of Shah Zamān, had been induced by Vazier Fath Khan to revolt in Kandahar, but he was defeated.

After settling the affairs of Kandahar, the Shah entered Sind at the head of a large army and recovered about 20 lakhs of rupees in settlement of arrears of revenue. From Shikarpur the Shah marched towards Peshawar, and from that place he proceeded to Kabul where he passed the summer. In the autumn, an expedition was despatched to Kashmir, where the governor had proclaimed his

[1] The deputation of notables was headed by the Mukhtār-ud-daulah.

[2] See Appendix III.

independence. The court moved to winter quarters in Peshawar, where the expedition returned, having proved successful, leaving a governor in the valley. Shuja-ul-Mulk had no peace. Kandahar was taken by Prince Kāmrān, and retaken by the Shah. The Vazier Fath Khan again submitted to the Shah, and a second time fled from his court and joined Prince Kāmrān. The escape of his brother Mahmud and the other princes from the Bālā Hisar produced further complications. The Chief Priest of Kabul was the moving spirit of the plot, and one Muhammad Ali, a tailor, was the instrument by which it was carried out. This man had been employed in the citadel, and he became acquainted with Prince Mahmud in the course of his daily avocations. Muhammad Ali by some means succeeded in setting the Princes free. He concealed Mahmud in his own house in the City, while the other Princes found shelter elsewhere. After some days, when the hue and cry had subsided, and it was comparatively safe to travel, horses were provided by the Chief Priest, and Mahmud and his liberator set out from Kabul. Travelling with circumspection and by unfrequented paths, the fugitives eventually made their way to Farah, where they found Prince Kāmrān and the Vazier Fath Khan Barakzai.

Prince Kaisar, who now governed Kabul, incited by the Mukhtār-ud-daulah[1], rebelled and attempted to seize Peshawar, and very nearly was successful (3rd March 1808). No sooner had this movement been put down than news was brought that Mahmud had seized Kandahar. Shah Shuja hastened to that city, and Mahmud and Fath Khan retired to Farah. The Shah went on to Sind, and was on his way northwards through the Derajat, when he heard from Bahawalpore of the advance of the British Mission under the Hon'ble Mountstuart Elphinstone. He hurried on to Peshawar to make preparations to receive the Mission. As soon as Shah Shuja had reached Peshawar, 10th of January, he set to work to collect as many men as possible for a great attempt on Kashmir where his governor had rebelled. The Shah's Vazier commanded the expedition.

The Mission which was despatched by Lord Minto, the Governor-General, arrived in Peshawar on the 25th of February. It was the beginning of official relations between the State of Afghanistan and the British Government, and the reasons for its despatch were the same as those which had prompted the Mission to Persia of Sir John Malcolm. The suspected intentions of Napoleon with regard to the middle east.

---

[1] In revenge for not receiving the Vazierate, he was killed in battle at Doaba, near Peshawar, where Kaisar was routed.

The expedition to Kashmir was a complete failure. The Vazier Akram Khan was very unpopular with his men, and in addition he had offended the Chief of Muzaffarābād, and whether owing to the road being blocked by snow, or the resentment of the Chief, the royal troops were unable to advance and the Vazier, in fear of being seized by his own men and delivered to the enemy, took to flight and reached Peshawar, where news of the reverse had arrived on the 23rd of April. Only some 2,000 men of the whole army returned in an evil plight to that place. To add to the Shah's perplexities news arrived that Mahmud had taken Kabul. A general panic prevailed in Peshawar. The King was at his wit's end to raise money, and the Vazier refused to lend or give his master any part of the hoards he had inherited from his father and had added to himself. Akram Khan, Bamizai, was a brave man, but his avarice, haughty and irritable disposition had rendered him generally unpopular, and his action in denying his Sovereign pecuniary assistance was inexplicable as their interests were identical. There was also a personal animosity existing between the Vazier Fath Khan and Akram Khan, which had determined the former to finally join Mahmud.

As it was not the policy of the British Government to take any part in the civil war, Lord Minto recalled the Mission, which left Peshawar on the 14th June 1809. The Royal Harem, and the Royal Treasure, was also sent with it for safety to Rawalpindi. Shah Shuja's efforts to raise an army proved successful, and the prestige he had acquired by the stay at Peshawar of the Mission had put his affairs into a highly prosperous condition. Some 14,000 men with artillery collected under his standard.

Shah Mahmud had marched from Kandahar, and Kabul had again been surrendered to him by the Kazzilbash tribes out of gratitude for the efforts made on their behalf, in the struggle with the Sunis. The governor of the city, Ahmad Khan, Nurzai, had also joined Mahmud with the garrison. From Kabul Shah Mahmud marched towards Jalālābād and Shah Shuja set out from Peshawar to meet him.

Treachery was rife in both camps. Alim Khan, Nurzai Sardar, had been instrumental in gaining possession of Kandahar, but at Kabul, owing to his attitude towards the Vazier, the latter had become suspicious of the Sardar's fidelity. Notwithstanding the fact that the Nurzai Chief was his son-in-law, Fath Khan determined to remove him; especially as Alim Khan was leagued with other Durani Chiefs who might be expected to follow him if he deserted. The Vazier recommended that this Chief should be executed; and when their camp was pitched on a ravine between Jagdalak and

Surkhpul, Alim Khan was put to death, and the locality has ever since been known as Alim Khan Kushta, the place where Alim Khan was executed.

On Shah Shuja's side, his baggage master had been bought by the Vazier Fath Khan, and had promised to act in a treacherous manner in return for a large sum of money. Madad Khan, the Sardar of the Ishakzais, also hated Shuja's Vazier, Akram Khan, and was only waiting for a favourable opportunity to go over to Mahmud. After the troops had passed the Khaibar and were approaching Jalālābād Shah Shuja's baggage master, in charge of the tents and baggage sent in advance, instead of forming the camp at Jalālābād, as he had been ordered, carried them to Nimla, thirty miles beyond that place. When Shah Shuja on an August morning set out from Ali Boghan, six miles to the east of Jalālābād, and did not find his camp at that place he became suspicious. The commander of his advanced troops also sent back alarming accounts of the Ishakzai Sardar's demeanour, which proved him to be in communication with the enemy. The Shah and his Vazier, Akram Khan, hastened on with their troops and eventually reached Nimla. At this place, about midway between Peshawar and Kabul, there was a famous old garden. It had been a stage on the Royal Route from Peshawar, and inside the garden, which was square, there were magnificent Plane trees and Cypresses. There were four raised platforms of masonry for the purpose of pitching tents, surrounded by great cypress trees planted at equal intervals.[1]

Late in the day while the Shah's troops fatigued after their long march were straggling into camp and putting up their tents, they were surprised by Vazier Fath Khan at the head of a smaller force of fresh troops. Taken at a disadvantage, notwithstanding their greater numbers, Shah Shuja's men were completely routed. Their Sovereign's guns, baggage, and a part of his treasury were lost, and he was compelled to take to flight. A dramatic incident took place during the confused struggle. Akram Khan, Shuja's Vazier, encountered Fath Khan. The former was armed with a double barrelled gun of a modern pattern, one of the presents made by the Head of the Mission a few months before. The former levelled the piece at Fath Khan and discharged both barrels; but one of the clansmen of the Vazier spurred his horse in front of his Chieftain and received the bullets destined for the latter and fell dead. In the mean-

[1] Shah Jahan in the 17th century encamped here. It was a stage on the Royal Road from Delhi and Peshawar to Kabul, and ordered the garden to be laid out. It still exists.

time another man of the Barakzai clan fired his pistol point blank at Akram Khan, who fell off his horse a corpse. The head of his Vazier raised on a spear and displayed before his men completed the discomfiture of Shah Shuja. He made his way to the south, and though he was put in possession of Kandahar four months later, he was unable to retain it, and was forced to retire to the Punjab by the Gomal Pass. After an interview at Sahiwāl[1] with Ranjit Singh, the Shah proceeded to Rawalpindi, where he joined his family. Here he rested for a year.

Mahmud was now king, but his reign was devoid of much importance. The Vazier carried on the government and Mahmud abandoned himself to self-indulgence, and gradually resigned his authority to his minister. In 1811 a meeting was brought about by the latter between Shah Mahmud and Ranjit Singh, while the Shah was proceeding (or was being taken by the Vazier) to Sind to re-assert Afghan supremacy.

Vazier Fath Khan again met Ranjit Singh, and it was arranged that the latter was to permit the Afghans to march by the Bhimbar route to Kashmir, and aid them in taking possession of the valley in the name of Shah Mahmud; in return for this assistance one-third of the revenue was to be paid to Ranjit Singh. In the previous year Shah Shuja had been made a prisoner by Jahandād Khan, whom he had placed in the fort at Attock as his representative. From that place the Shah was carried to Kashmir, where the governor, Ata Muhammad Khan, had detained him in confinement for 12 months. When the latter was conquered in February 1813, Vazier Fath Khan handed Shuja over to the Sikhs, by whom he was forwarded to Lahore. Attock was shortly after surrendered to the Sikhs, and Vazier Fath Khan, aided by his brother Dost Muhammad, was defeated in Chach, in an action fought on the 13th July 1813.

Vazier Fath Khan had left his brother Azim Khan to rule Kashmir, and the stipulation regarding the division of the revenue having been disregarded, a Sikh Army invaded Kashmir, but sustained a crushing defeat.

In Lahore, Shah Shuja, under pressure, had been constrained to part with the Koh-i-Nur diamond to Ranjit Singh for a consideration. He was nevertheless guarded carefully and kept a prisoner in his quarters. In December 1814 the flight of the ladies of the Royal Harem with the crown jewels to Ludhiana was successfully accomplished. Shortly after, the ex-Shah himself eluded the vigilance of his

[1] On the Jhelum river.

guards, and slipped out of Ranjit Singh's hands. With the aid of the Raja of Kishtwăr he very nearly succeeded in an ăttempt on Kashmir, but was driven back by exceptionally severe weather. After a variety of adventures, he reached Ludhianah in 1816, where he joined his family and the blind Shah Zamān. The allowance of 18,000 rupees originally assigned for the maintenance of the refugees, per annum, was raised to 50,000 rupees after Shah Shuja arrived. His minor and unsuccessful efforts against Shah Mahmud merit no description, and leaving him for the present in Ludhianah, it will be useful to return to the course of events in Afghanistan.

Fath Khan, the Vazier, was apparently very zealous in his master's interest, but in effect he was strengthening his own influence by providing his numerous brothers with governorships of Provinces, and also amassing great wealth himself. It is doubtful if this wily chieftain had ever forgiven the Sadozais for the execution of his father, but in the indolent voluptuary Mahmud he found a useful and most convenient stalking horse by means of which the right to the government of the Barakzais (of which their remote ancestor had been cozened) might be restored. Shuja's overweening conceit, autocratic bearing, and his persistent bad luck, coupled with the vices of Mahmud and his profligate son Kāmrān, were fast alienating the last of the adherents which the Sadozais possessed. So long as Mahmud enjoyed the means of gratifying his appetites and was not worried, the Vazier was allowed to do as he pleased.

Prince Kāmrān, however, took a different view of the situation. He can best be described as a human tiger. A debauchee of the worst type, there ran through his disposition a strong vein of ferocity and cruelty. On occasions, during his early manhood, he displayed determination and the courage of his race; but in later years, after all avenues of action had been closed to him, he became a tyrannical ruler, and gave himself up to horrible vices.

Hāji Prince Firuz-ud-din, who ruled over Herat, was suspected of aiming at independence, and it became necessary to take order with him. In 1817 the Vazier set out for Herat accompanied by Shah Mahmud and Prince Kāmrān. On this occasion so lavish was the Vazier in his expenditure that, although the expedition did not last more than six months, he is said to have disbursed ninety-six lakhs of rupees in advances to the soldiers and in presents to chiefs in his master's train. Such an expenditure of money alone would have rendered the Afghans glad to make Fath Khan their king. Mahmud waited at Kandahar with his son, while the Vazier went ahead to make sure of Herat. Prince Firuz-ud-din had reason also to apprehend a serious attack on Herat by the Persians as Husen Ali Mirza, son of Shah Fath Ali, was assembling his forces in Meshed. Firuz-ud-din nevertheless would not admit the Vazier's troops into the city. The latter pretended to acquiesce, but he set intrigues on foot, which resulted in the city and the citadel also being delivered up to him as well as the Prince himself. It was reported to the Vazier that the Prince's treasures were concealed in the apartments of the harem; but the sanctity of these chambers did not save them from spoliation. Dost Muhammad is said to have conducted this operation with very scant ceremony and to have roughly handled Rokya Begum, the wife of Malik Kasim (son of Firuz-ud-din), who was Shah Mahmud's daughter. Dost Muhammad was compelled to disgorge some of the plunder he was said to have obtained. At any rate, he fell out with his brother, and left him, having decided to join Azim Khan in Kashmir. On his way from Herat, he met Mahmud and Kāmrān, and paid his respects to them for the last time.

Meanwhile, the Persians had commenced their march on Herat, and the Vazier, aided by his brothers Purdil Khan and Kohandil Khan, advanced against them, and at the end of 1817, an action was fought at Kafir Kala between the opposing forces, in which the Persians were defeated, but in the moment of victory, Fath Khan was struck in the face by a spent bullet and fell off his charger. This accident disheartened his men who, regardless of their success, broke and fled. When Fath Khan regained his senses, he learned that his army had dispersed. He returned to Herat and found that Mahmud and Kāmrān had arrived, and were in camp in the garden known as the Bagh-i-Zāghān: there he repaired and paid his respects to his sovereign and the heir apparent.

The latter matured his plans to overthrow the Minister, whom he feared, and of whose influence he was jealous. His father, Mahmud, was won over to agree to this scheme. The Vazier was summoned to the private apartments of the Shah, on the pretence of discussing the affairs of Malik Kasim, son of Hāji Prince Firuz-ud-din. As soon as the Vazier appeared, he was seized, and a red-hot needle applied to his eyeballs destroyed his sight.[1] As soon as it was known that the Vazier had been arrested, Sardars Purdil, Kohandil, and Sherdil Khans and other brothers of Fath Khan, with their clansmen, effected their escape, and evading Kāmrān's myrmidons, they took the road to Kandahar. They assembled at the fort of Nad Ali on the Helmand river which the Barakzais had acquired by purchase. The father of the

[1] At the instigation of Ata Muhammad, son of the late Mukhtār-ud-daulah.

Vazier left twenty-one sons, so there was no lack of persons to carry on the blood feud with the Sadozais.

Sardar Azim Khan, in Kashmir, as soon as he heard of the affair, despatched his younger brother Dost Muhammad as his advance guard towards Kabul, and followed him in person to Peshawar. In the first flush of his rage he sent from Kashmir a Koran, to which he had affixed his seal, inviting Shah Shuja to occupy the throne. Owing to his strained relations with Ranjit Sing, the ex-King was unable to take the direct road to Peshawar, and he was compelled to make a wide detour by the Derajat. He overcame the Governor of Dera Ghazi Khan and took possession of that town, where he found two field pieces. The news of Shah Shuja's success brought several of the late Vazier's brothers to his side, including Sardar Purdil Khan, the brother; and Sarbuland Khan, the son of the blinded Vazier. In the meantime, however, Sardar Muhammad Azim Khan, on arrival in Peshawar, had discovered a tool more suited to his purpose in Prince Ayub (another son of Shah Zamān). As soon as Shah Shuja appeared on the scene he was attacked by the Barakzai, and after a severe conflict at the garden of Ali Mardān Khan, the ex-King was defeated and once more a fugitive. After hiding for two months among the hills of the Khaibar, he made his way south to Shikarpur, where his son Prince Timur was governor. He remained there a full year and more, and had begun to raise troops, having made a compact with the Amirs of Sind for help in his enterprise.

After they had worked their will on the Vazier, Shah Mahmud and his son Kāmrān left Herat in charge of Prince Seif-ul-Muluk, and taking their captive with them, they made for Kandahar with the utmost possible speed. Kabul was held by Prince Jahangir, Kāmrān's son, with Ata Muhammad Khan, son of the Mukhtar-ud-daulah as his tutor and adviser. The latter had been deprived of the government of Kashmir, and in consequence he was no friend of the Sadozais. Dost Muhammad had reached Jalālābād, and the sulky Ata Muhammad invited him to seize the capital. Although Dost Muhammad gained the City, Prince Jahangir held the Bala Hissar, staunchly supported by the Kazilbash tribes.[1] The regular garrison of Arabs and Abyssinian guards also were loyal. Dost Muhammad made strenuous efforts to capture the citadel. A mine was sprung

---

[1] Ata Muhammad was seized by Dost Muhammad, his sight was destroyed by Pir Muhammad, son of the Vazier.

See App. IV. Relations between the Afghans and Persians in 1816-17, which led to the downfall of Vazier Fath Khan, Barakzai, and of the Sadozais.

under the western bastion, which, however, was not completely wrecked, but an assault on the breach was repulsed with heavy loss. At the end of forty days, as no help arrived, Prince Jahangir with one of his adherents escaped from the Bālā Hisar, and fled by way of Hindkai and joined Prince Kāmrān in Kandahar.

In 1818 Shah Mahmud and Prince Kāmrān led 30,000 good troops from that city to attempt the recovery of Kabul. As the blind Vazier refused to further their designs, the Prince resolved to get rid of him; and in order to render their adherence to his father's cause beyond a doubt, he purposed that the Durani chiefs present in the camp should decree the Vazier's death, and also themselves execute the sentence. At Saiadābād (47 miles from Kabul) they were summoned to a council, presided over by Kāmrān, his meagre figure rendered imposing by scarlet robes, the "vestments of wrath", significant of death. This attire sufficiently denoted Kāmrān's fixed intention with regard to the blind Vazier, and also to any one in that council who should dare to thwart him. He was not one who would stick at trifles, and no one knew what the curtains of the council tent may not have concealed. The assembled chiefs obsessed by the venom of the Prince, in fear of their own lives—in dread of the searing irons (used to destroy the sight); or the less terrible sabre of the executioner, decreed the death of the Vazier, in accordance with the instructions of the Prince. Orders were issued forthwith, and the blind Fath Khan was led to the place of execution: round him the Durani chiefs took their stand. To each chief a certain stroke had been assigned, swords were drawn, and in a moment the victim fell beneath their blows; nothing could disturb his splendid fortitude, and except the creed of Islam, and verses of the Koran relating to a martyr's death, not a sound is said to have escaped his lips. Afterwards some reverent hands gathered up his manglod remains; they were put into a sack and carried away, and decently interred at Ghazni.

Dost Muhammad Khan with two thousand regulars, four thousand tribal levies and two field pieces took up a position at Chauki Arghandi, covering the approach to Kabul. Kāmrān on arrival at Maidān, two marches from the capital, heard that his enemy had strengthened a naturally strong position with field works, and retracing his steps he moved by Aobak into the district of Chaharāsia, compelling his enemy to take up a fresh position at Hindkai. The next day a partial action was fought, which terminated greatly in favour of Kāmrān. As the issue was very doubtful a council of war assembled in Dost Muhammad's tent, and it was decided to resort to the time-honoured ruse of sending concocted letters into the enemy's camp, to suggest the idea of there being traitors in his army. The blind Ata Muhammad, son of the late Mukhtar-ud-Daulah, a known adherent of the Sadozais, was a prisoner in Dost Muhammad's hands, and he was compelled, on pain of instant death, to indite the letters, which were sent by the Barakzai Chief by a trusty messenger who was carefully instructed to allow himself to be captured. The documents were seized and carried to Prince Kāmrān and were regarded by him as genuine. Knowing that he was detested, he dared not disregard them. He at once ordered the horses of the Royal stables to be prepared for a journey, and without bidding his chiefs farewell, he, with his father, and their personal followers, under cover of darkness, left the camp and fled towards the south. The next morning his chiefs were dismayed to find that their Sovereign had abandoned a half-won victory, and they followed on his footsteps.

At Shashgau, where Mahmud's party had been compelled to rest, he was overtaken by the remains of his army, and learned that he had been deceived. With heavy hearts the fugitives continued their course, hoping at Kandahar to be able to rally their men, and to collect fresh troops. At Kalat-i-Ghilzai, 147 miles further on, they heard that Kandahar had fallen. As soon as Kāmrān was out of the way, Purdil Khan had appeared before the place and blockaded it. The Governor refused to surrender until the result of the battle at Kabul was known, and both parties waited to hear what would happen. On the report of the flight of Mahmud from Kabul, Kandahar was delivered to the Barakzais.

The fugitives turned aside and entered the Derawat country where they lingered till Kohandil Khan, Barakzai, was reported to be on the march in their direction, with Malik Kāsim, son of Hāji Prince Firuzdin in his camp. Mahmud thereupon retired to Herat, where he was allowed to maintain a degree of authority by the Barakzai Chiefs.

In the same year, the branch of the Sadozais who had governed Multan for about thirty years were deprived of their government by Ranjit Sing, and the aged chieftain Muzaffar Khan died, sword in hand, on the day in which the citadel of Multan was stormed by the Sikh fanatics.[1]

Thus came to an end the Sadozai Dynasty. The Barakzai Chiefs at first made use of princelets of that family as puppets to conciliate any adherents they might still possess, but very soon they were able to dispense with this pretence, and as none of the princelets were men of character or ability, they were allowed to sink into obscurity in their own country, or they drifted away to Ludhiana.

[1] 2nd June 1818. Cunningham's Hist. of the Sikhs.

CHAPTER XIV.

THE MUHAMMADZAI AMIR OF KABUL. DOST MUHAMMAD BARAKZAI, AND RESTORATION OF SHAH SHUJA-UL-MULK.

HAVING disposed of Shah Mahmud and Prince Kāmrān, the Barakzai brethren became masters of Afghanistan. When Muhammad Azim Khan arrived in Peshawar, he found just the right person for his purpose in Prince Ayub, one of Shah Zamān's sons, who was content to surrender his rights into the Sardar's hands, provided he was assured of the title of King and enough for his pleasures. He was immediately made King, while Azim Khan assumed the position of his Vazier. As he was the eldest surviving brother of Fateh Khan, the other brothers acknowledged Azim Khan's authority as the head of the family. Dost Muhammad[1] in Kabul had set up his own puppet—Prince Sultan Ali Sadozai—but he was soon put aside; and when Azim Khan reached Kabul, Shah Ayub was advised to sanction his kinsman's execution, and he proved duly amenable.

Ranjit Singh took advantage of the condition of affairs in Afghanistan to invade Peshawar, but on this occasion he was content to garrison Khairabad, on the right bank of the Indus, and opposite Attock, so as to allow of his crossing the river whenever he wished to do so without opposition. Kashmir also was too strong a temptation to be withstood. On the 5th July a Sikh Army scaled the Passes, and annexed the valley, and Nawāb Jabbār Khan retired to Peshawar. Ranjit Sing continued to nibble at the outskirts of Afghanistan, and a few months later, Dera Ghazi Khan was attached, and in 1821 Dera Ismail Khan became a part of the Sikh Chief's dominions. In 1822 Yār Muhammad, another of the Barakzai brethren and Governor of

[1] As a boy he was employed in sweeping the famous Shrine of Mihtar Lam in the Lamghan district. At the age of 14; he is said to have been taken up by his brother Fateh Khan who employed him regularly afterwards.

Peshawar, considered it advisable to propitiate the Sikh Ruler with the gift of some valuable horses.

In the meantime, Muhammad Azim Khan, the Vazier, carried his puppet, Ayub, to Kandahar, and thence to Shikarpur, where Shuja-ul-Mulk had collected 5,000 horsemen, some infantry, and ten guns. The Amirs of Sind were anxious for him to leave Shikarpur, and when Azim Khan was marching from Kandahar, the forces of Sind threatened the fugitives' communications with India. Shuja disbanded his troops and retired to Ludhiana. Having removed this source of danger, for Shuja had been for over a year in Shikarpur, raising troops, and had been a rallying point for all who were ill-disposed towards the Barakzais, Azim Khan turned his attention to Peshawar and the Sikhs: he marched in person to that place. Ranjit Singh crossed the Indus on the the 13th, and on the 14th March 1821 he defeated the Barakzai chieftain in a pitched battle at Naushahro. Peshawar was sacked, and the country up to the Khyber Pass was overrun; but the Sikh ruler was willing to allow Yār Muhammad to retain the government of the place as his tributary. Azim Khan retired towards Kabul after this defeat, but on the road he fell ill, and died at Lataband.

The value of the estate left by the late Vazier was estimated at three crores of rupees (£3,000,000 sterling at that period). The division of this property became an additional source of trouble. The son of the deceased chief, named Habib-ullah Khan, was at once recognised as chief of the clan. In the turmoil that prevailed no one paid any attention to Shah Ayub, and he, finding his position to be an impossible one, wisely made his way to Lahore. Ranjit pensioned him till his death. The quarrels between the Barakzais grew to such a pitch that the distracted inhabitants of Kabul threatened to kill both Dost Muhammad and Purdil Khan, the leaders of the two parties who were wrangling over the estate of the late Vazier. Finally it was agreed that the whole of the property left by Azim Khan should be retained by the brothers Purdil and Sherdil Khans, and used to defray the cost of meeting foreign invasions. By the terms of this compact, these Sardars secured nine-tenths of the lands and revenues of Kandahar. The widow of the late Vazier was brought to agree to this arrangement, it was believed, by being told that, if she withheld her consent her only son, Habib-ullah, would be blown from a gun.

The other brothers held unequal shares of territory somewhat in the following proportions. Jabbār Khān was given the Ghilzai country;

Sultan and Yār Muhammad held Sukar, Lohgar, and one-half of Kabul. The other half of Kabul, with the Kohistan, and the Koh Daman, fell to the lot of Dost Muhammad. Jalālābād went to Zamān Khan, a nephew, and Ghazni was assigned to Muhammad Khan, own brother of Dost Muhammad. In about two years' time, the latter appropriated the Ghilzai country, and the other share of Kabul. Habib-ullah, who was a most unsatisfactory person, was turned out of Kabul by his uncle, and joined Yār Muhammad in Peshawar, who gave him an yearly allowance of 50,000 rupees (1824).

Neither Mahmud nor Kāmrān were in a position to intervene, and the only other enemies likely to prove troublesome were Ranjit Singh, and Shah Shuja. The English, with whom Dost Muhammad was fated to come into intimate contact, at this period were regarded by him, by his brother who governed Peshawar—and before the annexation of Kashmir by the Sikhs—by Jabbār Khan, in the light of possible allies against the encroachments of Ranjit Singh. The death of Mahmud in Herat in 1828, removed one source of danger.

In 1829 Yār Muhammad was defeated and mortally wounded by the famous Ahmad Shah. This person is said to have been a member of a Saiad family in Bareilly (United Provinces). He commenced life as a follower of the notorious free lance and robber, Amir Khan ; but when the latter settled down respectably as the Nawab of Tonk, Ahmad Shah adopted a religious life, and attained great distinction as a preacher. He left Delhi in 1826, and at the head of several hundreds of followers, he passed through Sind to Kandahar, where he was coolly received by the Barakzai Sardars. He then continued through the Ghilzai country, and eventually in the year 1827, he crossed the Kabul river into Panjtār in the Yusufzai country. The head of the Panjtar family welcomed the arrival of the Saiad, as his following of Ghazis formed a very useful reinforcement to the fighting men of that district.

Although Saiad Ahmad Shah had defeated Yār Muhammad, he was unable to seize Peshawar, owing to the presence of Sikh troops under Sher Sing and General Ventura. In 1830, this religious teacher was defeated by the Sikhs on the left bank of the Indus, and forced to recross it. He succeeded in gaining possession of Peshawar, which he handed back to Sultan Muhammad Khan Barakzai, on whom he imposed a tribute. In May 1831 Ahmed Shah was surprised and killed at Bālākot by the Sikh troops. His popularity with the Yusufzais had declined before this happened, as he was accused of marrying all the eligible heiresses in the country to his needy followers, and also on account of his lofty pretensions. His deputies were expelled after his death, the Ghazis were dispersed by the tribesmen, and his family was driven to find an asylum with his old master, the Nawab of Tonk.[1]

After the death of Yār Muhammad, the wretched creature Habibullah removed from Peshawar to Jalālābād, where his cousin Zamān Khan gave him a home. Here, the former fell in love with one of the ladies of his cousin's harem, and in order to satisfy his ill-regulated passions, he attempted to remove Zamān by poison. He was turned out of Afghan Territory, and he went off in a great rage, vowing he would join Shah Shuja. By the time he had reached Dera Ismail Khan, he became utterly insane, and signalized himself by murdering several of his slave-girls. He either died, or was put away soon after.

In 1832 Sir Alexander Burnes passed through Kabul on his well known journey to Bokhara. His writings and those of his native assistant, the Kashmiri Mohan Lall, have thrown considerable light on the affairs of Afghanistan. Long before this, towards the end of the 18th century, the adventurous Englishman Forster, had travelled overland, through Afghanistan, on his way to Europe from Hindustan. In 1826 Mr. Stirling of the Bengal Civil Service had spent some time in Afghanistan. In 1827 Masson drew attention to the antiquities he had discovered in Afghanistan. In 1828 Mr. Fraser, a Bengal Civilian, travelled in that country. He was followed in 1829 by the adventurous American Dr. Harlan. Dr. Wolff, attracted by the traditions of the Afghans, visited Kabul on his enterprising journey undertaken with the object of preaching Christianity to the Jews of Bokhara. He was disgusted with the Afghans, whose Jewish origin he appears to have scouted as a fabrication.

In 1833 Shah Shuja made his best planned independent attack on the supremacy of the Barakzais. He used his asylum in Ludhiana as a base of operations. On the 17th of February he left that place, and having come to an understanding with Ranjit Sing, the latter advanced him a lakh of rupees. The Amirs of Sind had promised their aid ; but when Shuja entered Sind they withdrew from their promises. Shuja, who had placed his head-quarters outside the town of Shikarpore, sent troops to seize Bhakkar, a romantic stronghold on an island in the Indus ; and on the 9th January 1834, the Sind

---

[1] A remnant of his followers, however, clung to the hills and they were soon after reinforced by Wahabi zealots from Bengal, Behar, and the United Provinces. Patna in Behar was the place of origin of these zealots and their doctrines. These formed settlements, first at Sitana, and then at Malka, in the Buner country. They assumed the name of Mujahidin or the Holy Warriors—a title which indicates very sufficiently their attitude towards the Indian Government later on.

troops were defeated with heavy loss about twelve miles from Rohri, the town on the left bank of the river and opposite Bhakkar. The Amirs paid 5 lakhs of rupees (£50,000), which was a welcome addition to Shuja's resources; for he had several disciplined battalions, the mainstay of his army, composed of Rohillas and other Hindustanis. These were 6,000 strong and commanded by a Scotsman, Campbell,[1] once an officer in the East India Company's Army, and afterwards in the Sikh Army. The pay of Shah Shuja's troops amounted to about a lakh a month.

The Barakzais offered no opposition to his advance, but shut themselves up in the City of Kandahar, and asked Dost Muhammad to help them. Putting aside his quarrel with his brothers, the latter responded to their appeal. At the end of two months, Shah Shuja gave a reluctant consent to an attempt to take the place by storm. The attack was unsuccessful, and he lost his best men in the assault. Dost Muhammad also was at hand, advancing rapidly to the succour of the beleagured town. Shah Shuja abandoned his good position, for another not so good among the gardens of Abbas-ābād, to the west of Kandahar, which gave him an uninterrupted line of retreat towards the west. Here he was attacked by the combined forces of Kabul and Kandahar. The result of two days hard fighting was favourable to the Shah, and quarrels had broken out among the allied forces; but in the hour of victory Campbell was severely wounded, one of his guns burst and killed several men, and exploded a magazine. A panic seized his Hindustani troops, which nothing could allay (2nd June 1834); his men broke, and the Shah fled to Lāsh on the shore of the Lake of Seistan. He disdained the proposal to seize Herat and to deprive his nephew of the Province; and he made his way across the desert to Kalat, where he found a temporary shelter with Mehrāb Khan, and then through Jesalmir[2] on his way to Ludhiana. Campbell was taken prisoner by Dost Muhammad and took service with him. The title of Sher Muhammad, and the following robes of an Afghan noble, concealed the identity of this gallant adventurer. He commanded the Afghan troops in Balkh and the districts beyond the Hindu-Kush, and is believed to have died in 1856-7—a Muhammadan.

The loss of Peshawar, which was taken on the 6th May 1834, by the Sikhs under the celebrated Hari Sing, was followed by a tender of

[1] According to some, he was of mixed parentage.

[2] Lieut. Boileau of the Bengal Engineers met Shah Shuja on the 2nd March 1835 at Koilath near Jesalmir.

friendship made by Dost Muhammad to the Indian Government; but the victory he won in July over Shah Shuja restored his confidence. On the 11th of May 1835, he was obliged to retire from the presence of a Sikh Army with the loss of two guns, and on the 30th May 1837, the Afghan troops under his eldest son, Muhammad Akbar, failed in their attempt on Jamrud, and were enticed into the open country and defeated with the loss of many guns. The gallant Hari Sing lost his life on this occasion, but the Afghans were unable to take advantage of this good fortune, and were forced to retire up the Khyber Pass.

Prince Kāmrān had become master of Herat after his father died in 1828; and in the same year a pestilence (either plague or cholera), was raging throughout Afghanistan, and the Vazier Ata Muhammad died of it—it had made its appearance in Herat. The Prince appointed his late minister's nephew, Yār Muhammad, to the vacant office. Early in 1832 the Shah of Persia, Fateh Ali, appointed his Heir-apparent to the government of Khurassan; and Abbas Mirza deputed his eldest son to lead the expedition against Herat. Prince Kāmrān sent Yār Muhammad to Meshed to interview the Prince Governor, and the latter placed the Vazier in arrest, and tortured him; in order to force him to agree to the surrender of Herat. Yār Muhammad, however, showed great fortitude under his sufferings, and Abbas Mirza having become dangerously ill, released the captive and recalled his son from Herat to his bed-side. In 1836 Kāmrān intervened in the affairs of Seistan on behalf of Malik Jalāludin. In 1837 he marched against Kandahar, but the Vazier was opposed to his scheme of meddling with the Barakzais, and after obtaining some trifling successes, the Prince retired; but he was allowed to amuse himself with laying siege to Lāsh and Juwein in Seistan, until he was recalled to Herat by the news of the advance of a Persian Army, led by the Shah in person. The siege of the city was commenced on the 15th November 1837.

The treaty of Turkomanchai[1] (signed on the 21st February 1828) introduced a new factor into the politics of the Middle, East, and Central Asia, which has influenced British relations with Afghanistan until recently. In 1835 Dost Muhammad sent a representative to the Court of Teheran, at a time when the successes of Ranjit Sing rankled in his mind. The invasion of Herat by the Persians was regarded with suspicion by the British Government, and when the demands of the British Representative at Teheran, to induce the Shah to re-

[1] Between Russia and Persia concluded the war between these countries, which was so disastrous to the latter.

linquish the siege, had no effect, on the 19th of June 1838, Indian troops under Colonel Sheriff were landed on the island of Karak in the Persian Gulf. The action thus taken was effectual. The Shah also had been unable to capture Herat, and the absence of discipline in his army had wasted the supplies of food in the country round the scene of operations. The faithful Colonel Semineau, a French Officer of Engineers, and an old soldier of the Empire, found his advice and efforts neglected by the vacillating Shah, who was swayed by an unprincipled Minister, and the incompetent Persian Commanders regarded him with jealousy, and active dislike, which neutralized his efforts. Eldred Pottinger, a British Officer, who had been travelling in disguise, and was in Herat, had been detained and impressed into the service of the Vazier and constrained to advise him. On the 9th of September 1838, the siege was raised, and the Shah retreated from Herat, having reduced the country to a condition of utter destitution. In the Persian Camp was Colonel Blaremburg, a Russian Engineer, and a member of the Mission, which had been despatched under Count Simonich.[1] The latter remained in Teheran. The Dragoman of the Mission, and Captain Vitkevich, also belonging to it, were present with the Persians. The last was a fluent linguist, and an active officer, and he continued to make himself very busy in Afghanistan.

In the month of March 1836, Lord Auckland relieved Lord William Bentinck as Governor-General in India. Dost Muhammad addressed a letter of welcome and congratulation to the new Governor-General, and was informed, in reply, that it was not the practice of the British Government to meddle in the affairs of other independent States. But in September 1837, Sir Alexander (at that time Captain) Burnes was sent on a professedly commercial mission to Dost Muhammad, which, however, was in reality a journey of political discovery. He was accompanied by Doctor Lord and Lieutenant Leech of the Bombay Engineers. From Kabul the last was despatched to Kandahar on a similar journey of discovery, also under a commercial disguise.

The Ruler of Kabul appears not to have made a secret of his dealings with Persia and the Russians, to which he professed British neglect of his overtures had driven him in despair. The situation was complicated by the appearance in Kabul of the energetic Captain Vitkevich[2], who posed as the envoy of Russia; he had been, it was

[1] A Dalmatian, taken prisoner while serving in the French Army, on the retreat from Moscow, he entered the Russian service. He arrived in Teheran in February 1833 as Minister to the Shah—Markham's History of Persia.

[2] Both Simonich and Vitkevich were disavowed by Prince Nesselrode. The former was superseded by Count Meden in 1839; and Vitkevich committed suicide. —Markham's History of Persia.

said, at the time, encouraging the Barakzai Sardars of Kandahar to strengthen their alliance with Persia. Burnes appears to have been strongly in favour of attaching Dost Muhammad to the British by strengthening his hands against foreign and domestic enemies. Calcutta and Simla, however, are a long way from Kabul[1], and in those days of dâk posts, he may have been unable to keep step with alterations in ideas and policy which had taken place. In his eagerness to detach the Chief of Kandahar from their Persian alliance, he exceeded his instructions, and made them definite promises of aid, and for this he was reprimanded, and he left Kabul thoroughly discredited in August 1838. It was finally decided to support Shah Shuja by force of arms, and on the 1st of October 1838, the Governor-General issued his proclamation declaring the object of the Expedition to Afghanistan and war was declared.

On the 10th of December 1838, the army of the Indus marched from Ferozepore and arrived at the town of Rohri on its banks, on the 24th of January 1839. The strength of the current, the depth, and the steady rise of the water, rendered the bridging of the river a very difficult task; but it was successfully carried out by Captain Thomson of the Bengal Engineers, and the troops crossed to the right bank on the 4th of February. The bridge of boats was swept away very soon after Shah Shuja forded the Indus seven miles up stream of Rohri, and his contingent of 6,000 men with its baggage, and animals, took seven days to cross. The Bombay Army under Sir John Keane had landed at Vikkar, at the mouth of the Indus, and was on its march to join the Bengal troops. The junction was effected at Kandahar.

On the 8th of May Shah Shuja was installed as sovereign in Kandahar; the Barakzai Chiefs having fled, on the advance of the troops, towards Persia. The attitude of the Durani Chiefs and the people was not all that could be desired, or had been expected. While the Army halted in Kandahar, Captain D'Arcy Todd was despatched to Herat on a mission to Prince Kāmrān. He carried with him treasure intended for the restoration of the defences of that place which had suffered greatly in the siege.

The move on Kabul was next made by Sir John Keane, and he was accompanied by the Shah. Dost Muhammad had provisioned Ghazni for a prolonged siege, had garrisoned it and placed his son Ghulam Haidar Khan in command. His idea was apparently that it should detain the invaders sufficiently to allow of his raising the Ghilzais and of recalling his son Akbar Khan and his forces from the

[1] Calcutta about 1,850 miles; Simla about 650 miles.

head of the Khyber. Ghulam Haidar had orders to brick up the gateways, and he had obeyed these instructions, except with regard to the Kabul gate, which had not been closed permanently in order to keep communication with Kabul. The defences of Ghazni proved stronger than they had been said to be, and as the heavy guns had been left behind, and provisions were almost at an end, it was decided to blow in the Kabul gate and storm the place. Before dawn of the 23rd July 1839, a party under Captain Peat of the Bombay Engineers, with Lieutenants McLeod, and Durand (afterwards Sir H. M. Durand), of the same corps demolished the gate, and Ghazni was taken by storm. Ghulam Haidar Khan was made prisoner.[1] Great stores of provisions were found, and were welcomed by the troops, who had been on reduced allowances of food. This success decided the Durani nobles, who had hitherto held aloof, to join Shah Shuja, and it upset all Dost Muhammad's plans. The latter had taken up a position at Maidān two stages in advance of Kabul; but on receiving news of the fall of Ghazni and the capture of his son, he gave up the idea of making a stand, and sent away his family towards Balkh. Akbar Khan also had fallen back before the advance of Sir Claude Wade, accompanied by a mixed force of Sikh auxiliaries and of locally raised levies, and by Prince Timur. Akbar Khan joined his father, and at the head of a band of resolute followers he covered the retreat of the Amir.

The progress of Shah Shujā from Ghazni to Kabul wore an air of triumph, owing to the crowds that thronged the road, and who had abandoned their villages and daily avocations, to witness the spectacle. To the people of the country, accustomed to the tumult of their national forces, the orderly movements of the foreign troops, which were bringing back Shah Shuja to his capital, must have appeared most wonderful. It was probably not the Shah whom they wished so much to see, as the white-faced strangers of whose existence the greater number of the spectators had never even heard. The State entry into Kabul was, however, the crowning event of the campaign. It was effected on the 7th of August. Everything that could render it imposing was done. An escort was furnished by mounted European Corps, the 4th Light Dragoons, the 16th Lancers, a squadron each, and a troop of Horse Artillery. The Shah was accompanied by the Envoy and Minister, by Sir John Keane, the Political and Military staff, and most of the officers of the Army, which had brought him back. It was a pageant that might well have recalled the visits of

---

[1] This was the first Military operation undertaken in the reign of our late Gracious Majesty Queen Victoria, and the first victory in her reign.

the Emperors of Delhi to this city in days long passed. The Jewels that decked the person of the Shah, and the brilliant uniforms of his imposing retinue, were seen to full advantage in the light of that summer afternoon, as the cavalcade paced through the streets of Kabul towards the citadel; the tread of the horses echoing between the buildings on either side of the narrow thoroughfares, and under the massive archways of the gate that had been thrown open to admit the King and his followers into the precincts of the Bāla Hisār. A candid witness, one who left Kabul before the troubles began, has recorded the fact that the dense crowds that lined the streets, and crowded the walls, and house tops, gazed at the procession with an impassive demeanour. Merely rising as the Shah rode by and sitting down at once after he had passed.[1] Shah Shuja-ul-Mulk had not seen the Bāla Hisār of Kabul for 30 years, and it is said that the tears streamed from his eyes, as he noted the ravages which neglect and the Civil wars had wrought, the signs of which were visible on every side; and as he recounted the splendours which as a young man he had witnessed, during the life-time of his father Shah Timur, and in the brief siege of his brother—the unhappy Shah Zamān.

[1] Major W. Hough, Depy. Judge Advocate-General of the "Bengal Column" of the Army of the Indus.

For the relations between the Amir Dost Muhammad and the Persian Government, which led up to the siege of Herat in 1837-38, see Appendix V.

CHAPTER XV.

THE FIRST AFGHAN WAR.—RESTORATION OF THE SADOZAIS.—NATIONAL MOVEMENT AGAINST FOREIGN INTERFERENCE IN THE GOVERNMENT, AND PRESENCE IN THE COUNTRY—MURDER OF SHAH SHUJA—FINAL ABANDONMENT OF KABUL, AND EXTINCTION OF THE SADOZAIS.

DOST MUHAMMAD, who had ruled for 13 years in the city which witnessed his rival's apparent triumph, had made good his flight to Balkh, where he collected his followers and made plans for the future. He had been in communication with the Rulers of Bokhara and decided to seek an asylum in his capital. In deference, however, to the opposition of his brother, the Nawab Jabbār Khan, the families of the Amir, and his sons, and their followers, were left in Khulm in the care of his brother. The fugitives received an honourable welcome in Bokhara; but after a time the demeanour of their host changed, and restrictions were placed on the movements of the refugees who were unable to leave the capital.

The restoration of Shah Shuja apparently had been successful. Nowhere had any serious opposition been experienced. The Army on which Dost Muhammad had expended the greater part of his slender revenue, had been stationed in the vicinity of the Khyber Pass fronting the Sikhs, and had not been available to oppose the invasion. The Kandahar Sardars, owing to their unpopularity, had been unable to offer any resistance to the Shah and his foreign supporters. Ghazni, which Dost Muhammad had hoped would delay the advance, and give time for the raising of the tribal forces, had fallen, and no opposition could be offered to the occupation of the capital itself. Left to himself, Shah Shuja might have been able to restore his authority, for the supremacy of the Barakzais had not been firmly established.

"The Shah was known to be by no means deficient in ability. Macnaghten himself described him to Rawlinson as a shrewd, cool, sensible, calculating character. His courage was of a doubtful hue" (the result probably of his reverses, the weakness of his cause and adherents—and the certainty of death, or of a more dreadful fate if he fell into the hands of his enemies); "but this natural timidity could not fail of receiving assurances from the presence of a disciplined body of foreign mercenaries—the contingent—well-armed and well-officered, whilst the occupation of the key points of his country would have enabled the Shah to maintain such a grip of Kabul, Ghazni, and Kandahar, that nothing but an army well provided with battering guns could have shaken his hold upon these important points. Shah Shuja might possibly, with such a bit in the mouths of the people, and with conciliatory conduct towards the chiefs, for whose restless but petty ambition he could have found scope in the Civil and Military service of the State, soon would have been in a position to brave the return of Dost Muhammad. Freed from the dictation of a British Envoy, and from the domineering presence of a British Army, provided that his financial measures had proved judicious, his popularity would have increased, and with it his real strength.

"He would have had the winter, which from its severity imposes rest and peace, as a season in which to consolidate his administration; it would have given him leisure to work on the characters and wishes of the chiefs, and raise an influential party favourable to his reign."[1]

In addition, there was a party in his favour, whom the severities of Dost Muhammad had alienated—led by an influential chief of the Popalzai clan. This would have proved a valuable nucleus round which to create a group of influential persons favourable to the restored government of the Sadozais. The revolutions, and bloodshed, of the past thirty years had probably rendered a large section of the population not sorry for a respite; and lastly an important factor in favour of the Shah was his previous friendship with the Ghilzais. A great part of these warlike, powerful, tribes had held aloof from the Barakzais. Against these advantages, however, there was the autocratic, and haughty character of the Shah himself, too deeply ingrained to allow of a change. The infirmities of mind and body, due to his advanced age, added to his difficulties. None of the younger members of the Sadozai Family possessed any force of character, or ability, and they were of no assistance at all to the aged Shah

[1] The first Afghan war and its causes; by Sir H. M. Durand, K.C.S.I., C.B., pp. 190-191.

in his critical position ; the Sadozais also had no clan at their back on whose devotion they could rely. The misfortunes, and the ill-success attending Shah Shuja, had probably caused men to be very chary of joining an unlucky Prince, and of supporting a dying cause. Every Barakzai on the other hand acknowledged Dost Muhammad's claim on his services ; and Afghans' reverence for a strong and brave man had been won by him.

The determination to occupy the country until such time as the government of the Shah had been sufficiently established to be able to dispense with the presence of foreign troops, proved fatal to our own influence in Afghanistan ; and to the Shah himself. The situation is summed up in a few words by one who was competent to pronounce a verdict :—" A mock king, a civil administration hated because, under foreign dictation and dissonant from the feelings of the Afghans, an envoy, the real king ruling by the gleam of British bayonets, and thus enabled to impose his measures, however crude or unpalatable. A large army, raising by its consumption the price of provisions and preying on the resources of a very poor country."[1]

As early as October 1839, the Khyberis, who had once been Shah Shuja's very good friends, were in rebellion on account of reductions of the subsidies which they received. In the following month, Lord Keane, with the troops returning to India, had to fight his way through the Pass. The Ghilzai rising (the spring of 1840) was quieted by the rough handling they received at the hands of a small expeditionary force despatched from Kandahar, and an annual subsidy of £3,000.

The surrender of Nawab Jabbār Khan, with the families in his charge, on the 3rd of July, was the result of the operations of British troops and the Shah's local corps in the valleys to the north of the Hindu-Kush. The escape of Dost Muhammad from Bokhara and his appearance on the left bank of the Oxus, was followed by revival of intrigues in his favour. His agents were busy in the Kohistan and in the capital, and two of his sons were stirring up the Ghilzais in Zurmat. A column under Sir Robert Sale, in the Kohistan, met with determined resistance. But the measures taken to counteract the efforts made by Dost Muhammad's partisans, and by him in person, proved so effectual that he decided to avoid an ignominious betrayal into the hands of his enemies by the more dignified course of a voluntary surrender to the envoy in person, which he put into effect on the 3rd of November. It showed his own opinion as to the con-

---

[1] The first Afghan war and its causes ; by Sir H. M. Durand, K.C.S.I., C.B pp. 193-194.

dition of his affairs. On the 12th he marched to India with Sir Willoughly Cotton, and for a time he resided in Ludhiana, from where he was removed to Calcutta.

Prince Timur governed Kandahar as his father's representative, but the officials about him owed their selection to the sole qualification of having shared the exile of the Shah. They were the creatures of Mulla Shakur (the Ishakzai), an ancient adherent of the Shah, whom the latter had appointed to be his first Minister. The tardy removal of Mulla Shakur, and the appointment of Muhammad Usman Khan[1] in his place, however, did nothing to mitigate the popular feeling of dislike that was rapidly gaining strength. The rapacity and venality of the Kandahar officials soon provided Major Rawlinson, the Political Officer, and General Nott, Commanding the troops at Kandahar, with grave cause for apprehensions of impending troubles. With the support afforded to the Government by the presence of British troops, the right hitherto enjoyed by the Afghans of rebelling against their sovereign's tyranny, could not be exercised with impunity. In December 1840, Akhter Khan, an Alizai Chief of the Zamindawar, drew together the bolder spirits among the discontented in Southern Afghanistan, and the native Royalist party had been driven from the field. The victories of Wymer, on the 9th May, over the Ghilzais, and of Griffin on the 17th of August, and the success won by Chambers over the Ghilzais once more on the 5th of August, had cowed for time the insurgents in the south. But neither the Political nor the military officers in Kandahar were deceived by the success of the operations. Under the surface the evil spread in all directions, but the warnings from Major Rawlinson in Kandahar and from Pottinger in the Kohistanere failed to disturb the false sense of security that prevailed in Kabul.

Other causes also created a bitter feeling against the foreigners, who were occupying their country, and inspired the Afghans with a deadly hatred towards them. The reduction of the subsidies paid to the Ghilzai tribes, who occupied the country between Kabul and Jalālābād, caused these tribesmen to break out into open rebellion. Amin-ullah Khan, Chief of Lohgar, had been threatened with removal by the Vazier (whom the Shah had created Nizam-ud-daulah), and this brought matters to a crisis at the capital, where a report had been circulated that certain influential persons were to be removed to India, when Sir William Macnaghten left Kabul, to take up the appointment of Governor of Bombay, and the time of his depature was drawing

[1] Son of the Vazier to Shah Zamān, Wafadār Khan.

near. The indecisive actions fought by Sir Robert Sale, against the Ghilzais, were magnified into victories by the nationalists; and a colour was given to the reports by the ill-advised Treaty of Tezeen made with the insurgents by Major Macgregor. Moreover, Akbar Khan, the second son of Dost Muhammad, had escaped from Bokhara, and was now at hand to direct the national movement, and lead the insurgents. The people of the Kohistan were thoroughly disaffected, and resolved to avenge the destruction of their forts and villages. Foremost among them was the Saiad Mir Masjidi, who had rendered himself famous for the defence of his fort at Tutamdarra. The preachings of the Mullas, and the exhortations of Akbar Khan, roused the Kohistanis to action.

On the night of the 1st November they entered Kabul. They were met by insurgent Ghilzais, and by the local malcontents headed by the Chief of Lohgarh—the Kazilbash held aloof from the movement,—who was deep in the confidence of both the Shah and the Envoy: they determined to act at once. On the morning of the 2nd November 1841, the storm burst, and Kabul was in an uproar. Burnes was killed and the Treasury containing £170,000 in cash was plundered. The Shah who knew the temper of his people called for aid to the British troops in Cantonments, and the blundering attempt to save Burnes, and the Treasury, made by Campbell at the head of the Shah's Hindustani corps was unsuccessful, and was defeated with heavy loss.

There were some 4,500 good troops in Cantonments, a force sufficient under an able commander to have crushed the rising effectually. Ability, however, was lacking, and that which followed is too well known to need repetition—well might the Shah, as he saw from the Bala Hisar the melancholy spectacle presented by the inaction of our troops, exclaim—"the English are mad."[1]

"There was an unearthly faintness upon their hearts; and it was as though some great crime had caused the wrath of God to settle down upon the host, withering the hearts of its leaders, unnerving the right arms of England's soldiery, and leaving them no power to stand before their enemies.[2]" On the 23rd of December 1841 the British Envoy was murdered at an interview with Muhammad Akbar, and on the 6th of January the disastrous retreat towards Jalālābād was commenced; a week later, Dr. Brydon brought the news to the garrison of Jalālābād that "Elphinstone's army, guns, standards, honour, all being lost, was itself completely annihilated."[3]

---

[1] The first Afghan War and its causes; by Sir H. M. Durand, K.C.S.I., C.B. 357.

[2] *Ibid.* 372.

[3] *Ibid.* 378.

The retreat of the British troops from Kabul, and the efforts made by Muhammad Akbar Khan to effect the destruction of Sale's force in Jalālābād, either by treachery or by force, had drawn most of the turbulent spirits of the national party from the capital, and Shah Shuja made frantic efforts to create a party in his own interests. The Prince Shahpur was so far successful that he induced the Chiefs in Kabul to visit the Shah, who gave them a formal reception on the 19th February. Muhammad Akbar did not relish the turn that affairs had taken in the capital, combined with his ill-success at Jalālābād; and he vehemently urged the leaders to force the Shah to declare himself openly on the side of the nationalists. Mir Hāji, son of the Chief Priest of Kabul, was elected as their leader, and a great crowd of Ghazis streamed out of Kabul with banners displayed, to reinforce their countrymen round Jalālābād, and the Shah declared his willingness to accompany them. On the 2nd of April 1842, his tents were pitched at Siah Sang,[1] and the next day he held a reception of the leading men at that place. In order to be prepared for another term of exile, he is said to have concealed on his person, a bag containing his choicest jewels, the value of the gems was estimated at 50 lakhs of rupees. After the reception was over, he was left to be the prey of his melancholy forebodings, and in his perturbation, he decided to return to the Bāla Hisār. After a restless night, he finally made up his mind to return to camp. At the last moment he is said again to have hesitated, but in the end he entered his litter and passed out for ever from the gate of the citadel.

The Shah's movements had been made known to Shuja-ud-Daulah, son of that Zamān Khan Barakzai, whom a faction of the nationalists had made their Amir at the commencement of the outbreak. Shuja-ud-Daulah had waited all night in the cemetery between the Bala Hisar and Siah Sang, and when the litter of the aged Shah approached, the conspirators opened fire on the party. The Shah sprang from his conveyance and ran for his life and took shelter from the bullets in a dry irrigation channel. When the Chief rode up to the litter, which the bearers were hurrying towards the Bāla Hisār, and found it empty, he lost his nerve, and was about to fly, when his principal adherent Jafir Khan, a Murād Khāni Kazilbash, whom the Vazier had proscribed, seized his bridle and adjured him to complete the task he had undertaken. A careful search revealed the Shah crouching in his shelter and with their weapons the conspirators set him free from the cares of this life. His corpse was stripped of the jewels he wore on his

[1] About 2 miles to the east of the Bala Hisar

clothes, and when all was quiet, one of his personal attendants, who was concealed close by, crept out of his hiding place and carried his master's body to the Bāla Hisār. Shah Shuja was murdered in the morning of the 4th April 1842; in the 65th year of his life. He was a scholar, and had attained to some distinction in literature. His poems are still admired in India, and in his own country. He amused himself in his exile by writing his memoirs in Persian. His fidelity to his foreign allies gradually became doubtful. His position as a puppet must have galled his autocratic and proud nature, and he must have seen that he was regarded with contempt by those whom his foreign allies held down by force, and he may have tried hard to remove this feeling, and to create a party that would be not inimical to him, in case of a general rising of his countrymen: the extreme probability of which he was quite able to foresee.

Prince Fath Jang was raised to the throne of the Sadozais in the Bāla Hisār, by the members of the Royal Family, and their adherents. He obtained some trifling successes over the partisans of Zamān Khan, but he was eventually forced to shut himself up in the citadel, and his cause was weakened by the defection of the Lohgar Chief Amin-ullah Khan, who joined Muhammad Akbar, when that redoubtable Chief reached Kabul, wounded alike in body and in his pride by his complete defeat in the open field by the despised garrison of Jalālābād on the 7th April.

The relief of Jalālābād and the advance of British troops on Kabul from that direction and from Kandahar, had tamed Akbar Khan's pride, and he agreed to recognise Fath Jang as his sovereign, claiming the position of Vazier for himself. This was a short-lived arrangement, for the latter obtained possession of letters written by his master to General Pollock, and these gave the Barakzai an opportunity to depose the puppet King, who was stripped of the remains of Shah Shuja's wealth. He made his escape from the Bāla Hisār, and a solitary Afghan, clad in filthy rags, who rode into the British camp at Gandamak in September 1842, announced himself as Fath Jang, King of Kabul.

After the re-occupation of the city, he was restored to the throne, with Ghulam Muhammud Khan, the Bamizai, son of the late Mukhtar-ud-Daulah, as his first minister. Prince Shahpur accompanied Sir John McCaskil's column into the Kohistan, which dispersed the formidable gathering of the tribesmen headed by the Naib Amin-ullah Khan Lohgari, and burnt Istalif. On the withdrawal of the British troops, Prince Fath Jang very wisely seized the opportunity of removing the family of the Sadozais from Afghanistan, and of resigning a position he saw no prospect of retaining after that army had retired; and on the 11th October he abandoned Kabul. Prince Shahpur, however, was advised by some of the Chiefs, for he had become popular with a party of the latter, to make an attempt to govern the country. The Sadozais had been thoroughly discredited, and their cause was recognised as dead. The Vazier Ghulam Muhammad was intriguing for the return of Akbar Khan, who had been lurking behind the Hindu Kush at Tashkurgan. Prince Haidar, who tried to govern Bamiān, fled before the redoubtable Barakzai and arrived at Kabul without a single follower. Prince Shahpur, wisely followed his friends' advice, and while there was yet time to escape, he made off with his family by the Karkagh Pass, across the hills towards Jalālābād, where the ill-omened Muhammad Usman Khan, Sadozai, was still the governor. The Jabbar Khel Ghilzais, who inhabit the Assarah (Hisarak) district, captured the fugitives, but owing to the good offices of Azimgul Khan, the Prince was allowed to pass on to Peshawar, while the Jabbar Khel escorted his family with all due respect to that place.

In the occupation of Afghanistan by foreigners, and especially by pork-eating Europeans, the Afghans professed to recognise the fulfilment of that vision of the holy Ako, in which he had seen the skin of a hog spread in the dwelling of his host; and in the retreat, and massacre, of the foreign troops the prediction of the Shekh that it was not to be regarded as altogether an unfavourable omen. The belief in the fulfilment of the vision was greatly strengthened by the coincidence that the invasion of Afghanistan by British troops, occurred in the year of the Hog, according to the Turkish mode of reckoning in which each year in a cycle is named after an animal.

The effect of the recovery of the British captives, and the destruction of the Bazar in Kabul as a retributive measure calculated to restore lost prestige, was completely neutralized by spectacles that everywhere met the eye of travellers along the dreary mountain track from Gandamak to the end of the defile of the Khurd Kabul, where the remains of brave men, helpless camp followers (16,000 souls) lay thick; in some places paving the narrow way between the steep hillsides that formed the defiles. In the cool and dry climate of this region, the melancholy evidence of the greatest blow that England had ever experienced to her honour and prestige, endured for years; and only very slowly were they resolved into their elemental dust. Succeeding generations of Afghans were able to gloat over the proof (from their point of view) of the success that had crowned the efforts of the

Ghazis, and of Akbar Khan, over the hated foreigners whom Providence had delivered into the hands of the holy warriors of Islam. The destruction of the bazar in Kabul faded from the minds of all, but its peaceful occupants, who had been friendly to our presence ; but every Afghan, who traversed this route—one of the high roads of the country —could not help but feel his national pride and religious fanaticism stimulated, as his heavily shod foot, or the hooves of his ponies or mules, crushed the bones with which the path was strewn, and which were to him a testimony of national prowess, and the fulfilment of the ancient prediction of the saintly Ako, the Pir of the Alizais.

The disaster at Kabul terminated the career of the debauched Prince Kāmrān, whom the astute Vazier had allowed to retain a semblance of authority, as long as he thought the puppet was likely to be of any use. Yār Muhammad had been intriguing with all his neighbours—he Persians at his gates, the British in Kandahar, and even with the ulers of the remote Khanates along the Oxus. When, however, he found that no more money was to be obtained from the British authorities (who had disbursed some £200,000 in Herat), he turned Major Todd out of the city[1]. As soon as it became quite certain that no effort would be made on behalf of Prince Kāmrān by the allies of the Sadozais, he seized him and his sons, and the Prince was sent away to Kuhsan, where lands had been assigned for his support. The presence of the Sadozai Prince was, however, inconvenient, and the Vazier despatched two of his creatures—the Alakozais Taj and Daud—to put an end to Prince Kāmrān at Kuhsan. Kāmrān's sons who were quite worthless, found an asylum in Persia. These degenerate descendants of the great Ahmad Shah, were Jahangir, Seif-ul-Muluk, Saadat Muluk, Alamgir, Nādir, Ahmad Ali, Jalāludin, Sikandar, and Shihab. The doles which they received from the Shah enabled them to lead lives given up to low pleasures, and the indulgence of their depraved appetites. Alamgir and Ahmad Ali are said to have made their way eventually to India.

The Sadozais disappeared from History.

---

[1] Major Todd's proceedings at Herat were disapproved by Lord Auckland. He was remanded to his regiment (Bengal Artillery) and was killed in the battle of Firuzshah (Sikh War).

CHAPTER XVI.

THE AMIR DOST MUHAMMAD, MUHAMMADZAI, BARAKZAI.— CONSOLIDATION OF HIS GOVERNMENT IN AFGHANISTAN.

THE Sadozai Princelets having proved failures, the Amir Dost Muhammad was allowed to return to his country, and while the army of retribution was returning through the Punjab to take part in the pageant at Ferozepur, Dost Muhammad was passing through that Province bound for Kabul. The Barakzai Chiefs, who had possessed Kandahar, emerged from their obscure retreat in Persian territory and took possession of that city again. Even the change-loving Afghans may have had a surfeit of alterations of fortune, and a stable government may not have been unwelcome to allow them to recover their breath after the violent excitement of the past three or four years. Dost Muhammad held only a fourth part of Afghanistan after his return to Kabul. The petty Chiefs to the north of the Hindu-Kush were independent, or under the influence of the Ruler of Bokhara. The Barakzai Sardars were independent Rulers of Kandahar, and the Vazier Yār Muhammad held the Province of Herat. The Amir of Kabul had enough to do to reorganise the government of his small territory, and for some time he was unable to enter into disputes with the Kandahar Chiefs or the Ruler of Herat. His task was materially helped by his relations with the Indian Government. His residence at the seat of Government in Calcutta, had probably a very much greater effect on him than his Afghan pride wouid allow him to acknowledge; and the experience he had gained of the resources and real strength of that government, undoubtedly influenced his conduct at a time when his attitude towards the Indian Government had become a matter of very great importance. His native ability could not have failed to appreciate all that he saw during his short term of exile, for in 1843 he was back in Kabul.

Of the four parties, who were concerned in the late war, he alone had benefited. Shah Shuja was dead. The British Government had poured out blood and treasure, and the loss to its prestige barely had been recovered by the achievements of the avenging army. His old enemy Ranjit Sing, was dead, and his State was on the verge of destruction. With Yār Muhammad in Herat and his own brethren in Kandahar, Dost Muhammad was quite able to deal; and the Ruler of Bokhara was of no account. From the Persians he had nothing to fear. The intervention of the Shah's government, his alliance with the Indian government, had rendered impossible. The quality of the Persian troops placed their government in the position of an enemy which the Afghans might well despise.

Dost Muhammad is said to have been the twentieth son of Sardar Sarfarāz Khan Barakzai, and with the exception of the eldest Fateh Khan; and the next in seniority, Sardar Azim Khan, he was the ablest and most capable member of the family. The unambitious character of Nawāb Jabbār Khan, rendered him an invaluable counseller to his younger brother the Amir, who was said to have highly appreciated the Nawab's ability, foresight and prudence. The mother of Dost Muhammad belonged to the Siah Mansur, one of the tribes of Tajik or Persian origin, near Kandahar, and the wisdom and intellect of her famous son was probably inherited from her. Although on account of her Tajik origin, her co-wives very likely looked down on her, she was said to have been the favourite of her husband; and to have always accompanied him on his expeditions. Her son's education, probably for this reason, seems to have been neglected, for he is said to have only learnt to read the Koran at a comparatively late age. After the execution of Sarfaraz Khan, a cousin of the Sardar, Abdul Majid Khan, asserted his right, according to the well known Afghan custom, by which the nearest relation can claim to marry a widow of a deceased kinsman, and married the mother of the future Amir. A brother of Majid Khan married one of Dost Muhammad's sisters at the same time. After the remarriage of his mother, Dost Muhammad lived in Maruf, or the Toba plateau, in one of the forts belonging to his step-father. The eldest sister of Dost Muhammad married Shah Shuja, to whom she bore several children, her only son is said to have died while the Shah was in Kabul. A third sister was a widow at the time of the occupation of Kabul. She obtained permission to remain with her sister in Kabul, when the Amir's family was deported to India. She became a very active canvasser in her brother's interests, and was said to have gained many adherents to her brother's cause in Bamiān and the Kohistan. She successfully evaded all attempts made to seize her, and finally escaped to Jalālābād, and thence to Peshawar. As the youngest but one of a large family of brothers, the Amir was brought up in a hard school, his elder brothers making use of his services very freely. He got his chance at last when Sardar Azim Khan was unable to leave Kashmir at a moment's notice, to avenge the cruelties practised on the Vazier Fath Khan, and he was obliged to send Dost Muhammad to seize Kabul.

Dost Muhammad appears to have had none of the morose, and fanatical qualities of the Afghan nature in his composition. The strain of Persian blood inherited from his mother modified very greatly the rude Afghan temperament in her son. He is said to have possessed an equable and good temper, a lively imagination and ready speech. He is said to have been gifted with an extraordinary taste for music and to have attained to great proficiency as a performer on the Rabāb (a description of the guitar). At social gatherings he unbent freely, and entertained his friends with songs—ballads of his native land or the more elaborate odes of Persian Poetry. Even after he returned from exile, his favorite resort was the picturesque village of Nanachi, near the capital, surrounded by vineyards, and gardens, and pleasantly situated on the banks of a small lake. He used to repair to this place with his intimate associates and pass the time with music and songs, while flasks of the famous Kabul wine (made by the Armenians settled there) circulated, and warmed the hearts of the company and diverted their minds from the cares and recurring problems of state craft. It is not to be wondered at, if as it was said, the bounds of moderation were sometimes exceeded in these assemblies even at the risk of offending his gloomy and bigotted subjects. His frank and courageous bearing, and his accessibility endeared him to his subjects, and it is said that any man might stop him when he rode abroad, and demand redress for wrongs or speak his mind freely to the Amir without incurring any risk of offending him.[1]

[1] The title of Amir which is still used by the Barakzai Rulers of Kabul, has a peculiar significance. It denotes the possessor of delegated authority. Sultan from an Arabic root also, which signifies predominance, denotes a ruler who holds that position by right of conquest. The Sultan of Turkey owes his presence in Europe to the conquests of his ancestors. Shah on the other hand signifies a despotic sovereign ruling by virtue of Divine Right, an autocrat. The Sadozais by virtue of the prediction relating to their ancestor Asadullah claimed this right; but it was established by the great Ahmad Shah at great risk of offending his turbulent nobility; whom his successful foreign campaigns alone rendered complaisant. It implies a power over the persons and property of the subject, repugnant to the character of the Afghan people.

Within his jurisdiction, roads were safer than they had been in former days. Two and a half per cent. was the duty levied on merchandise passing through his territory, and in the later period of his government after the war, M. Ferrier was informed in Kandahar, and Herat, that even including illegal gratifications to venal officials, the duty was not more than four per cent. This brought in revenue (according to the notorious Mohan Lall, who professes to have obtained the figures from Mirza Samiullah the Amir's Minister), estimated at 4,15,500 Kabuli rupees, or about £40,000 at that time. The whole revenue at the Amir's disposal from the territory that acknowledged his authority was 25 lakhs of Kabuli rupees, said to have been equivalent to 24 lakhs of the East India Company's rupees, or to about £226,000 at exchange of that period. As the Amir is said to have expended 21 lakhs on his army, there was not much money available for other purposes. The Amir was obliged to have recourse to arbitrary measures to find the means to meet his expenditure—forced loans which rarely or never were repaid. Notwithstanding the security of the roads, and low transit dues, owing to these irregular demands trade had declined below what it had been during the troubled reign of Shah Mahmud. Even during the second period of his reign, before he took Kandahar from his brothers, the revenue at the disposal of Amir Dost Muhammad was estimated at a little more than 32 lakhs, and the assistance he received from the Government of India was vitally necessary to the maintenance of his administration—a necessity which has not disappeared in the days of his successors. The revenue of Kabul had fallen below the amount realized in the 17th century by the Moghul Emperors, but the decrease was due very largely to the loss of districts in the time of the Amir Dost Muhammad, which in the earlier period had been part of the Province of Kabul.

The decrease in the revenues of the Kandahar Province under the rapacious Barakzai Sardars was still greater. In the 17th century, the revenue under the Moghul administration had been 15 lakhs of rupees. At the end of the 18th century, when the traveller Forster passed through the country during the reign of Shah Timur, Sadozai, 18 lakhs was the revenue of the Province. Under the Barakzai Sardars only 80,000 rupees were realized. Holding as they were supposed, nine-tenths of the land round Kandahar, they acted in a most arbitrary manner in their dealings with the more peaceful section of their subjects. In several of the districts the power of the tribes were too great to allow the Sardars to oppress them ; but wherever it could be done with impunity the country was taxed according to the pleasure of the rulers. The revenue was farmed, and the contractors with the aid of soldiers extracted all they could get from the people. After these demands had been satisfied "shoals of hungry soldiers and followers of Chiefs are let loose on the villages to gather for themselves what they can pick up."[1]

After the Amir Dost Muhammad had taken possession of Kandahar, his heir Ghulam Haidar Khan governed the Province, but under him the cultivator found no relief. In the height of the summer "when water to the cultivator is worth any money, the Sardar frequently puts all the water in a canal up to auction, and has been known to realize as much as 70 rupees (Kandahari) for one day's supply of water to a promising vinery." [2]

These exactions fell on the Tajik section of the population. "The result is, that in the immediate vicinity of towns, and close to the ruler the agriculturist continues to till the land; but in many parts of the country you approach large and apparently flourishing villages, enter them, and no human voice greets or curses you there, as the case may be. Once rich vineyards are dried up, and all around is desolation. This is especially the case in the Kandahar district, where every fresh change of rulers has only brought increased taxation, until the population has been decimated and tax gatherers, enraged at not being able to squeeze money out of mud walls, have seized and sold into slavery the last wretched inhabitant of a once prosperous and influential village."[3]

The revenues at the disposal of Ahmad Shah, according to the Mizan-ul-Mamalik, of Muiz-ullah Mohmandi, of Peshawar, who prepared it for the Minister Shah Wali Khan, is said to have been, or was estimated, at a little more than thirteen crores and thirteen lakhs. Kashmir contributed, it is stated, 29,90,800 rupees (of Ahmad Shah's period), and Sind, about 26 lakhs. Nothing is mentioned of any revenue from the Persian territory held by that monarch, nor from Herat or Kandahar. In those days, the Sutlej and the Indus formed the eastern limits of the Afghan Kingdom, but the Durani monarch also held districts on the left bank of the Sutlej, governed by his representative in Sirhind. The greater part of the land on the Kandahar and Herat Provinces was probably held by the great Afghan clans, who gave in return their services in the field; and who were

---

[1] Mission to Kandahar, 1857.

[2] *Ibid.*

[3] *Ibid.*

too powerful to be meddled with. The burden in those times also of the taxes, fell on the peaceful Tajik and Indian sections of the subjects of Ahmad Shah.[1] As Province after Province was lopped off during the lifetime of Ahmad Shah's degenerate successors, and as the tribute from Sind declined to what the Suzerain was able to take, the revenues of the Sadozais fell away, but even in the disturbed reign of the indolent voluptuary, Shah Mahmud, the revenue of his kingdom is said to have amounted to ninety-six lakhs of rupees or just short of £1,000,000 sterling; what part remained in the hands of the Vazier of course no one ever was rash enough to ask; but if Fath Khan was able as he is said to have been to disburse ninety-six lakhs in advances, before the ill-fated expedition to Herat, and his brother to have left property valued at three crores of rupees (over £3,000,000) the office of Vazier must have been very lucrative, and it accounts for the eagerness with which it was sought.[2]

The western Ghilzais, after a fruitless struggle for years against the authority of Amir Dost Muhammad, at last were forced to submit, and their leader Muhammad Shah Khan was living in 1857, a prisoner at large in Kabul, but under strict surveillance. His contemporary, Malik Shahdād, another of the same clan, held out in the fastnesses of Tagao where he found shelter and continued to defy the Amir, who was unable to capture him or restrain his raids, though the nephew and rival of the outlaw had been put into possession by the Amir of his uncle's lands and chiefship.[3]

About August 1855 Amir Dost Muhammad deprived his brothers and their sons of Kandahar; and Sardar Rahmdil Khan with the Amir's consent retired to Persia.

The Kandahar Sardars were of the lower type of Afghan character, but Yār Muhammad, the Alakozai, who had taken possession of Herat, was quite a different person, and showed great ability in governing his Province. He summoned his clansmen to Herat and gave them lands in the districts which were under his sway. He styled himself Vazir-i-Kabir, the Grand Vazier. He put down disorders with a firm hand. The year after he assumed the government, he invaded Ghor, and extended his authority as far as Tizli and Karz

---

[1] Moorcroft, the famous traveller, estimated the value of the shawl manufacture, for which Kashmir was famous, at as much as 300,000 £ in the earlier part of the last century (1822).

[2] The Punjab had been the most valuable portion of the Durani kingdom, and its importance to the sovereign of Afghanistan accounts for the frantic efforts of Shah Zamān to regain possession of at least some portion of it.

[3] Mission to Kāndahar.

districts of the Zamindawar. He brought the Hazara Zaidnats to his feet, and having reinstated their chief Karimdād Khan as his governor, and fixed an annual tribute on the tribe, he returned to Herat. At the close of the winter he set out to add Maimanah to his possessions; but for several reasons he decided to return to Herat (1846), and the next year he sent Mir Hashim Khan, the Alakozai Chief, to subdue Hikmat Khan, the Chief of Maimanah. The reason of Yār Muhammad's return to Herat was his desire to arrange for the departure of his daughter to Kabul, where she was to be married to the famous Akbar Khan, second son of the Amir.

The Chief of Ghor had given shelter to two of Prince Kāmrān's sons, and one of these Chiefs, Din Muhammad, had visited Kandahar and had tried to induce Major Rawlinson to take up Kāmrān's feud with the Vazier. The outbreak at Kabul had just taken place, and it was out of the question to undertake fresh adventures in the direction of Herat. Yār Muhammad remembered this, and by the end of 1846 he had the Chiefs of Ghor under his heel. The death of Muhammad Akbar, in 1847, gave him cause for anxiety, but he was re-assured by the news that his daughter had been given in marriage to Sardar Ghulam Haidar, another son of the Amir.

Yār Muhammad sought the friendship of the Persians with great ardour, but the Shah regarded the Vazier with a virulent personal dislike, and decided to encourage the Barakzais in their design against Herat. The death of Shah Muhammad Shah, on the 4th of September 1848, owing to which the army destined to co-operate with the Sardars of Kandahar was disbanded, saved Yār Muhammad any further anxiety on this account. The latter had been in person aiding Prince Hamza Mirza, who was blockaded in Meshed, which had been beseiged by the son of the late Asaf-ud-Daulah with the help of the Turkomans of Merv, after he had rebelled against the Shah. The city continued to hold out against the attacks of the beseigers who numbered 8,000 men. When the news of the Shah's death arrived and became known, two battalions which had garrisoned the citadel, joined the beseigers; the former, however, were suffering from the effects of a famine which was raging, and the assaults of the enemy increased their sufferings. Yār Muhammad marched the Persian Army into his own territory, and entertained them with the greatest hospitality for the whole of the winter. Prince Hamza was recalled to Tehrān in the beginning of 1849. Before he left Kuhsan, where the Persian troops had wintered, he presented Yār Muhammad with four pieces of cannon as some return for the entertainment of his troops. Shah Nāsir-ud-din, after he ascended the throne in the summer of that year, presented Yār Muhammad with a richly jewelled sabre, and a patent of nobility, with the title of Zahir-udaulah. The Vazier also depatched offerings to the Court of the Shah; and a collossal elephant (the remains perhaps of the Regal Paraphernalia of the Sadozais), presented by him to the Shah might be seen (wrote M. Ferrier), promenading the streets of Tehran. Towards the north Yār Muhammad annexed Andikhui, and Shibarghan, to his territories; and his authority was acknowledged almost up to Balkh. He transplanted 7,000 families of Taimunis from Ghor, and also Hazaras from Kala-i-Nuh to replace those inhabitants of the Herat valley who had perished or been forced to emigrate during the siege of 1838. Trade was encouraged, and an unskilful attempt was made to work silver and iron ores existing near Herat; and it was even said that he was desirous of establishing machinery to work the raw produce of wool and cotton raised in his territory. He was a most exacting ruler, and his stern measures created enemies, who revenged themselves by accusing him of bartering his subjects to the Turkomans—five men in exchange for one Turkoman horse valued at 100 tomans.

In 1851 he marched to Lāsh and reduced the fort at that place, the chieftain of which had been coquetting with the Sardars of Kandahar. Sardar Sher Ali, son of Mihrdil Khan, was at Lāsh; an army from Kandahar designed to frighten Yār Muhammad had advanced to Girishk, while Muhammad Sidik Khan, son of Sardar Kohandil Khan, had taken possession of Chakānsur in Seistan. Yār Muhammad, however, was not dismayed, and he pointed out to the Kandahar Sardars that it would be unadvisable for him and for them to fall out, who had a common enemy in Kabul, and that he was going to punish Ahmad Khan, brother of Sālu Khan, the Ishakzai chieftain of Lāsh. The Kandahar Sardars hesitated; and the Ruler of Herat brought the rebellious chief to his senses. He had been unwell when he started from Herat, and as his indisposition grew on him, Yār Muhammad left his son, Saīd Muhammad, to march the troops back, while he hurried on to reach Herat. He died on the way, at the Rabat of Mir Mirhulah, on the 1st June 1851.[1] His corpse was carried to Herat; and buried on the south side of the shrine of Jam'i. Yār Muhammad reigned for eleven years as an independent Ruler.

---

[1] Sir Clements Markham, in his History of Persia, p. 498, says, 8th of June 1851. The date in the text is from the Tarikh-i-Sultani.

His son and successor Saīd Khan was a worthless person, and tainted morever with insanity. The Chiefs put up with him for some time, till at last his Naib or Deputy, Isa Khan, a Bardurani, invited a grandson of Hāji Prince Firuz-ud-din, Sadozai, to Herat, and put him in possession of the seat of authority on the 15th September 1855. Saīd Khan was murdered at once without an effort on the part of any one, but Hāji Khairullah, an Alakozai headman, to defend him. This solitary partisan of the unworthy son of Yār Muhammad was overpowered and mortally wounded. Naib Isa, the Bardurani, and the Sadozai Prince, next compelled the Alakozais to disgorge some of the wealth they had acquired during Yār Mahammad's life-time.

On learning what had taken place, the Shah of Persia assembled an expedition force, commanded by his uncle the Hisām-us-Sultanah Sultan Murād Mirza, and despatched to reduce Herat and to avenge the death of the son of Yār Muhammad. The siege of Herat was begun early in April 1856.[1] Isa Khan and his protegé, Prince Yusuf, sent to Kandahar and also to the Amir Dost Muhammad for aid. The latter would have nothing to do with the matter, and Isa Khan, offended at the treatment he received from his nominee, seized him and gave him up to the Persians, by whom the Sadozai Prince was at once despatched to Tehran and later on executed to avenge the murder of Saīd Khan. Finally, after a prolonged blockade, owing to famine within the walls, Isa Khan surrendered Herát to the Persians. A short time after he was assassinated by a man suborned for the purpose (it was believed, by the Hisam-us-Sultanah), as he was returning from the Persian Camp to the City.

The confusion in Herat after the death of Yār Muhammad had rendered the Amir Dost Muhammad very eager to intervene, but after he had taken possession of Kandahar in August 1855, the Persians had forestalled him. In 1851 the Amir had asserted his influence beyond the Hindu-Kush, and in the same year he obtained possession of Balkh. Herat alone remained out of his possession, and prevented the realisation of an united kingdom of Afghanistan. On the 30th March 1855, Sardar Ghulam Haidar Khan met the Chief Commissioner of the Punjab, Sir John Lawrence, and a treaty of friendship was the

---

[1] Abbas Kuli, a Persian, in April 1852 had occupied the citadel of Herat, leaving a Persian force at Ghurian, reinforced later by Sam Khan, Ilkhani of Deregez. The latter was recalled in January 1853, but Abbas Kuli remained in Herat as Vazier to Said Muhammad.

The British Ambassador at Teheran remonstrated and threatened the Sadr-i-Azam, in consequence of which on January 25th, 1853, an engagement was contracted and signed in Teheran by the Persian Government binding themselves not to interfere in Herat. Abbas Kuli was recalled.—Markham's Hist. of Persia.

result. Dost Muhammad appealed to the British Government with regard to the seizure of Herat, and he followed up his appeal by descending the Khyber to Peshawar and there a treaty was concluded between the British and Afghan Governments, on 6th of January 1857, Sir John Lawrence representing H. E. the Viceroy and Governor-General in India.[1] Shortly before the Amir had started from Kabul for Jamrud, war had been declared with Persia (1st November 1856), and an Expeditionary Force under Sir James Outram landed on the Persian Coast and humbled the pride of the vainglorious Shah. One of the conditions on which peace was made with Persia, (4th March 1857) was the evacuation of Herat by the Persian troops.[2]

On the 13th March 1857, a Mission under Major (afterwards Sir Henry) Lumsden of the Corps of Guides, accompanied by Lieut. Lumsden of the Quarter Master General's Department, and Surgeon-Major Bellew, a small staff of native officials, and a weak representative escort, left Peshawar, and reached Kandahar on the 26th of April. The Afghans were elated at the events of the short campaign in Persia; but at the same time the news spread up the passes of the "breaking out of the mutiny of the Bengal Army; and for months all men's thoughts were concentrated on Hindustan. As the storm thickened, urged by the preaching of bigotted Muhammadan zealots, pressed on by the secret machinations of the "Peshawari Brothers," Sirdars Sultan Muhammad Khan and Pir Muhammad Khan, the Afghan nation called on the Amir to put himself at the head of the faithful, raise the green standard of "Islam," to which thousands would flock, and pouring down the passes to sweep the infidel *Faringi* from the contaminated soil of Hindustan; and thus once more re-establish Muhammadan supremacy throughout Asia. The excitement throughout the country was intense, and the moment a most critical one; for the resolution of the aged ruler seemed for an instant to stagger; and his better judgment was on the point of being swept along with the popular torrent, when his son Sirdar Muhammad Azim Khan had the moral courage to come to the rescue and exposing himself to the full tide of popular disappointment, he reminded the Sirdars of the power of the British nation, of the many storms which had already burst

[1] In consideration of an annual subsidy of 12 lakhs of rupees during the continuance of hostilities with the Persians, he was to keep up a certain number of regular troops for the defence of Afghanistan, and British officers were to be deputed to see that this was done and to help the Amir in every way in military matters when called on to do so.

[2] Signed at Paris and ratified at Baghdad on May 2, 1857 —Markham's History of Persia.

harmlessly over their heads; and that failure would be to the Amir, the certain loss of his Kingdom; and openly accused the "Peshawari Brothers" of getting up the agitation in the hope of ruining his father for their own aggrandizement. The step was a bold one, and caused a momentary estrangement between the Amir and his son; but the former on a little reflection recalled Sirdar Azim Khan to his councils, approved of and acted on his advice, and being materially strengthened by the cool and determined bearing of our frontier authorities in the Peshawar district, the Amir weathered the storm, which entirely subsided on the fall of Delhi. Throughout that anxious period, I was in daily intercourse with the heir-apparent (Sardar Ghulam Haidar Khan, who was governor of Kandahar), who having had the advantage of seeing the signs of our power during his visit to Bombay, Madras and Calcutta, was fully convinced of the necessity of controlling the hasty rashness of his countrymen; and frequent expresses passed up, in hot haste, to Kabul, imploring the Amir to pursue a determined policy, adhesive to the British alliance."[1]

"On the 27th July, the Persians ostensibly evacuated Herat in accordance with the terms of the treaty, placing that government in the hands of a creature of their own, Sirdar Sultan Ahmad Khan, better known as Sultan Jan, a son of the late Sirdar Muhammad Azim Khan, and nephew of the Amir." "He selected for his minister Sirdar Sher Ali Khan,[2] second son of the late Kandhari Sirdar Mihrdil Khan; and in October Colonel R. Taylor, with a British Commission, arrived from Bagdad at Herat, and in the name of the British acknowledged the *de facto* government. The Persian forces all the while hovered in strong masses about the Herat frontier; and it was generally believed that under the pretext of concentrating preparatory to a move against the Turkomans, they were only watching the progress of events in India; and it was not until the tide of fortune was seen to have turned decisively in our favour that they advanced towards Sharukhs" (Sarakhs).[3]

---

[1] The Mission to Kandahar.

[2] Afterwards he was appointed by the British Government as Wali of Kandahar in the second Afghan War.

[3] The Persians after taking Sarakhs and leaving Shah-Daulat Khan (a fugitive Afghan Sardar) to rule the Province, pushed on to Merv. "Shahzadah Sultan Murad-Mirza after an ineffectual blockade for upwards of a month, finding his army starving, and reduced to living on their baggage donkeys, commenced a retrograde movement on Meshed. The retreating Persians were surrounded by the Turkomans and the Commander was the first to take to flight, leaving the great mass of his army to be taken prisoners and carried off into hopeless slavery. A strong body of Persian reinforcements advancing from Tehran under Jafir Kuli Khan received a like check at Mazinan, the leader escaping with difficulty.—The Mission to Kandahar.

Colonel Taylor's party left Herat about the 1st March 1858, although the Jews and Hazaras carried off from Herat had not been given up, and Lāsh Juwein still remained in the hands of Persia, and Sultan Jan acknowledged the sovereignty of the Shah over Herat by having the "Khutbah" read, and coinage struck in the name of the Shah; and on the departure of these officers, the Sirdar gave out that he had dismissed the Mission, having made up his mind to have nothing to say to infidels. He, however, received and hospitably entertained the Russian Scientific Mission under M. Khanikoff in 1858.

The recognition of Sultan Ahmad Khan by the British Government, put Herat for a time out of the reach of the Amir Dost Muhammad, but he occupied himself with the annexation of the district of Kunduz, on the northern slopes of the Hindu-Kush, which he is supposed to have effected in 1859. Sultan Ahmad Khan turned out the children of the late Yār Muhammad Khan from Herat, where provision for their support had been ordered by the Shah. Sardar Ali Khan and the other children found an asylum in Kabul. The ruler of Herat waxing bold next wrested Farah[1] out of the keeping of Seif-ullah, the deputy of the son of the Amir, Sharif Khan, and installed as his representative in Farah, Afzal Khan, son of the late Sarda Purdil Khan Barakzai, who had fled from the Amir's Court to Herat. This act gave the Amir an opportunity for regaining possession of Herat. He swooped on it from Kabul, and after a siege or blockade of ten months, he captured the place. By this success he attained his long cherished desire—the consolidation of Afghanistan—for the realization of which he had worked and waited so long. He was not fated to enjoy the fruits of his labours, for he died in Herat on the 9th June 1863.

---

[1] Said to have been seized by the Amir, with Sabzawar and Lāsh, Andikhui and Maimanah as late as 1857.—Markham's History of Persia.

NOTE.

On the 27th October 1862, Mr. Eastwick was told by the Hisām-us-Sultanah, Prince Murad Mirza, that the revenue of Herat was 100,000 Herati tomans =38.000 £. Not less than five regiments of infantry and 4,000 horse must be kept up to maintain peace. In addition there were the civil charges. Hence there was a deficit. Yār Muhammad made this up by extracting 18,000 tomans from Seistan and a like sum from Ghor.

For a summary of events leading to the Treaty of Paris, and the fall of Herat to the Amir Dost Muhammad, see Appendix VI.

CHAPTER XVII.

AMIR SHER ALI.

TWELVE sons survived the late Amir; of these, the eldest Muhammad Afzal Khan, Governor of Afghan, Turkistan and Balkh, and Muhammad Azim Khan, who governed the Kuram Khost and Zurmut, were by the same mother, a daughter of the Turi Malik of Shaluzan, in the Kuram.[1] Sher Ali Khan, Heir-Designate, and Muhammad Sharif Khan, Governor of Girishk, were by the same mother, a daughter of Haji Rahmat-ullah Khan, another of whose daughters had been one of the wives of the Shah Shuja.[2]

Muhammad Amin Khan was governor of Kandahar: and his mother belonged to the Popalzai tribe.[3]

Wali Muhammad Khan and Faiz Muhammad Khan by the same mother, Ahmad Khan and Muhammad Zaman Khan by another wife, were stationed in Turkistan under Afzal Khan's orders, the first-named having been commandant of Akchah. Lastly, there were Muhammad Aslam, Hasan and Husen Khans by one mother.

Afzal Khan, the eldest son, was reputed to be the bravest of all the sons of the late Amir, and endowed with a natural aptitude for military affairs, and a character for liberality; while the flourishing condition of his territory bore witness to his capacity as an administrator. These qualities, however, were marred by an unfortunate predilection for dissipation of all sorts. His brother, Azim, was also notorious on account of his dissolute life and vices of the most degrading description.[4]

The Heir-Designate appears to have imbibed at an early date a dislike to the English, and in 1857 Major (afterwards Sir H. B.)

---

[1] Mission to Kandahar, Major H. B. Lumsden, 1857.

[2] *Ibid.*

[3] *Ibid.*

[4] *Ibid.*

Lumsden described him in the following terms. "Sirdar Sher Ali is said to have a great deal of intelligence and aptitude for business; but is frequently an invalid from attacks of gout, to which all this branch of the Amir's family are subject. He is a man of violent temper and cruel disposition, and is well known to be but ill-pleased with the British alliance, and in passing through his district we, in several instances, saw signs of his ill-will towards us."[1]

Each of the sons who had been intrusted with important governments had under his orders a body of troops, and thus was in a position to support by force of arms any claim he might consider he possessed to the throne. Sher Muhammad (ci-devant Campbell), was Sipah Salar or Chief Commander under Muhammad Afzal Khan, and the preceptor of Abdur Rahman, the son of the latter. Afzal Khan was also credited with having given his daughter in marriage to the eldest son of the Amir of Bokhara, a sufficient indica-ion of his probable course of action with regard to the throne.

Sardar Sher Ali Khan had left his eldest son Muhammad Ali as Governor of Kabul when he accompanied his father to Herat; and as soon as the funeral ceremonies had been completed, he hastened to the capital where he had been summoned by his son who feared a revolt.

A struggle for the throne at once commenced. The first to show his disaffection was Amin Khan at Kandahar, and by the time Sher Ali had reached Girishk, on his way to Kabul, about the end of July 1863, the family discord was complete. Early in 1864, the Amir who had been recognised by the British Government, sent an envoy, Muhammad Rajik Khan to India to negotiate a new treaty, to apply for aid in warlike material, and to obtain the recognition of[2] the eldest son of the Amir, Muhammad Ali Khan, as Heir-apparent. It was held that a new treaty was unnecessary, as the one concluded with the late Amir Dost Muhammad Khan was still in force; and the envoy returned to Kabul without waiting for a reply to the other requests.

In the meantime, attempts to compose the differences among the brothers had failed, and preparations for a civil strife continued in active progress. On the 20th April 1864, the Amir ordered the advance of a body of 10,000 men and 10 guns under Muhammad Ali Khan towards Bamiān to meet the invasion of Muhammad Afzal Khan from the north. Simultaneously another division of 6,000 men with

---

[1] Mission to Kandahar, 1857.

[2] Treaties, Engagements and Sanads. Afghanistan, Vol. XI, 4th Edition 1909.

8 guns, led by the Amir's youngest son, Muhammad Ibrahim Khan, and Muhammad Rajik Khan moved towards the south to cope with Muhammad Azim Khan's expected revolt in the Kuram. A collision was precipitated by the capture of the fort at Gardez, but after one slight skirmish Azim Khan was abandoned by his troops, and obliged to seek refuge in British Territory. He was permitted to reside at Rawalpindi.

Afzal Khan had proclaimed himself Amir in Turkistan, and had marched against the heir-apparent at the head of 25,000 men. An indecisive action on the 3rd June 1864, in the defiles of the Hindu-Kush, was followed by a reconciliation; on the basis of the restoration to Afzal Khan of the government of Turkistan, which, however, was shorn of the districts of Maimana, Kunduz and Katāghan.

This compact was soon broken. Alarmed at the menacing language used by the Amir; Abdur Rahman, son of Afzal Khan, fled to Bokhara, where he met with an honourable reception. On hearing this, the Amir turned all his wrath upon the father, whom he caused to be placed in irons.[1] Muhammad Sharif Khan, another brother, had been left in Kabul, who fearing lest he should fall into the hands of the Amir, determined not to wait his return to the capital, and joined Muhammad Amin Khan, who was making strenuous efforts to put Kandahar into a state of defence.

Fateh Muhammad Khan (a son of the famous Sardar Muhammad Akbar Khan and a grandson of Amir Dost Muhammad) was appointed to govern Turkistan, and Amir Sher Ali commenced his retreat to Kabul in October 1864. After a short delay, caused by a rumour that the Amir of Bokhara was about to invade Afghanistan in the interest of Abdul Rahman, the Amir entered the capital, with his prisoner Muhammad Afzal Khan, in the following month.

With the opening of the season of 1865, the Amir turned his attention towards Azim Khan (who had quitted British territory in March); and in order to secure the Kuram and Khost districts, and also to crush the more dangerous coalition at Kandahar. It was Muhammad Azim's policy to avoid an engagement till the Amir's approaching necessity at Kandahar, should give him an opportunity for action. On the 5th and 6th June,[2] severe fighting took place at Kajbaz, about 8 miles to the S.W. of Kalat-i-Ghilzai, in the course of which the Heir-apparent, Muhammad Ali Khan, was shot by his uncle, who also

---

[1] *Ibid.*

[2] Treaties, Engagements and Sanads—Afghanistan, gives the 3rd June as the date of this action.

lost his life. The Kandahar force was routed, and Muhammad Sharif Khan fled.

While these events were taking place in the south, Abdur Rahman Khan, with the countenance of the Ruler, had left Bokhara, crossed the Oxus without opposition and encamped at Akchah. Fateh Muhammad Khan marched to oppose him, but his troops mutinied, and he was obliged to save himself by flight. By the 12th August 1865, Abdur Rahman was master of Turkistan without striking a blow and commenced to make preparations for an advance on Kabul, in the name of the Amir of Bokhara.[1]

The loss of his son at Kajbaz appeared to shake the reason of the Amir Sher Ali, and on his arrival at Kandahar, he gave himself over to the indulgence of his grief, and shut himself up for several months, and at one time, he was believed to have been actually out of his mind. The Turkistan disaster failed to rouse the Amir, and he refused to leave Kandahar, or to take any part in the management of affairs. Abdur Rahman marched without opposition to Bamiān, where he was joined by his uncle Azim Khan, who had made his way into Badakshan, through Chitral[2], and had crossed the Hindu-Kush by the Dora Pass. From Bamiān, uncle and nephew continued their advance to within ten miles of Kabul, from where negotiations were set on foot with Ibrahim Khan, the eldest surviving son of the Amir Sher Ali, who was governor of Kabul. All state prisoners were to be released, and their property restored, and an armistice was agreed upon, pending the ratification of these terms by the Amir. His consent was refused. Abdur Rahman thereupon advanced on Kabul, and on the 3rd March, Ibrahim Khan was obliged to capitulate, under promise of safety and freedom for himself and for all the members of the Amir's family in Kabul. Muhammad Azim Khan was proclaimed Amir. These events at last roused Sher Ali to action, and on the 26th April he marched from Kandahar towards Kabul at the head of 14,000 men and 25 guns. Fateh Muhammad was directed by him to make a simultaneous advance from Jalālābād. Muhammad Azim remained in Kabul to meet this attack; while Abdur Rahman advanced to arrest his uncle's progress. On the 10th May 1866, a severe battle was fought at Shekhabad on the road to Ghazni, where Abdur Rahman's army was entrenched. Sher Ali was completely defeated and fled from the field, leaving his camp and artillery in the hands of the enemy. Ghazni fell and Muhammad Afzal Khan was

---

1 *Ibid.*

2 Sardar Azim Khan had again found an asylum in India.

released from confinement in that fortress. He was conducted in triumph to Kabul and proclaimed Amir. Throughout these events the policy of the British Government was that of strict neutrality.

The tyrannical conduct of the government in Kabul alienated the troops and the principal men of note, and revolts and defections occurred on every side, strengthening the cause of Sher Ali. He rejected the proposals of the party in power in Kabul to leave him in undisturbed possession of Kandahar and Herat, while they retained Kabul and Turkistan. He again marched on Kabul only to meet with a second crushing reverse near Kalat-i-Ghilzai in January 1867. He retired to Herat, and in a short time his rivals gained possession of Kandahar.

Muhammad Afzal Khan having thus become *de facto* Ruler of Kabul and Kandahar, was recognised as such by the British Government, which also declared, in pursuance of the policy of neutrality, its determination to acknowledge Sher Ali Khan as Ruler of Herat as long as he retained possession of that place and preserved his friendship for the British Government. Before the action of Kalat-i-Ghilzai, Sher Ali had been joined by his brother Faiz Muhammad Khan, who had quitted Afzal's party on being refused the government of Turkistan, to which he considered himself entitled for the assistance he had rendered Abdur Rahman Khan on his arrival from Bokhara. Sher Ali left Herat in May 1867, and in company with Faiz Muhammad he advanced on Kabul. After some trifling initial successes, they were defeated in September of that year at Kila Allahdad.[1]

Faiz Muhammad was killed; and Sher Ali again fell back on Herat. Muhammad Afzal Khan died on the 1st October 1867, and was succeeded by Muhammad Azim Khan, his brother, who was recognised as Amir of Kabul and Kandahar by the British Government.

Not disheartened by his reverses, Sher Ali Khan busied himself in preparation to renew the struggle. In April 1868, Kandahar was gained by his son Muhammad Yakub Khan. Later on Sher Ali himself advanced towards Kabul. Muhammad Azim Khan was deserted by his troops and fled to Turkistan, and Sher Ali entered Kabul in triumph on the 8th September 1868.

The British Government regarded with satisfaction the re-establishment of a consolidated administration in Afghanistan; and, in order to strengthen the Amir's authority and enable him to meet the more pressing demands on the exhausted revenues of the country, practical assistance in the shape of a gift of six lakhs of rupees and 6,000 stand of arms was afforded to him.

---

[1] *Ibid.*

In the meantime, Muhammad Azim Khan and Abdul Rahmān Khan had collected their forces and marched from Turkistan on Kabul. A decisive engagement took place at Tinah Khan, where the Amir obtained a complete victory. His opponents fled to the Waziri hills, from whence, through Nushki and Chagai, they made their way into Persia. Muhammad Azim Khan died on his way to Teheran on the 6th October 1869.

Immediately after his restoration to power, the Amir Sher Ali had expressed a wish to have an interview with the Viceroy, Sir John Lawrence. The troubles in Turkistan prevented for a time the fulfilment of this intention; but after the victory at Tinah Khan the proposal was renewed, and an interview between the Amir and the Earl of Mayo, Sir John Lawrence's successor, took place at Ambala on the 27th March 1869.[1]

The Amir was informed on this occasion that, while the British Government had no desire to interfere in the internal affairs of Kabul, yet it would view with severe displeasure any attempt on the part of the Amir's rivals to disturb his position and rekindle civil war. The Amir returned to Kabul on the 21st April 1869, taking with him as a further present from the British Government a sum of six lakhs of rupees, and one heavy and one mountain battery of Artillery.

For some time the relations between Muhammad Yakub Khan[2] and his father had been the reverse of cordial. Disappointed in his efforts to obtain recognition as heir-apparent, he fled from Kabul with his younger brother Muhammad Ayub Khan, in September 1870, and attempted with a small force to take possession of Ghazni. Finding that the gates had been closed, he invested Kandahar, but was repulsed, and his attempt on Girishk was equally unsuccessful. Here negotiations for a reconciliation were commenced, but were broken off by the arrival of troops from Kabul to act against him. Yakub Khan took to flight, and during the early part of 1871 wandered about the Seistan Border, committing raids, and intriguing equally with the Persian authorities, and the officials of the Amir. In April 1871, having collected a sufficient force, he invested Herat, which fell on the 6th May following. The chiefs of that Province, through whose assistance and treachery he had obtained possession of the city, assumed control of the finances, and Yakub Khan found his position as ruler, and his ability to reward his followers, merely nominal.

---

[1] *Ibid.*

[2] His mother was a daughter of Saadat Khan, Chief of the Momands—Mission to Kandahar.

Under these circumstances, he proceeded to Kabul, and with some difficulty was reconciled to his father, who appointed him Governor of Herat, subject to the general control of trusted officials from Kabul. The check exercised by them was slight, and Yakub Khan retained all the real power; but he was much hampered by the impoverished state of that Province.[1] The reconciliation between father and son was not sincere ; and reports of Muhammad Yakub Khan's intrigues and of the measures he was taking for strengthening his position in Herat, were a constant source of displeasure to the Amir. The estrangement on the son's side was completed by the formal nomination of Abdulla Khan, the youngest son of the Amir, as Heir-Apparent, in 1873 ; no actual rupture, however, occurred. Yakub Khan's main object now was to secure for himself the independent government of Herat and money for carrying on the administration. With this object in view, he suddenly resolved on a visit to Kabul. Before doing so, he stipulated that he should return to Herat ; should not be detained at the Capital more than ten days, nor be compelled to wait on or to see the Heir-Apparent, and should be allowed to take back all his adherents. These stipulations were agreed to by the Amir's agents, Asmatullah Khan and Arsala Khan Ghilzai, who had proceeded to Herat to conduct Yakub Khan to his father's presence. On his arrival on the 1st November 1874, he was treated ostensibly with kindness ; but the policy to be pursued towards him was debated in the Amir's council chamber, and resulted in his being placed under surveilance, the alleged reason being the Amir's fear that he would make over Herat to Persia. Muḥammad Ayub Khan, who had been left by Yakub Khan at Herat, retaliated by imprisoning some of the Amir's officials at Herat, and making preparations for the defence of the city against the troops which the Amir had sent after Yakub Khan's arrest to take possession of it. Herat, however, fell without resistance, and Ayub Khan, deserted by his followers, was compelled to take refuge in Persia.[2]

For many years after Herat was evacuated by the Persian troops in 1857; Persian troops had occupied posts in Seistan, and their title to the possession of the country had been disputed by the Afghans, whose claims were based on a condition of affairs which had come into existence about the middle of the 18th century. Previous

---

[1] The impoverished condition of the whole country is illustrated by the decrease of the revenue in Amir Sher Ali's reign. The collections from all the Provinces of his Kingdom are said to have amounted to no more than about sixty-six lakhs of rupees (Indian).

[2] Treaties, Engagements, Sanads. Vol. XI, 4th Edn., 1909.

to this date, Seistan had been for many centuries a part of the Persian Empire. Persia had more than once invited the interference of the British Government, notably at the time when the Amir Dost Muhammad had recovered Herat in 1863. Then the British Government was not prepared to intervene, and the Persian Government was informed that it must be left to both parties to make good their possession of Seistan by force of arms. As Persia was bound by article 6 of the Treaty of 1857, not to take up arms against Afghanistan without first inviting the friendly offices of the British Government, the effect of this refusal to interfere was to authorise an appeal to arms. The Persians had occupied the delta of the Helmand, in consequence of which disturbances were continually occurring, raids and reprisals took place, which were most injurious to the prosperity of the country and to the subjects of both claimants in the neighbouring districts. At length both Governments agreed to refer the question of the sovereignty and boundaries of the whole of Seistan to the British Government, on the understanding that both ancient right and recent possession were to be taken into consideration. It was also agreed that the decision of the British Government should be binding on both parties.[1]

Accordingly, in the spring of 1872, Commissioners on behalf of the parties concerned and the British Government assembled in Seistan; examined the lands in dispute, and heard the evidence produced on both sides. An award was finally pronounced by Major-General Goldsmid, the chief of the Mission, which, after some demur, was eventually accepted by Persia and Afghanistan and confirmed by the British Government.[2]

---

[1] *Ibid.*

[2] The substance of General Goldsmidt's arbitral award is as follows :—

"That Seistan proper, by which is meant the tract of country which the Hamun on three of its sides, and the Helmand on the fourth, cause to resemble an island, should be included by a special boundary line within the limits of Persia; that Persia should not possess land on the right bank of the Helmand; that the fort of Nad Ali should be evacuated by Persian garrisons, and the banks of the Helmand above the Kuhak Band given up to Afghanistan; that the main bed of the Helmand below Kuhak should be the eastern boundary of Persian Seistan, and that the line of frontier to the hills south of the Seistan desert should be so drawn as to include within the Afghan limits all cultivation on both banks of the river from the Band upwards, the Malik Siah Koh on the chain of hills separating the Seistan from the Kirman desert appearing to be a fitting point; that on the north of Seistan the southern limit of the Naizar should be the frontier towards Lash-Juwein; that Persia should not cross the Human in that direction, her possession being clearly defined by a line to be drawn from the Naizar to the Koh Siah hill near Bandan; finally that no works were to be carried out on either side calculated to interfere with the requisite supply of water for irrigation on both banks of the Helmand."—*Ibid.*

At this time and for many years subsequently the boundary between Afghanistan and Baluchistan, from Seistan eastwards, was the Helmand, up to

Concurrently with the question of the Seistan Boundary in 1869, the advance of the Russians into the Central Asian Khanates, caused the British Government to enter into negotiations with that power, with the object of defining the north-west frontier of Afghanistan. In 1872 the British Government proposed that—

(1.) Badakshan, with its independent district of Wakhan, from the Sarikul (Wood's Lake) on the East to the junction of the Kokcha river with the Oxus (or Panja), forming the northern boundary of this Afghan Province throughout its entire extent.

(2.) Afghan Turkistan, comprising the districts of Kunduz, Khulm and Balkh, the northern boundary of which would be the line of the Oxus from the junction of the Kokcha river to the post of Khojah Saleh inclusive, on the high road from Bokhara to Balkh. Nothing to be claimed by the Afghan Amir on the left bank of the Oxus below Khojah Saleh.

(3.) The internal districts of Akchah, Siripul, Maimena, Shibarghān and Andikui, the latter of which would be the extreme Afghan Frontier possession to the northwest, the desert beyond belonging to the independent tribes of Turkomans, were to be regarded as belonging to Afghanistan.

(4.) The western Afghan Frontier between the dependencies of Herat and those of the Persian Province of Khorasan are well known, and need not here be defined.

This somewhat vague settlement, known as the Clarendon-Gortchakoff agreement of 1872-73, was concluded without any reference to the Amir.

Landi Wali Muhammad, and from this place to the Pishin Lora river between Nushki and Sharawak, following that river up to the junction of the stream which drained the Shal valley which belonged to Kalat. Over the tract to the west of Nushki, the influence of Azad Khan, Chief of Khārān was paramount. When in 1884-85, Sir Robert Sandeman caused Azad Khan to recognise the Khan of Kalat as his overlord, and granted the Khārān Sardar an annual allowance from the Indian Government, any possible extension of British influence up to the Helmand was forestalled by Amir Abdur Rahman's far-sighted move, of taking possession of Chagai (of which he held effective possession for ten years) in the winter of 1885.—G. P. T.

The Boundary Commission of 1885 was formed to demarcate Afghanistan and Russian Territory, according to the agreement of 1872.

The Seistan Boundary Commission, 1903-05, had to lay down a Boundary according to the Award by General Goldsmidt of 1872.

Both the Agreement of 1872 and the Award were drawn up without an accurate knowledge of existing geographical conditions, and the task of both Commissions was rendered very difficult in consequence.

CHAPTER XVIII.

AMIR SHER ALI—THE RUSSIAN ADVANCE IN CENTRAL ASIA—THE WAR WITH AFGHANISTAN, 1878—81.

THE petty tyrants who ruled the Central Asian Khanates had earned an evil reputation from their traffic in slaves, and the Khan of Khiva was the first of those rulers to feel the resentment of the Russians who had been harassed by the Nomads, nominally the subjects of the Khan of that State. It was impossible to restrain the depredations of these tribes without occupying that State, and in 1839, an expedition had started from Orenburg for this purpose. Owing to the severity of the winter, and the inhospitable nature of the desert, General Perovsky had been compelled to fall back on Orenburg, after losing a quarter of his army and 10,500 camels.

The Kirghiz, who were the subjects of the Khan of Khokand, tried to drive the Russians back from the Lower Syr Daria, with the result that the number of Russian fortresses was increased, and Fort Perovsky was built in 1853 as the most advanced post. After a long period of inactivity, caused by the Crimean war, the eastward advance was recommenced, the town of Turkestan fell on the 23rd of June 1864, and Chimkent on October 4th.

Taking advantage of a war that had broken out between Bokhara and Khokand, the Russians under Tschernajev took possession of Tashkend in June 1865. A war between them and the Amir of Bokhara was the result, and the Bokhara Army was routed by the Russians near Irjar, on the 25th of May 1866, and immediately afterwards General Romaniski marched against Khokand, now a dependency of Bokhara, and took possession of the town of Khojent.

Muzaffar-ud-din, Amir of Bokhara, urged by the fanaticism of his subjects, made preparations for war against the Russians, notwithstanding the refusal of the Khans of Khiva and Khokand to take a part in this enterprize[1]. Before he was able to take the field, an army under General Kaufman advanced on Samarkand, defeated the superior forces of Bokhara, and entered the city on the 14th May 1868. This was followed by efforts to establish communications with Yarkand. Kuljar was occupied in 1871, and a commercial treaty was concluded with Yakub Beg in 1872.

After the annexation of Khokand (March 3rd, 1876), and the final reduction of Khiva, and of its Khan, to the position of a Russian vassal, Russia had become paramount in Central Asia, and the subjugation of the independent Turkomans, who infested the region between the Oxus and the ill-defined limit to which the influence of Persia was supposed to extend, was clearly the next step to be taken.

The prestige enjoyed by the Central Asian Principalities, subdued by Russia, was very great, and the resistance of their loosely knitted forces having been overcome without a check by Russia caused the fame of her power to obsess the minds of all Asiatics, and it was the theme of conversation in every bazaar in the east. It is not to be wondered at, therefore, if the morose Afghan who sat on the throne in Kabul, was impressed by the Russian victories to such an extent as to cause him to forget the friendship he had professed (probably unwillingly and caused by his necessities rather than predilection), for the British Government. It is popularly believed that he was disappointed most grievously, at the result of the Seistan Commission, and perhaps the conclusion of the Clarendon-Gortchakoff agreement without his being given an opportunity of expressing his views, may have fanned his disappointment into an active resentment. The introduction of the Amir as a third party into the negotiations probably would have had the effect of prolonging the discussion indefinitely, while the situation in Central Asia was such as to render it imperatively necessary to obtain from Russia an early acknowledgment that certain districts belonged to Afghanistan, and as such were to be regarded as out of bounds for Russian troops, and beyond which no encroachment in the direction of that country would be permitted by Great Britain.

From 1872 onwards the relations between Afghanistan and the British Government became increasingly cold and strained, while the antagonism or rivalry between Great Britain and Russia in Europe caused a fresh outburst of activity in Central Asia, and gave the movement of Russian troops in that continent a definite object—to menace India. The question of abating the nuisance of marauding

[1] The Russian Advance on Central Asia. Harmsworth's History of the World, p. 1518 *et seq.*

Turkomans was a secondary object, and Russian statesmen considered the new move as a check to England. The military party avowed their belief that the surest way of settling the Eastern question in Europe was to frighten England by advancing to the gates of India. Military men and Civilians alike thought that, at the least, an advance was the only means of neutralizing hypothetical British intrigues with the Princes of Central Asia.[1] Relations between Great Britain and Russia were strained almost to the point of an open rupture by the Treaty of San Stefano (March 3rd, 1878), and an expeditionary force of British and Indian troops was despatched to the Mediterranean from India [2]; but the war clouds that had been gathering in Europe were dispelled by Russia's consent to submit the Treaty to a conference of the Powers in Berlin, and in July 1878, Lord Beaconsfield returned to London the bearer of Peace with Honour.

In 1873 the Government of India had presented Amir Sher Ali with 15,000 Enfield rifles, 5,000 Snider rifles and with 200 rounds of ammunition for each of the latter. In addition, 10 lakhs of rupees was set aside for him, of which 5 lakhs was regarded as a contribution towards the amount to be paid to the Seistan sufferers, and the remainder as a contribution towards the general expenses of the Amir, which he might, if he thought fit, expend in arrangements for the settlement of Seistan, or otherwise, as he thought best. The ten lakhs of rupees was deposited in the Kohat Treasury, pending the Amir's instructions. The money was never drawn.[3]

The unchecked progress of Russia in Central Asia, and the memory of the tragedy enacted in the Passes leading to Jalālābād in 1842 must have led to comparisons unfavorable to the British Government by a semi-barbarous Ruler, such as Sher Ali was ; and his still more ignorant subjects, could not be expected to appraise rightly the small military value of the undisciplined levies, which alone the Rulers of the conquered Principalities could oppose to western science and training. Both the Amir and his subjects probably regarded Russia as omnipotent, and friendship with that power as likely to be more profitable to them than friendship with the British Government.

Matters came to a crisis when, on the 11th August 1878, the Amir gave an official welcome to a Russian Mission at his capital.

---

1 The Russian advance on Central Asia. Harmsworth's History of the World. p. 1518 et seq.

2 The troops sailed from Bombay, 25th April 1878. Malta was reached 28th May. Troops embarked again for Cyprus 18th July. Returned to Bombay 18th September 1878.

3 Parliamentary papers.

The Government of India thought it necessary to insist upon a similar reception being accorded to a British Mission, and preparations were accordingly made for the despatch of a party of British and Native officers of rank, under Sir Neville Chamberlain ; but on the 21st September 1878, by the Amir's orders, his officers at Ali Masjid, refused to allow the British Envoy to travel through the Khyber Pass.

In spite of this public affront, it was still deemed to be desirable, before proceeding to extremities, to give Sher Ali a *locus penitentiæ.* An ultimatum was accordingly addressed to him, threatening him with war, unless, by the 20th November 1878, he signified his willingness to comply with the demands of the British Government ; no answer having been received by the prescribed date, British troops crossed the frontier on the 21st November by three main lines of advance, by the Bolan Pass on Kandahar, the Kuram Valley, and by the Khyber Pass towards Kabul.

The Afghan forces were everywhere defeated, the principal action being fought at the Paiwar Kotal on the 2nd December, which opened the way to the capital. Sher Ali, unable to contend against the troubles he had brought on himself, fled from Kabul on the 10th of December 1878, and in company with the remaining members of the Russian Mission, took the road to Turkistan. Yakub Khan was released and left as regent at Kabul.

Communications passed between Yakub Khan and the British officers, but the troops continued to advance, till, towards the end of January 1879, they were in military occupation of a considerable part of Afghanistan. On the arrival of the news that Sher Ali had died at Mazār-i-Sharif on the 21st February, negotiations were opened with Yakub Khan which ended in the Treaty of Gandamak, signed by him in the British Camp, on the 26th May, and which was ratified by the Viceroy four days later. By this Treaty the districts of Kuram, Sibi, and Pishin were assigned and to remain under British administration, any surplus revenue over expenditure was to be handed over to the Amir. The Khyber and Michni Passes were to be controlled by the British Government, who were to retain the control of all relations with the independent tribes inhabiting the territory directly connected with these Passes.[1]

Article 4 provided for the residence at Kabul of a British Agent, and Sir Louis Cavagnari was selected to fill this appointment. On the 6th of July that officer left Simla and reached Kabul on the 24th of

---

[1] Treaties, Engagements and Sanads, Vol. XI., 4th Edn., 1909.

the same month, accompanied by British Officers and a suitable escort, and was installed in the Bālā Hissār close to the Palace of the Amir.

There may have been many eye-witnesses of the calamitous retreat of the British forces in 1843, alive at this time, and very many more who had viewed with their own eyes, clear evidence of the destruction of British troops in the passes that lead to Jalālābād. The arrival of the Herati regiments, which Ayub Khan had despatched to Kabul, appears to have given an impetus to the inflated idea of their own prowess, which the memory of 1843 had created in the minds of the Afghans, and to their dislike to the residence of foreigners in their capital. That which had been done in 1843, they probably considered could be repeated in 1879. Once more Kabul was in uproar. Gandamak was several days' journey from that city, the troops were being withdrawn to India, and the Amir was unwilling or unable to control the outburst of feeling against the foreigners. The residence of the British Agent was surrounded by a horde of infuriated Afghans, thirsting for the blood of foreigners, and conspicuous among them were the men belonging to the Herati regiments. After a heroic defence, the small garrison in the Residency was annihilated (3rd September).

This tragedy arrested the evacuation of the country and the second phase of the war was opened by an advance on Kabul. Yakub Khan hastened to meet the advancing troops under General (Lord) Roberts, at Kushi, on the 28th of September. On the 12th October the day on which the Bālā Hisār of Kabul was formally occupied, he signified his intention of resigning the throne of Afghanistan; his tents and those of his personal attendants were removed to the Head-Quarter Camp. On the 28th, as he was contemplating a flight to Turkestan, he was placed under close arrest. On the 29th orders were received from Simla for his immediate deportation to India, and at 6-30 A.M. on the 30th of October Yakub Khan left the camp on his way to Peshawar.[1]

At Chahārāsia, in the Logar Valley, the troops which had participated in the massacre of the British Agent and his devoted companions, aided by large numbers of the disaffected townsmen of Kabul, and local tribesmen, had attempted to oppose the advance of our troops on Kabul. They had been conspicuously defeated in the open field; their organisation was at an end, and their leaders had taken to flight. The army which Sher Ali had endeavoured to create had failed him at

[1] The Second Afghan War, 1878-80, Abridged Official Account.

his need. Time was, however, necessary, before the jealousies and enmities of the clans and their chiefs could be composed, and the latter induced to subordinate their personal aims and resentments in order to allow a national movement being set on foot to drive the foreigner from their country. The occupation of Sher Ali's unfinished cantonments in the vicinity of Kabul, the dismantling of the Bālā Hisār, and the deportation of Yakub Khan, coupled with the absence of any member of the family who could be raised to the throne with any prospect of retaining possession of it, unaided by foreign troops, proved that an immediate evacuation of Afghanistan was not contemplated. The memories of 1842-43 revived; and only jealousy and distrust of each other, prevailing among the leaders of the people, prevented them from making common cause against the enemy in their midst. At length the exertions of the Mulla of Ghazni, Mushk-i-Alim, seconded by the appeals of Yakub Khan's family, who had remained in Kabul, and of the priesthood generally, succeeded in causing all other considerations being set aside in favor of combined action against the invaders. The rising tide of popular feeling was evidenced by the appearance of large numbers of armed men in the country round Kabul, which afforded constant occupation for the troops in Sherpur, the defences of which were being strengthened in view of the attack which was impending, and which, in course of time, became known to have been fixed for the morning of the 23rd December 1879. During the dark hours of the night, the armed bands of the national militia gathered in the shelter of gardens and villages, drawing in towards the hastily erected defences of Sherpur[1] as the hours passed, under the leadership of Muhammad Jān, the Wardak Chief, and Mir Bacha, of the Kohistan. The aged Mushk-i-Alim fired the beacon with his own hands, on the summit of the Asmai hills at 5-30 A.M. which had been agreed upon as the signal for a general advance on the position held by the foreigners. The latter, barely more numerous than the force which had occupied the cantonments near Kabul in the winter of 1842-43, were animated with a very different spirit, and by midday, when the British troops were able to take the offensive, the assailants were in full retreat; their rapid movement and the depth of the snow saving them from the pursuit of the cavalry. On the 24th December not a single Afghan was to be found in the villages near the Capital, or on the surrounding hills.

The defeat of the nationalists proved that the British grip on their country was not to be loosened by force, yet the Afghans were

[1] The Second Afghan War, 1878-80, Abridged Official Account.

far from being subdued. And though Kabul was retained under direct British administration until its future government could be settled on some basis which would have a reasonable prospect of stability, the invading forces held only the ground on which they stood. There were tracts into which British troops had not penetrated, and though communication with India was safe, the presence of an enemy in their midst, camel trains passing to and fro, and the warlike spirit of the people, urged them to reprisals, which provided ample scope for the display of the valour and discipline of the British troops. The premeditated and deliberate insult offered by Sher Ali to the British Government had been avenged, and the last and lingering effects of the disaster of 1843, on the prestige of Great Britain, had been completely effaced by the successful invasion of Afghanistan. In Southern Afghanistan, the Ghilzais who had drawn to a head under Sahib Jān, son of an influential Taraki Malik, were dispersed after a spirited combat at Shahjui on the 24th October 1879, by a detachment from Kandahar.

After witnessing the failure of the rising at Kabul which he had incited, the Mulla Mushk-i-Alim had carried away Musa Jān, Yakub Khan's young son to Ghazni. That place had become the provisional capital, and the child had been proclaimed there as the ruler of the country. Ayub Khan remained undisturbed in Herat, but the eyes of all men were turned towards Abdur Rahman, who, in the spring of 1880, had left his refuge in Russian Territory and had made his appearance with a considerable body of followers in Afghan Turkistan. He had been cordially welcomed by the leading chiefs and had established his authority on the northern side of the Hindu-Kush. The Sardar had a few adherents of note in the country to the south of the mountains, more especially in the Kohistan, where considerable excitement had been manifested after his arrival in Kunduz. Upon the announcement of his intention to cross the mountains, Khoja Jān, Mir Bacha, and other chiefs of the Kohistan, and the Koh Daman, withdrew their support, hitherto given to the cause of Yakub Khan, and to his son Musa Jān ; and transferred their allegiance to Abdur Rahman. There seemed to be reason to believe, from the character of the latter and his reputation for ability, that, with the countenance of the British Government, he might be able to establish himself more firmly upon the throne of Kabul than any of the other possible candidates for the Amirship.[1]

The dispersal of the adherents of Musa Jān in Ghazni was carried out by the division of troops which had been originally

[1] Treaties, Engagements and Sanads, Vol. XI, 4th Edition, 1909.

drawn from the Bengal Presidency, permission having been given to move in relief to India, either by the Bolan Pass or by way of Ghazni. After Kalat-i-Ghilzai had been passed, on the northward march, it became apparent that opposition was being organised to the advance of this division; and on the 19th April 1880, a force of armed tribesmen, estimated at 15,000 men, were discovered in position on the heights overlooking the road at a place about 16 miles from Ghazni. The greater part of this gathering was drawn from the Ghilzai tribes, but the rear of the column had been dogged by contingents of Duranis from Kandahar, and of the Alizais from Zamindāwar, who had kept out of sight, but who had doubtless joined the Ghilzais at this point. The latter displayed their usual courage, and disdain of caution; and 1,000 dead bodies on the field of Ahmad Khel, attested the valour of the gallant clansmen, who withdrew after a desperate struggle lasting an hour. Ghazni was occupied on the 21st April 1880, and no further opposition was offered to the progress of the division to Kabul.[1]

The negotiations with Abdur Rahman having been sanctioned by the Secretary of State for India, on the 1st April, the chief Political Officer in Afghanistan despatched a letter to Abdur Rahman who was then at Kunduz. Preparations were steadily going on for the withdrawal of the troops to India when, on the 29th July, the bazaars of Kabul, which were full of armed supporters of the future Amir(who had reached Istalif on this date), were thrown into a state of the greatest excitement by news of the defeat at Maiwand, on the 27th July, by Ayub Khan, of a small force detailed from Kandahar to oppose his advance. Neither the concentration of the troops in Sherpur, nor the disturbing news from the direction of Kandahar, were allowed to interfere with the negotiations on foot with Abdur Rahman. Though the Sardar had at first made some attempt to assert his position, as Amir in his own right, he readily accepted the position offered him by the Government of India, namely, that of Amir of Kabul; the Kandahar Province being severed from Kabul and made into a separate principality. Matters having been satisfactorily settled, he was formally recognised as Amir, at a Durbar held in Kabul on the 22nd July 1880. On the 31st of July and the following day, a conference was held at Zimma (near Ak Sarai, and about 16 miles from Kabul), at which the wishes and intentions of the British Government were fully explained to him. No formal treaty was drawn up, but it was understood that he was to be assisted with money and arms by the

[1] Second AfghanWar, 1878-80, abridged official account

Government of India to such an extent as might appear to them to be necessary; that he was to be recognised by them as Amir of Kabul, and its dependencies; that he might take such measures as he pleased to bring Herat under his control, but that he was not to interfere with the Wāli of Kaṇdahar; that Pishin, Sibi, and the Kuram were to be no longer regarded as belonging to Afghanistan; that the British Government were to control the Khyber and Michni passes and all relations with the independent tribesmen inhabiting the hills directly connected with the passes; and that the foreign relations of Kabul were henceforth to be conducted subject to the approval of the Government of India. No mention was made, at this time, of Khost; but at the Amir's request, he was allowed to take possession of the district, a few months later.[1]

On the 8th of August 1880, the division organised for the relief of Kandạhar, began its famous march towards the south, accompanied by representatives of the Amir Abdur Rahman, to demonstrate to the tribes along the route, that he was in complete accord with the British Government in this matter. The prestige gained by Ayub after Maiwand, rendered him a formidable competitor for the Amirship, whom the new Amir would have had great difficulty in disposing of at this time. Ayub's prospective defeat was likely to prove very useful to the Amir, as it would give him time to arrange his affairs. On the 11th August General Sir Donald Steward received the Amir Abdur Rahman at a formal Durbar, handing over to him the capital, which had been in the hands of British Officers for ten months. The fortifications constructed by the British Army of occupation were also made over to him intact, with thirty of the guns belonging to Sher Ali, which had been captured at Kabul; and more than 5 lakhs of rupees which remained in the Treasury at that place.[2]

The withdrawal of the troops towards India had commenced at 5-30 A.M. and they were accompanied by several Afghan notables, who considered it advisable to leave Kabul; and by many Hindus. The retreating columns were followed by large droves of cattle belonging to private owners, going down to India. That night the troops encamped at Butkhak and the occupation of Kabul had been brought to a close.[3]

---

[1] Treaties, Engagements and Sanads, Vol. XI, 4th Edition, 1909.

[2] The Amir received 39½ lakhs of rupees in all.

[3] The original intention of withdrawing part of the force *via* the Kuram Valley was eventually discarded, owing partly to the necessity of despatching a large force from Kabul to Kandahar and partly to the desirability of using the most direct route in order speedily to leave Northern Afghanistan to the Amir. (The second Afghan war, 1878 to 1880, Abridged Official Account).

Ayub Khan, after a great deal of vacillation and lengthy preparation, had started from Herat in the preceding June, with the intention of annexing Kandahar to his own principality. On the 27th of July, he met and defeated a British force at Maiwand. This unexpected success, very greatly increased his prestige, and as he advanced towards Kandahar he was joined by large number of tribesmen, and the garrison of that city was shut up within the walls. On the 24th of August a great stir was perceived in Ayub's camp, and intelligence was brought in that he was retiring to Bābā Wali, as he had received news of the arrival at Kalat-i-Ghilzai, of the relieving force, and of the proclamation, as Amir, of Abdur Rahman. At noon a heliograph was seen twinkling through the haze, from the summit of a far-off hill to the east of Kandahar; announcing the approach of the succours from Kabul. On the 31st Lord Roberts arrived at Kandahar, and on the 1st of September Ayub Khan was completely defeated, and took to flight, shorn of the reputation he had accidentally gained at Maiwand; losing all his artillery—thirty pieces, excluding the two guns which he had taken at Maiwand, and all his baggage. The dead body of Lieut. Hector Maclaine, R.H.A., who had been made prisoner at that place, was discovered outside the tent he had occupied close to Ayub's quarters.[1]

Ayub Khan made his way to Herat, and remained quiescent there whither it was not considered advisable to follow him. It would have been well for him had he remained there in 1880; as the loss in material, and reputation at Kandahar, directly contributed to his over-throw by Amir Abdur Rahman; when in the next summer

[1] Towards the end of January 1890, I was at Dizak, in Persian Baluchistan, and while breakfasting (prior to my departure) with Dilawar Khan, the Chief of that place, I was introduced to one Sarwar Khan, a Popalzai Afghan, who said he had been one of Ayub's Officers. He had accompanied the Sardar in his flight to Persia after the latter had been defeated by Abdur Rahman, and again, when in 1887, the Sardar had attempted to enter Afghanistan, to join the insurgent Ghilzais. When (9th November 1887), Ayub Khan surrendered to General MacLean, the British Representative in Khorasan, Sarwar Khan had hung back as he dreaded being sent to India. He had found a refuge in Dizak and was trying very hard to make his peace with Amir Abdur Rahman. This man asseverated that Ayub Khan had given strict orders to the guard over Lieutenant Maclaine, that they were to make their prisoner over to the first British troops that appeared. In the confusion of the flight, at the end of the battle, the infuriated Ghazis swarmed into the camp, and exasperated by the reverse they had sustained; and in order to glut their appetite for the blood of infidels, they over-powered the guard and murdered the prisoner in their charge.

Sarwar Khan also said that Ayub Khan had not intended to fight at Maiwand, as he knew that a collision with British troops would prejudice his claims to the Amirship. The Mullas who had given him their support and the Ghazis who had joined him in response to their call, openly declared that, unless the Sardar made war on the infidels, they would abandon his cause. After much discussion, it was decided to continue the advance—"and the decree of fate was fulfilled."

the former had for a time succeeded in taking possession of Kandahar.

The course of events had made it quite clear that the Wali of Kandahar, Sardar Sher Ali Khan, son of Mihr Dil Khan, Barakzai, could not hope to maintain himself in the Principality created for him, without the assistance of British troops ; and it was impossible to keep troops there for an indefinite period. He was accordingly allowed, at his own request, to retire to British India on a pension, and the Government of India thereupon offered Kandahar to Amir Abdur Rahman. His Highness was not at first prepared to accept the offer, urging the want of ammunition, arms and transport. Eventually, however, he consented to the proposals made to him. On the 19th of April formal instructions reached the General Officer Commanding at Kandahar regarding the withdrawal of the troops from Southern Afghanistan. On the morning of the 16th, Sardar Muhammad Hashim Khan, the Governor appointed by the Amir, entered Kandahar, and in the course of the day he paid a formal visit to Colonel St. John, the Chief Political Officer, with whom he discussed the details of the evacuation, and the handing over the charge of the city. The burial places of British soldiers in the neighbourhood of the city were committed to the care of the Amir's governor ; and the families and property of certain persons, who had been in the employ of, or friendly to the British, were also commended to the care of the governor. General Ghulam Haidar Khan was within two marches of the city, and a detachment of Afghan Infantry were at Deh khwaja in readiness to take charge of the gates and citadel, and at noon precisely, on the 21st of April 1881, the Union Jack was hauled down under a salute of thirty-one guns and the last of the British troops quitted the cantonment and citadel, and encamped on the plain to the north of Kandahar.[1]

The withdrawal of the troops continued without interruption or incident, and each post along the line was handed over in turn to the Amir's officials, and with the arrival of the retreating forces at Chaman, on the 27th April 1881, the evacuation of Afghanistan was completed.[2]

Once more the renewed activity of Russia in Central Asia synchronised with the invasion of Afghanistan by British troops; operations at this time having been undertaken by the former against the Akhal Tekke Turkomans. Under-rating the resistance likely to be offered by these

[1] Second Afghan War, 1878-80, Abridged Official Account.

[2] The total estimated expenditure entailed by the war, on the British Government, up to 31st May, was £ 9,500,000 ; of which the exchequer bore a share of £ 5,000,000, the remainder being defrayed by the revenue of India.—*Ibid.*

ferocious marauders, a force which proved unequal to the task, had failed to capture the Turkoman intrenchments at Dengil Teppe on the 9th September 1879. The reverse, however, merely checked for a short time the Russian advance, and the storming of Geok Teppe on January 24th, 1881, completed the subjugation of the northern, or Tekke Turkomans, and the Turkomans of Merv soon after submitted to the inevitable, and voluntarily became subjects of Russia. The progress of Russia had brought her up to the western undefined boundary of Afghanistan, and the foresight which had led to the conclusion of the Clarendon-Gortchakoff agreement of 1872-73 was amply vindicated.

CHAPTER XIX.

AMIR ABDUR RAHMAN—AFGHANISTAN, THE BUFFER STATE.

SARDAR AYUB KHAN made a bid for the throne after our troops had withdrawn from Kandahar. He defeated the Amir's men in an action at Karez on the 20th July 1881 and seized Kandahar. Leaving his son Sardar Habibullah, with Parwana Khan as Commander-in-Chief, in Kabul, Amir Abdur Rahman took the field in person and advanced on Kandahar. Ayub abandoned the city on his cousin's approach, and was completely defeated on the 22nd of September, in an action fought in the ruins of Old Kandahar. In the meantime, Sardar Abdul Kudus Khan, a cousin of the Amir and his Governor of Afghan Turkistan, advanced on Herat and seized the place on the 4th of August 1881. Ayub Khan retired to Persia, and for six years he resided in Tehran.

"When I first succeeded to the throne of Afghanistan my life was not a bed of roses." [1]

In these words the Amir described his position after the evacuation of Afghanistan by our troops. Beset on all sides "by difficulties of all kinds," he surmounted them, owing to his great qualities as a man and as a ruler, which were governed by a cool head and an iron resolution. If his methods would not be approved by the civilized world, they were the only methods which his stiff-necked countrymen understand or respect in their rulers.

"High stands thy Kábul citadel where many have room and rest ;"
"The Amirs give welcome entry, but they speed not a parting guest ;'
"So a stranger needs safe escort, and the oath of a valiant friend ;"

* * * * *

"Wilt thou send the Jamsheedee Aga, who was called from the Western plain ;"
"He left the black tents of his horsemen, and he never led them again ;"
"Shall I ask for the Moollah, in Ghuzni to whom all Afghans rise ?"
"He was bid last year to thy banqueting—his soul is in Paradise ;"
"Where is the Chief Faizulla, to pledge me the word of his clan?"
"He is far from his pine-clad highlands, and the vineyards of Kohistan :"
"He is gone with the rest—all vanished ; he passed through thy citadel gate."

[1] Life of Abdur Rahman, Amir of Afghanistan, Vol. I, Chap. IX, p. 210. John Murray, London 1900. By Sultan Muhammad Khan.
The first eleven chapters are said to have been written by the late Amir.

[2] Verses written in India—Sir Alfred Lyall, London, 1896. "The Amir's Message," p. 65.

One of the most important events in the reign of the Amir was the delimitation of the North-Western Frontier of his kingdom. For this purpose, as far back as 1869, in the reign of Amir Sher Ali, negotiations had been commenced between the British and Russian Governments, and the Clarendon-Gortchakoff Agreement of 1872-73 had been concluded.

The steady advance of Russia in the direction of Merv, and the frequent reports which were received as to the occupation of that district, caused the British Government to suggest the demarcation of the Afghan Boundary, certain details regarding which had been left unsettled by the Agreement of 1872-73. Numerous communications passed between the two Governments, but without decisive results, till in February 1884, while the matter was still under consideration, official information was received that the Merv Turkomans had made their submission to Russia, and that the Czar had determined to accept them as his subjects. Upon this a memorandum was despatched to the British Ambassador at St. Petersburg to communicate to the Russian Government, in which it was observed, that the occupation of Merv seemed entirely inconsistent with the hitherto uniform assurances of the Russian Government that they had no intention of occupying that district.[1]

In their reply (March 1884) the Russian Government explained their action with regard to Merv; adding that, if the British Government should find it useful and practicable to complete the arrangements previously concluded between the two Governments, by a more exact definition of the countries, separating Russsian possessions from Afghanistan, Rџssia could only repeat the proposals of 1882, to continue from Khojah Saleh westwards, the line of demarcation agreed to in 1872-73. The British Government accepted (29th April 1884), and suggested the appointment of a Joint Commission, which should commence operations the following autumn; and after considerable correspondence, it was arranged that General Sir Peter Lumsden, the British Commissioner, and General Zelenoi, the Russian Commissioner, should meet at Sarakhs about the 13th October 1884.

Sir Peter Lumsden duly arrived from England on the Frontier and joined his escort which had marched to meet him from India. Difficulties however arose, the Russian Commissioner did not appear; and by the time it had become necessary to retire into winter quarters, no progress had been made. Russian troops, however, had already

[1] Treaties, Engagements and Sanads, India, Vol. XI, Part V, pp. 326-7. 4th Edition, 1909.

advanced and occupied Pul-i-Khatun, on the Hari Rud; and Pul-i-Khisti on the Murghāb River. Shortly before this, Afghan troops had occupied Panjdeh, and the Russian Ambassador had called the very serious attention of the British Government to this fact.[1] On the 30th of March 1885, discussions were interrupted when a Russian Force attacked and defeated a considerable body of Afghan troops, at Pul-i-Khisti, near Panjdeh. The Amir was at Rawalpindi on his visit to the Viceroy at this critical moment. War, however, was averted, and the negotiations were resumed in London. Sir Peter Lumsden was recalled to England to assist in the negotiations there, and the charge of the Mission devolved on Colonel Sir West Ridgeway. It was not, however, till the 10th of September 1885 that final arrangements for the demarcation were concluded between the two Governments.[2] On the 10th of November the Joint Commission met, as arranged, at Zulfikār, and work was commenced; good progress being made, till shortly after Christmas both parties were driven into Winter-quarters. Work was resumed on the 1st of March 1886, and by the 18th of June, the frontier had been definitely fixed, and pillars had been built from Zulfikār on the Hari Rud to the meridian of Dukchi, a group of wells to the north of Andikhui, and within forty miles or the Oxus.[3]

Unfortunately the Joint Commission found it impossible to agree as to the spot at which the Frontier Line should enter the cultivated tracts in the vicinity of the river, or actually meet it. All the old papers bearing on the subject had mentioned Khojah Saleh as being the Frontier; but no place on the river could now be found which both sides would admit to be the Khojah Saleh of the Agreement of 1872-73. In consequence the Commission dissolved itself, at Khāmiāb, early in September 1886. The British party returned to India through Kabul, where they were honourably entertained by the Amir for about a week.

In the following year, negotiations were resumed, and eventually a settlement was reached by mutual concessions. Afghanistan restored to the Sarik Turkomans most of the land of which they had been deprived between the Khushk and Murghāb rivers; and Russia withdrew her claims to all districts then in possession of the Afghans, on the Oxus; and to the wells and pastures necessary to

---

1 *Ibid.*

2 In the meantime British Officers belonging to the Mission visited Herat, and examined its defences, and the approaches to that place.

3 Treaties, Engagements and Sanads, India, Vol. XI, Part V., 4th Edition, 1909.

the prosperity of the Uzbegs of Afghan-Turkistan. Early in 1888 the demarcation was completed of the revised portion of the boundary between the Khushk and Murghāb rivers and between Dukchi and the Oxus.[1]

While the British Commission was in the neighbourhood of Herat, a local dispute regarding the boundary between Persia and Afghanistan, in the Hashtadān Valley, was brought to notice and investigated. After protracted correspondence between the two governments, both referred the matter to the decision of the Viceroy. The compromise suggested in the report, submitted to him by Major-General MacLean (the Agent to the Governor-General in Khurassan), was accepted by both parties, and was put into effect by actual demarcation, on the spot, during the months of March, April, and May 1891.

In 1891 and in the following year, the Russian Government complained that the Afghans had infringed the provisions of the Protocol of the Afghan Boundary Commission, of the 22nd July 1887, by irrigating lands on the left bank of the Khushk River by means of canals taking off from that stream. A Joint Commission of a British, Russian and Afghan Official investigated the matter on the spot; a settlement was made after inquiry, and effect was given to the Joint Commissioners' decision on the spot.[2]

This concluded the delimitation of the north-western boundary of the kingdom of Afghanistan; and there remained a settlement of the questions that had arisen with regard to the spheres of influence of the Amir and his friends, the British Government, in the opposite direction.

The annexation of the Punjab and of Sind had carried the boundary of the British Empire in India up to the foot of the hills to the west of the Indus. Immediately beyond lies the mountainous region known as the Roh, composed of ridges and valleys descending from the western watershed of the Indus. It was the homeland of tribes who always had been practically independent of control, and whose poverty drove them to prey on the peaceful inhabitants of our lowland border districts. This region can be divided roughly into three sections, each of which is inhabited by tribes of as many origins. To the south of the Bolan Pass, and between it and the Arabian Sea, lies Baluchistan; the largest of the three sections. To the north of this is the Pathan Section and north again of the latter lie the small

[1] *Ibid.*

[2] *Ibid.*

Dard States of Hunza, Nagar, and others, of which Gilgit had been the ancient capital.

Over Baluchistan, with the exception of Kalat, Persia had exercised a fluctuating control down to a recent period. The Pathan Section was nominally subject to the Ruler of Afghanistan, while China regarded one or two of the Dard Principalities as being under her influence.[1]

The steady advance of Russia from the Caspian had led to considerations for the protection of the North-West Frontier of India, and the celebrated Frontier Official, Colonel John Jacob, had foreseen the necessity of entering into arrangements with the tribes adjoining the Sind Frontier, and for the occupation of Quetta at the head of the Bolan Pass. In 1867, Sir Henry Green, Political Superintendent and Commandant of the Sind Frontier, placed the matter before the Government officially. The scheme involved the occupation of Quetta, and it was carefully considered by the Government of India, and was rejected in the most decisive terms.

On the question of border management, there grew up two schools, one of which believed the "close border" policy, as a general principle, to be the better. By this all unnecessary interference with the tribes was to be avoided, treating them in a friendly manner when they behaved well, and punishing them when they molested us; but no attempt to occupy their territory or to send British Officers among them should be made, nor to establish any sort of control over them. The other school held that our officers should be encouraged to enter into close personal relations with the tribesmen, to enter their country, and efforts should be made in course of time to establish permanent control over the tribes, and to introduce something like peace and order among them.[2] For some time the advocates of the "close border" policy had their way; but even before the second Afghan War, the Government of India had been compelled by force of circumstances to depart from this policy. As early as 1864 the establishment of a Political Agency in Kalat (Baluchistan) had been mooted, but till about 1871 the matter had remained in abeyance. Then recurring quarrels between the Ruler and his Chiefs led to the appointment of a Political Agent in Kalat, to compose the differences and quarrels which distracted that country and which re-acted injuriously on our territory adjoining the boundary of that State. Owing to the anarchy which prevailed, the Political Agent was with-

[1] Indian Frontier Policy; Edinburgh Review, January 1898.

[2] *Ibid.*

drawn on the 23rd of April 1873, and the question of Military intervention was under consideration. Captain (afterwards Sir Robert) Sandeman, however, was deputed to put into effect his suggestion, that an effort should be made to arrange a peaceful settlement of Kalat affairs before resorting to the military expedition recommended by the authorities in Sind. The occupation of Quetta followed, and with it began the extension of our influence and control over the tribes, Baluch and Afghan, within reach of that place. In 1877 the Indian Government had to remind the Amir Sher Ali that they had never recognized his claim to allegiance from Chitral, Dir, Bajour or Swat; and that any attempt on his part to enforce such a claim would be regarded as an unfriendly act by us.

The Government of India at the same time was fully alive to the importance of securing an effective control over the northern passes leading into the Dard Section; but it was determined that this should be done, if possible, through the Maharaja of Kashmir, a body of whose troops had been stationed in Gilgit to control, to some extent, the tribes and to check their raids upon settled Kashmir territory. The Maharaja had been encouraged to tighten his hold upon the Dard country. Although, owing to their altitude the passes leading from the north into the valleys of this country are blocked by snow for a great part of the year, yet in 1881, Mr. Gladstone's Government had observed that this part of the Frontier was especially exposed to intrigues. The open gap, which existed in this region between China and Afghanistan, offered a very strong temptation to adventurous spirits to explore the valleys to the south of the Hindu-Kush and Karakoram Ranges. Russian Officers, in 1889, had actually penetrated into the Dard States; and even, in 1891, the Chieftain of Hunza had openly declared that he was under Russian protection. The Government was obliged to take action for the exclusion of Foreign influence from these tracts.[1] The Political Agency at Gilgit had been withdrawn in 1881; but it was necessary in 1885 to send Sir William Lockhart to Chitral, to thoroughly examine the country with a view to defensive measures; and in 1889 a Political Agent again was placed in Gilgit.

For a long time both the Amir of Afghanistan and the Government of India claimed the right to exercise control over some of the tribes in the Roh or Pathan Section. There was incessant correspondence with Amir Abdur Rahman about the Afridis, the Turis of Kuram, and the Waziris, and at times some very sharp letters were written.[2] In

[1] *Ibid*, pp. 267-68.

[2] *Ibid.*

1893, both the Indian Government and the Amir being weary of this perpetual friction, Lord Lansdowne sent his Foreign Secretary, Sir Mortimer Durand, to Kabul. An amicable settlement on this subject was reached, and the respective spheres of influence within the tribal belt were defined. The actual delimitation of the boundary between the two followed. The Amir was given a free hand with regard to Kafristan. He retained Asmār, and was given the Birmal Valley; but on the south, Chagai was relinquished by him. He also engaged to refrain from exercising any interference in Swat, Bajour or Chitral.[1]

For some time past communications had been exchanged between the British and Russian Governments, regarding their respective spheres of influence on the Pamirs, and about the Clarendon-Gortchakoff Agreement of 1872-73, making the River Oxus the north-eastern boundary of Afghanistan up to Lake Victoria (Sar-i-Kul). This boundary had been fixed at that time on insufficient information, and it had been discovered afterwards, that Shighnān and Roshān, portions of which lie to the north of the Oxus, formed part of Badakhshān, a province belonging to the Amir of Afghanistan, while the district of Darwaz, the greater portion of which lies to the south of the river, was tributary to Bokhara. Russia, however, claimed the literal fulfilment of our agreement of 1872-73; and it was necessary to explain to the Amir the terms of the agreement of 1872-73, and the extent of the Russian claim which involved His Highness' withdrawal from trans-Oxus Shighnān and Roshān.[2]

---

[1] The work of determining the actual boundary between the spheres of influence was divided into sections, and was carried out for the most part by Joint Commissions during the years 1894-96, the only portion of the Frontier line remaining undemarcated being a small section in the vicinity of the Momand country and the Khyber. The Afghan-Waziristan Boundary from Domandi to Laram was demarcated by British Officers at the special request of the Amir.—Treaties, Engagements and Sanads, India, Vol XI, p. 331, 4th Edition, 1909.

This boundary has now come to be regarded, as the Indo-Afghan Boundary. But in the agreement, "the line was not described as the boundary of India, but as the eastern and southern Frontier of the Amir's dominions, and as the limit of the respective 'spheres of influence' of the two Governments. At one point the boundary of 'British territory' is mentioned, but this was actual British territory, not tribal territory. With regard to the latter, the extension of our authority, not the extension of our Frontier, was evidently the course of action contemplated".

Indian Frontier Policy; Edinburgh Review, January, 1898, p. 264.

[2] In the spring of 1892, a party of Russian troops cut off the Afghan outpost at Somatash on the Yashikul (Yellow Lake) in trans-Oxus Sighnān, on the northern tributary of the Oxus—the Alichur River. The Russians were commanded by a Colonel Yanoff.

In the month of September 1893, while the Durand Mission was on its way to Kabul, a collision between Russian and Afghan troops took place at Murghab, in Afghan-Badakhshān. The Russians were beaten off on this occasion.

Life of Abdur Rahman Amir of Afghanistan, Vol. I., (pp. 285-287).

Sir Mortimer Durand had been instructed that this was to be his primary duty, and the negotiations resulted in the conclusion of two agreements, both dated the 12th of November 1893. By one of these, the Amir bound himself to abandon all districts not then held by him to the north of the Upper Oxus, on condition of receiving in exchange all the districts to the south of the river. The other agreement referred to the boundary between Afghan and British spheres of influence. To mark their sense of the friendly spirit in which the Amir had entered into the negotiations, the Government of India raised his annual subsidy to eighteen lakhs of rupees; he was granted full permission to import munitions of war, and was promised some help in this respect. The Amir agreed that the Frontiers of his dominions, from Wakhan to the Persian border, should follow the line shown in the map attached to the Agreement; the Amir also received from Sir Mortimer Durand a letter, dated the 11th November 1893, informing him that the assurance given him by the British Government, when he had come to the throne in 1880, remained still in force, and was applicable to any territory which might come into his possession in consequence of his agreement with the British Government regarding the Upper-Oxus Frontier.[1]

On the 11th March 1895, after prolonged negotiations, notes were exchanged between the British and the Russian Governments concluding an agreement in regard to the spheres of influence of Great Britain and Russia on the Pamirs; and the demarcation of the boundary line by a Joint Commission composed of British and Russian Delegates. The Amir being informed by the Government of India of the terms of this agreement, expressed his pleasure with the settlement.

The British and Russian Commissions met at Lake Sari-Kul (the former having completed the distance from Bandipur, in Kashmir, in exactly one month) on the 22nd of July 1895. On the 28th of July, the first pillar was erected at the eastern end of Lake Sari-Kul, and before the middle of August the line had been demarcated as far as the Orta Bel Pass. The Commissioners decided that Lake Sari-Kul should henceforth be known by the British as well as by the Russians as "Lake Victoria," the range to the south as the "Chaine-de-l'Empereur Nicholas II" and the peak nearest to the Lake, as "Pie-de-la-Concorde."[2] Difficulties, however, arose regarding the line from Orta Bel onwards. It appeared that, while the lattitude of Lake

---

[1] Treaties, Engagements and Sanads, India, Vol. XI, 4th Edition, 1909.
[2] *Ibid.*

Victoria had been correctly determined to be 37°-27′, the positions of Kizil Robat, the Orta Bel and Baiyik Passes were inaccurate, and about six minutes south of their true positions.[1] It was found to be impossible to adhere strictly to the terms of the Anglo-Russian Agreement and the British Commissioner recommended the acceptance of a line proposed by the Russians, running southwards to the watershed of the Taghdumbash, which the Russians acknowledged to be the Chinese Frontier. The British Commissioner considered this to be the only natural Frontier south of the lattitude of Lake Victoria. He was empowered to accept this line, and the sites of the final pillars were fixed accordingly. The final Protocol was signed on the 10th September 1895, and the Joint Commission was dissolved on the 13th September 1895.

The Amir was supplied by the Indian Government with copies of the map signed by the British and Russian Commissioners, with a description of the boundary of Afghanistan in the direction of Wakhan and the Pamirs.

In accordance with the terms of the Anglo-Russian Agreement of the 11th March 1895, Bokhara evacuated Cis-Oxus Darwaz in October 1896. The Amir had retired from trans-Oxus, Shighnān and Roshan in 1894.[2]

By the agreement arrived at by the Pamir Boundary Commission, Eastern Wakhan was formally acknowledged by Russia as forming part of the territories of the Amir of Afghanistan. To enable him to carry on the administration of this strip of country properly, the Government of India granted him an additional subsidy of rupees fifty thousand a year, with effect from the 1st March 1897.

The Ghilzai rebellion in 1886 and 1887 was a widespread and dangerous movement, an expression of the feud which this important section of the people of Afghanistan nourish against the supremacy of the Duranis. After some successes at the commencement, the insurgents suffered a decisive overthrow on the 27th July 1887. Ayub Khan fled from Tehran and attempted to join the rebels, but the Amir's Frontier Officials were on the alert and unable to evade their vigilance, and after suffering great hardships in the desert, the Sardar and his followers surrendered to General MacLean on the 9th of January 1887. The Sardar with a very large number of followers was sent to India, where a suitable provision has been made for their

[1] On this parallel of latitude, equivalent to about 7 miles.

[2] Treaties, Engagements and Sanads, India, Vol. XI, 4th Edition, 1909.

support, and he has undertaken to make no attempt to disturb the peace of Afghanistan.

This insurrection was barely suppressed, when the Amir's cousin, Sardar Muhammad Ishak Khan,[1] who was Governor of Afghan-Turkistan, threw off his allegiance; proclaimed himself Amir, and began his march on Kabul. He was, however, completely defeated on the 29th of September 1887, in the Valley of Ghazni Gak, three miles south of Tāshkurgān, and fled across the Oxus. He is now living in Samarkand, where he receives a small allowance from the Russian Government. The Amir visited Turkistan. He was delayed there for some time, and did not return to his capital till the 24th July 1890. In the month of December 1888, the Amir's life was attempted. He was fired at by a soldier while reviewing his troops at Mazar-i-Sherif.[2]

The Hazaras had shown signs of disaffection in 1890 and in 1891 a widespread rebellion of these tribes against the Amir's authority broke out. It was not till July-August 1893 that the tribesmen were compelled to make their submission, and their country was settled. If there was any truth in the very circumstantial stories, which drifted across the border into Quetta, the punishment which the Hazaras received must have been terribly severe. It was openly said that pillars were made at points on the highways of the heads of slaughtered Hazaras, as a warning to others who might contemplate a trial of strength with the existing Government. The bazars of Kandahar and of all the principal towns were said to be full of Hazara prisoners of both sexes who were sold as slaves; and at that time Hazara slaves were very cheap. The first insurrection of 1891 was followed by a more extensive rising in 1892. On this occasion Muhammad Azim Khan, Hazara, the Amir's Governor of the Hazara country, threw in his lot with his countrymen. His defeat was effected by another Hazara notable, Muhammad Husen Khan, a personal enemy of the rebellious Governor. On his return to Kabul Muhammad Husen Khan was received with distinguished favour by his master and was

---

[1] Son of Sardar Azim Khan (uncle of the Amir) by an Armenian Christian slave girl. Ishak Khan had joined the Nakhsbandi Sect, to curry favour with the Turkomans, who were his subjects and who are specially devoted to this sect. The holy men of Mazar-i-Sherif told him that the Saint had bestowed the throne of Kabul on him.

In June-August 1888, the Amir was suffering from a long and severe attack of gout, for which he was treated by Miss Lillian Hamilton, M. D., and a report was circulated that he was dead.—Life of Abdur Rahman, Amir of Agfhanistan, Vol. I, pp. 261-267.

[2] *Ibid.*

appointed Governor of the Hazara country; nevertheless he also rebelled soon after, and thirty thousand of the Amir's troops had to be employed to subdue the tribesmen. Muhammad Husen Khan was made prisoner, with other Hazara Chiefs, and these persons with their families were sent to Kabul.[1] They were replaced by men on whom the Amir was able to depend, and who were imposed on the tribesmen as their Chiefs. The Jamshidis and Hazaras as Shiahs were more rigorously treated than the Ghilzais and the other tribes, who were reluctant to submit at once to the stern rule of the Amir.

In 1895 the Amir, whose state of health prevented his undertaking a journey to England, deputed his second son, Shahzada Nasrullah Khan, to pay his respects to her late Majesty Queen Victoria. Leaving Bombay on the 29th of April, the Shahzada arrived in England on the 23rd of May, and was received by the Queen at Windsor, on the 27th. He left England on the 3rd of September, and after visiting Paris, Rome and Naples, he arrived in Karachi on the 16th October 1895. He returned to Kabul through Quetta, Chaman and Kandahar.

About this time the dignity of Knight Grand Cross of St. Michael and St. George was bestowed upon Sardar Habibullah Khan, as well as upon his younger brother, Sardar Nasrullah Khan. The Grand Crosses of the Orders of the Bath and Star of India had been bestowed previously on their father, the Amir.

In 1896 Kafristan was conquered and annexed to the dominions of the Amir, never before had any of his predecessors been able to impose their authority on this people, nor had Afghan troops ever penetrated into the sanctuaries of the Kafirs in the valleys of the Hindu-Kush.

The Amir's authority now was acknowledged in every part of his kingdom within the boundaries which girdle the country. In the same year, he assumed the title of Zia-ul-Millat-wa-ud-din (The Light of the Nation and of Religion).

Amir Abdur Rahman died in Kabul on the 3rd of October 1901, aged about 57 years.[2] Not an old man in point of time, but for twenty eventful years he had toiled and planned unceasingly to consolidate his power over the unruly Afghans, and until his eldest son was old enough to assist him in the routine of the Government, Abdur Rahman had laboured single-handed. In addtion, during the latter part of his life-time, he had suffered greatly from gout. He had

---

[1] *Ibid.*

[2] Life of Abdur Rahman, Amir of Afghanistan, Vol. I, p. 1, Note .

no brothers; but this was an advantage, as he was relieved of all dangers from family intrigues, which might have seriously embarassed him in his dealings with the refractory tribes. His cousins were very inferior to him in character and ability, and with the exception of Sardar Muhammad Ishak Khan, they have served him loyally; dominated by the master-mind which guided the affairs of their country through many critical periods, when mistakes might have entailed serious consequences. The recognition of the integrity and independence of Afghanistan, by the two Powers, who had become his neighbours, gave him a free hand in his dealings with his subjects; as secret malcontents and his open enemies were deprived of all hope of being countenanced or assisted from outside in their struggles with the Amir. His death was immediately followed by the peaceful accession of his eldest son, Sardar Habibullah Khan.

It was not till 1885 that the late Amir found time to devote attention to establishing manufactures, and then it was to provide arms and ammunition for a million soldiers. The first European who entered his service was a M. Jerome, a Frenchman, whom the Amir picked up in Rawalpindi in 1885. This person was succeeded by Mr. (now Sir Salter) Pyne, who arrived in Kabul early in April 1887, and the foundation stone of the first factory was laid on the 7th of that month. Other factories were established as time went on, the number of Englishmen in the service of the State was increased, and in 1894 the first hospital was opened by Miss Hamilton, M. D.[1] The residence of Englishmen (and women) in Kabul has resulted in the publication of several books, describing the personal experiences of the authors; the conditions of life of the small European community at the capital, the circumstances under which they have worked, and the difficulties they have had to overcome. Incidentally, however, light is cast on the Political situation at the capital. The facts emerge that the progress made appears to depend very greatly on the exertions and the life of the Ruler, who is very far in advance of his countrymen; and that there exists a strong conservative or reactionary party, even at the capital and near the throne, who view with grave doubt, if not with actual disfavour, the policy of the Ruler with regard to domestic affairs and his relations with foreigners.

A great advance has been made in Engineering, especially with regard to bridging and the manufacture and repair of arms;[2] and in these matters the Afghans display considerable aptitude. But the

---

[1] *Ibid*, Vol. II., p. 70.

[2] Afghanistan: the Buffer State. Captain Gervais Lyons, 1909, p. 177.

progress made is due to the energy and foresight of the Rulers; and it is not the outcome of a desire for progress that has originated and grown upwards among the people at large. Their appreciation of the benefits of civilization is manifested in a direction which threatens the tranquility of their country—a keen desire to equip themselves with fire-arms of modern patterns. This is due primarily to a feeling of nervous apprehension as to the ultimate fate of their country, placed as it is between two Great Powers, and of the overwhelming strength of both, the Afghans are fully aware. With any rising of the tribesmen, to which the possession of serviceable breech-loaders may tempt them, the Amir with the resources at his disposal, would be able to deal successfully, provided he was not seriously embarrassed by grave family dissensions. As each year passes without disturbances, his position is strengthened and the likelihood of a successful rising diminishes. No foreign capital is invested in Afghanistan, and no Power would be compelled to intervene to protect the interest of its subjects, in the event of serious disorders breaking out in that country. The effects even of complete anarchy might possibly be confined within the boundaries that enclose the country. For this reason the linking up of the rail heads at Chaman and at Kushk (about 450 miles apart), the cost of which the Amir could not defray from his revenues, would appear to introduce a certain element of danger into the existing relations with Afghanistan that would outweigh all the prospective, commercial and other advantages, which are urged in favour of establishing Railway communication between India and Europe, through the territory of His Majesty the Amir.[1]

> "For never did Chief more sorely need Heaven for his aid and stay"
> "Than the man who would reign in this country, and tame Afghans or a day."[2]

---

[1] *Ibid*, p. 146.

[2] Verses written in India. Sir Alfred Lyall, London, 1896. "The Amir's Soliloquy," p. 58.

CHAPTER XX.

THE LANGUAGE AND LITERATURE OF THE AFGHANS.

THE language of the tribes who style themselves Afghans, is Pashto; and it belongs to the Aryan sub-family of the Indo-European Family of languages. In the irregularly-shaped area included by the boundaries of Afghanistan, the population is, however, by no means entirely Pashto-speaking. "Roughly speaking, we may say, that the country in which the majority of the population use Pashto as their language is Southern and Eastern Afghanistan, the country to the west of the Indus from its southward bend to Dera Ismail Khan, and a strip of Northern Baluchistan." There are only two dialects; but several sub-dialects, the differences, however, are not so great as to render any one unintelligible in a district where another dialect prevails. In His Majesty the Amir's territory, there is a great admixture of races, including Tajiks, Hazaras, Kazilbashis, and Kafirs, who speak the languages of the countries of their origin. With the exception of the Hazaras and Kafirs of the more remote districts, Pashto is generally understood, and the Afghans also understand the mother-tongue of their fellow-subjects, who are brought into contact with them. In the Hazara country the inhabitants do not, among themselves, employ Pashto, but either Persian, or a language of Mongolian origin. The Tajik population use Persian, their mother-tongue, from which the name of Farsiwān or Persian-speaking[1]—another appellation of this section of the people of Afghanistan—is derived. In Seistan, the Tajik population understand and prefer to use the Baluch language, which belongs to a distant group of the Aryan sub-family. The Baluch language is also understood in Southern Afghanistan to a greater extent than is believed.

"The rugged character of its (Pashto) sound suits the nature of the speakers, and of the mountains which form their home; but they

[1] Farsiwān, a corruption of Farsi-Khwān, Persian speaking. Some authorities, however, favor the derivation from Farsi-bān—Persian *men* as being more probable.

are most inharmonious to the somewhat fastidious oriental ear. Tradition tells us of the earliest linguistic survey on record, in which a Grand Wazir brought to his king specimens of all the languages spoken on the earth; but the specimen of Pashto consisted of the rattling of a stone in a pot. According to a well-known proverb Arabic is science, Turki is accomplishment, Persian is sugar; Hindustani is salt; but Pashto is the braying of an ass! In spite of these unfavourable remarks, though harsh sounding, it is a strong, virile language, which is capable of expressing any idea with neatness and accuracy. It is much less archaic in its general characteristics than Baluch, and has borrowed not only a good deal of its vocabulary, but even part of its grammar from Indian sources." Pashto is written in a modification of the Arabic-Persian Alphabet. It has received considerable attention from scholars both in India and in Europe.

"Pashto exhibits many points of connection with the Ghalchah languages of the Pamirs, but still more closely related to these last is the curious isolated little speech, known as Ormuri or Bārgista (the speech of Barak), which is the tongue of a few thousand people near Kanigoram in Waziristan * * *. They have an impossible tradition that they came from Yaman in Arabia, and that their language was invented for them by a very old and learned man named "Umar Labān" some four hundred years ago. They claim to be descended from a certain Mir Bārak, from whom one of the names of their tribe and of their language is derived. The language is certainly an East Iranian one, and deserves more study than it has yet received. It does not appear to have any literature, but the Arabic-Persian Alphabet, as adapted for Pashto, has been employed for writing it."[1]

The first person, who is believed to have used Pashto for literary purposes, is the famous Pir Roshan, Mian Bayazid[2], the founder of the heretical sect of the Roshanis or Ihdàdis; and he used the national

---

[1] Census of India, 1901.—Languages.

It may be interesting to note in this connection that Ormur (Persian, Chiragh-Kush) or the "light extinguishers," is the name of an heretical sect, possibly allied to the Yezidi schism, who are said to hold their religious celebrations in complete darkness. The Roshanis also (another heretical sect), celebrated their festivals in darkness, and were accused of gross immorality on these occasions.

In the 9th and 10th centuries, Multan was the headquarters in India of the Karmathian heresy, whence the doctrines may have been introduced into the fastnesses of the Waziri country into Kainguram, where professors of these doctrines may have found a refuge on the overthrow of their seats in Multan. Mian Bayazid may have imbibed these heretical opinions in his youth, which led him to promulgate the Roshani doctrines in maturer years (16th century).

[2] His famous opponent, the Akhun Darwezah Baba, also wrote in Pashto a refutation of these heretical teachings.

language to present his doctrines direct to the people of Afghanistan with the view of making proselytes.

The intense pride of the Afghan in everything that pertains to his country, very soon led to the growth of a national literature. This movement began at a period when Arabic and Persian were the media through which alone learning and accomplishments could be acquired, and which constituted the whole course of education. Arabic, the language of their sacred book, was the most important branch of study for those who proposed to enter into the priesthood. Persian, the language of secular writers, was also the official language in the middle east, and indispensable to all who desired to enter the Civil and Military professions or to pose as refined and educated persons. The authors, who wrote in Pashto, were not ignorant persons, unacquainted with other languages and unable to express themselves in any other than their rugged mother-tongue ; but the majority were educated persons, who by reason of their social position, it is certain must have had a liberal education in the classical languages ; but who impelled by their patriotism, deliberately and of their free choice, selected their native language as the medium in which to express themselves in prose as well as in metre. The great classical authors of Persia, Shekh Sadi of Shiraz and Hafiz, have always delighted the learned leisure of the educated classes in the middle east, and their admirers have translated their works into Pashto for the benefit, presumably, of those of their countrymen who have no Persian, but such translations are excluded from the brief notice of Pashto literature, which is all that is permitted in this place.

The sentiments that pervade this indigenous literature are chiefly those of love—and a burning desire for martial fame and a lofty mysticism, akin to that of the Persian Sufis. A fervid tone of patriotism also distinguishes many of these compositions. The persons who composed these works were either Mullas or members of the families of Chiefs, such as Fath Khan, the Yusufzai, who was a soldier of some considerable reputation. He served in the wars n the Deccan under the Emperor Aurangzebe, and also in Gujarat. The famous Chief of the Khataks, an Afghan tribe, on the right bank of the Indus to the south of Peshawar, is celebrated equally as an Afghan patriot, an inveterate enemy to the Emperor of Delhi, and as a poet, whose fame has eclipsed that of his contemporaries. Both these authors lived about the same period, 17th century. This period seems to have been rich in authors, who wrote in their native language ; or another Afghan poet also flourished in the long reign of the

Emperor Aurangzebe. Mulla Abdur Rahman, who shares the popularity of the Khatak Chieftain with his countrymen, belonged to the Goria Khel Sept of the Momands in the Peshawar District; and his works are principally of a religious and mystical character. The poetry of the Khatak Chief has been translated into English. It breathes a martial spirit, suitable to the position of the author, and probably inspired the general rising of the tribesmen against the Emperor Aurangzebe, whose treatment of his brothers and his father, the indulgent Emperor Shah Jahan, was universally execrated, even by the Afghans with whom the deposed monarch appears to have been very popular.[1]

Another Mulla, one Abd-ul-Hamid, composed his poetry in the reign of Shah Timur, the Sadozai King of Afghanistan. He is regarded as the Shekh Sādi of Afghanistan. A late author was Kasim Ali, an Afridi; his writings bear the stamp of mysticism. He was born in Farrukhābād (in Oude), and seems to have added a little English to the languages he professed to have acquired. He has

---

[1] Khushal Khan is mentioned in the Chronicles dealing with the first ten years' events of the reign of the Emperor Aurangzebe. According to his poems, he was seized by the Governor of Kabul in Peshawar. As Peshawar was generally visited in the winter, the seizure must have taken place in the winter of 1663-64. The mention made of him in history is in April 1667. He could not have been detained very long, and as he was able to write poems, which are diatribes of invective against the Emperor, his imprisonment could not have been severe.

Shortly before the month of April 1667, a serious rising took place among the Yusufzais, organised by a Mulla with a fakir as the principal mischief-maker, named Muhammud Shah, whom the tribesmen regarded as a saint. The Governor of Attock called on the land-owners and chiefs in his jurisdiction to muster their levies and join him in opposing the Yusufzai, who had crossed the Indus by the ford of Hārun (Hoond?). The Gakkhars are mentioned as auxiliaries, and also Khushal-Khan and Ashraf (his son).

The name of the Khatak Chief does not appear in the great rising that terminated in a desperate battle fought by the associated Afghan Clans with the Royal Troops, perhaps in the Tezin Valley. While Khushal Khan was detained in Rantipur in India, Ashraf was detained at Kabul.

Khushal Khan was born A.D. 1613, his father Shahbāz Khan died from the effects of a wound he received in a fight with the Yusufzais in the year 1650, when Khushāl himself was wounded. The Emperor Shah Jahan confirmed the latter in the chieftainship of the Khataks. Khushal Khan seems to have joined his friends Ismal Khan and Darya Khan in the great rising of the Afghans, which had for its object the expulsion of the Moghul's authority from Afghanistan. On the death of his friends, Khushal resigned the chieftainship in favour of his eldest son Ashraf, and eventually retired for safety to the Afridi country, where he died aged 78 years.

He was the father of very many sons. Ashraf, the eldest born in 1634, was also a poet. He fell a victim to the intrigues of his younger broher Bahram, who betrayed him into the hands of Aurangzebe in 1683. He died in 1693 in the Fortress of Bijapur where he had been a prisoner.

Abdul-Kadir, a younger brother of Ashraf, was born in 1652. He was as distinguished as a warrior as a man of letters. He was desirous of being recognised as chief of the clan, so when Afzal Khan, son of Ashraf, was raised to that position by the tribesmen Abd-ul-Kadir, and ten of his brothers were put to death with a number of their sons at the village of Zaman Garrai in one day, and the tribe had peace.

devoted one entire ode to the abuse of the English in India, whom he stigmatizes as "a nation of shopkeepers", who, in Hindustan, have turned into soldiers, anticipating the verdict of a more famous person. Two other Indian Afghans, the Nawabs Hafiz Mahabat Khan and Allah Yar Khan, Rohillas, were the authors of works of some value, but of a very opposite character. They are the authors of two lexicographical works. The former compiled his treatise in 1805-06 at the request of Sir George Barlow, (who was the British Resident at the Court of Oude), and the latter in about 1808.

Important events in the history of the tribes, and especially the memory of heroes, whose martial exploits they celebrate, form the theme of the ballads so popular among the Afghans. These keep alive the martial spirit of the clans, and are the cause of the frequent epidemics of turbulence which render them such bad subjects—far more than the preachings of the Mullas who are credited with being the cause of the troubles, but who take advantage of the trend of popular feeling to keep up their influence, guide its manifestation and lend it the colour of religious movement. After a long period of peace (from an Afghan point of view), the wilder spirits of the clans become desirous of emulating the deeds of heroes sung at every camp fire; and the intense vanity of the Afghan is roused and impels him to actions which may give him a similar and undying fame among his countrymen. The ballad that was composed on the battle of Naushahra, in which the Sikhs defeated the Afghans and in which the Khatak Chief, Abbās Khan, was slain, has been translated by Major Raverty, and is a good specimen of this class of poetry. A perusal of this stirring poem shows how well calculated the ballads are to inflame the vanity of the tribesmen and stir them up to emulate the actions of the famous dead. With the infidel at their gates plunder, fame, and religious merit, may be earned together. The results are Frontier Expeditions involving on our part a great outlay of money and the loss of valuable lives; and, as owing to the unprofitable nature of the country permanent occupation is out of the question, no lasting effect could (till lately) be produced on a people who are taught to believe that no man can live for a moment beyond the time that has been allotted to him, nor perish a moment earlier than the day which has been foreordained by the Almighty for his death, among whom human life is lightly esteemed, and who by reason of the country they inhabit can inflict far heavier losses on an invader than they suffer themselves.

The Pir Roshan, who has been mentioned several times, was descended from a family of distinction in Medina, a member of which was the famous Abu Ayub, who was killed in the siege of Constantinople, and whose tomb there is regarded as a shrine by the Ottoman Turks at the present day. The branch of the family to which Pir Roshan belonged was domiciled in the 13th Century at Mastoi, in the country of the Barkis, in the Lohgar valley near Kabul. From there the grandfather of Shekh Bayazīd (the Pir Roshan) migrated to Kaniguram in the Waziri country,[1] where the latter was born among the Ormur tribe alluded to. The doctrines preached by this schismatic teacher was akin to that professed by the Ismailians (assassins).[2] The Afridis, Orakzais, Khalils and Yusufzais became his followers. As the Pir Roshan proclaimed that God had given him the Kingdom of Hindustan, he was brought into collision with the Mogul Emperors. Pir Roshan, his son, and his grandson, were killed in battle, either with the Imperial troops, or with other Afghan tribes, who had not embraced his doctrines, which found adherents chiefly in the Roh. After these reverses, the sect of the Roshanis gradually fell into disrepute, although here and there, both in Afghanistan and India, there are still those who observe its doctrines in secret. A branch of this family settled in Julundhur in the Punjab in 1609 A.D.; and in 1635-36, Hazār Mir, an Orakzai, a leader of this sect, visited the Court of Shah Jahan and made his submission. He was given the rank of a commander of 1,000 horse and lands near Panipat, north of Delhi.

The influence of such teachers and of the orthodox priesthood in Afghanistan has always been very great owing to the profound knowledge they possess of the foibles and weak points of the national character. They have ever been intolerant of every kind of authority but their own. The most barbarous and the most ignorant, the poorest, and the most priestridden, of the tribes of Afghanistan are those of the Roh. Here the influence of the Mullas has always been very great and political matters have given the Mullas greater power over these tribes, than their brethren possess over other tribes, which are more remote from the boundary which separates British and Afghan territory. But even among the tribes of the Roh, the influence of the Mullas now is not as great as it has been.

A reference to any recent map of India will show that the unproductive tract of the Roh lies on the British side of the demarcated frontier, and that along the Tochi and Kuram valleys, this tract has been pierced

---

[1] To escape the ravages of the Moghols of Chingiz Khan.

[2] Mian Bayazid (born in Kaniguram) is believed to have been initiated into this form of heresy in India. He had visited Kalinjar (in Bandelkand) with horses for sale, and met at that place, a Mulla, who became his preceptor.

by the extension of British Administration up to the present boundary. The Roh is now divided into three irregular blocks, and from the valleys of these streams the sanctuaries of the tribes, in the most remote valleys, are enfiladed, and can be reached with comparative ease and rapidity. It is now possible to concentrate against a group of malcontents, and to crush the movement before the evil has spread, and infected the tribesmen in the adjoining blocks. A general insurrection against law and order throughout the Roh has been rendered almost impossible. Service in the Border Police, and Militia Battalions, provides incomes, and honorable employment, consonant with the character of the tribesmen who enrol themselves gladly. The cost of the simple form of administration in these areas is an insurance against the recurring expenditure of money and lives, which was entailed by strong punitive expeditions in the past. Then our troops had to fight their way across a series of very strong positions, before the further valleys were reached, where alone, by the destruction of towers and villages, the crops on the plots of cultivated land round them, and the felling of orchards, some punishment could be inflicted for wanton and unprovoked aggression on the part of the tribesmen.

The punishment which it is possible to administer now is swifter and heavier than before. There is a vein of common sense and shrewdness in the Afghan character, which enables them to balance the practical drawbacks and possible advantages attending a blind reliance on the exhortations and promises of their Mullas. The national tendency to become berserk—and vanity, are however easily roused, and then these failings obscure the better judgment of the more experienced members of a tribe and render the rank and file of the latter deaf to reason.

Unless other causes conspire to excite these failings and move the tribesmen to take up arms, the preachings of the Mullas of the benefits that may accrue from a holy war with infidels, are coldly received and fall on unresponsive hearts; and as time goes on their baneful influence will probably decrease still more, and they will at last be obliged to confine themselves to those secular duties and spiritual ministrations, which render the Mullas so indispensable to their illiterate and superstitious countrymen.

NOTE.

Major R. Leech, C.B, Bombay Engineers, was the first person, after Elphinstone, to draw the attention of European scholars to Pushtu and the dialects or languages spoken in the countries adjoining Afghanistan. In 1838 he published an epitome of the grammars of the Brahui, Baluchi, and Punjabi languages, with vocabularies of the Baraki, Pashai, Laghmāni, Kāshgāri, Tirahi, and Dir dialects, and of the language of the Moghal Imaks. His untimely death in 1845, cut short a promising career.—G. P. T.

APPENDIX.

APPENDIX I.

The Vesh or Distribution of Lands and Holdings.

In Southern Afghanistan, the distribution of lands and tenements alluded to in Chapter I (at p. 8), does not appear to exist. During the progress of the settlement of the Pishin districts, inquiries were made as to whether the system had ever been in force, and the result was a negative. Among the Barech Afghans in Shorawalk, however, a modification of this custom apparently does exist. The reason for the absence of the custom is probably the extent of country over which the great tribes of Southern Afghanistan are distributed and the fact that irrigation is only possible within a comparatively restricted area along the banks of the larger streams and rivers, and the foot of the mountain ranges where alone it is possible to have recourse to Karezes. The area of pasture lands, and those on which crops depend altogether on moisture derived from the snow and rainfall, is very much larger than those where irrigation is possible. The conditions, therefore, on the former are very much the same everywhere, and the owners of sheep, goats and other live-stock, is quite as well off as, and in some cases richer than the persons who occupy the irrigated portions ; and their mode of life is more congenial to their dispositions. The inconvenience that would be entailed by periodical redistributions of tribal lands and holdings would not be compensated by any probable increase of individual wealth or comfort. The reason, therefore, for such redistribution does not exist, and the custom has either disappeared or has never been in force among the tribes who occupy this part of Afghanistan.

APPENDIX II.

Kandahar and the Indian Government of the Moghul Emperors of Delhi.

Kandahar had been for centuries in the possession of the rulers of Herat ; and it continued to form a part of the widespread Empire bequeathed to his successors, by Shah Rukh, the son of Timur. In course of time, as the rulers of Herat degenerated, the governors of provinces became virtually independent in the tracts which they governed, nominally, on behalf of the rulers of Herat. In the beginning of the 16th century Kandahar was in the hands of the Arghun Family. Baber, the founder of the dynasty of the Indian Moghuls, deprived the Arghuns of Kandahar in 1522. After his death, the town and province was in turn held by the Uzbegs and the Persians, and was taken from the latter by Prince Kamran (the second son of Baber), who eventually held undisputed possession of the countries dependent on Kabul, Ghazni and Kandahar to the south of the Hindu-Kush, and also of Badakshan, Kishm and Kunduz, to the north of the range (1542).

Kandahar was the price which Humayun agreed to pay, for the hospitality and assistance he had received from Shah Tahmasp, the Safavi Monarch of Persia. Humayun arrived in Seistan in 1545, where he found 14,000 horse waiting for him, and he marched along the banks of the Helmand towards Kandahar. On his arrival at Laki (on the ford of the Helmand above the modern village of Landi Muhammad Amin Khan) he was met by Kamran's governor of the Garmsir district, who surrendered it to Humayun. Kandahar was besieged (21st March 1545) and it surrendered on the 3rd of September. It was handed over to the third son (an infant) of Shah Tahmasp who had accompanied Humayun, as the nominal commander of the Persian auxiliaries

After the death of Shah Tahmasp, the internal affairs of his Kingdom fell into great disorder, and his successors were unable to maintain their authority in Khurassan, which had been over-run by the Uzbegs; until about 1598-99, when Shah Abbas I was able to devote his undivided attention to this part of his Kingdom. In the meantime, that branch of the Safavi family, to whom Khurassan had been conveyed as an appanage, had been gradually disposed of Herat and of all, but Kandahar and Ghazni, of their inheritance. At last their descendants were unable to retain even these districts; and in 1597 Rustam Mirza took refuge in the Court of Akbar, the famous grandson of Baber (he arrived at Court on the 12th August), and he was followed soon after by his brother Muzafar Husen Mirza, Safavi. Shahbeg Khan was ordered to proceed from Multan with 10,000 men and to take possession of Kandahar and the outlying dependencies.

When news of Akbar's death got about, the Persian Governor of Herat despatched a force under one of the Maliks of Seistan, and other frontier chieftains to take possession of Kandahar, having been urged to take this step by a disaffected section of the population, who were unfriendly to the Indian officials. Shahbeg Khan proved too formidable an antagonist, the attack was a failure; and Shah Abbas I disavowed the whole proceedings. This was in 1605. In 1622 Shah Abbas surprised Kandahar, which was ill provided for repelling an attack, and the Indian Governor, Abdul Aziz, the Nakshbandi, was compelled to surrender. He was allowed to retire to India and the Emperor Jahangir ordered him to proceed to Mecca, but on the road to the Coast, Abdul Aziz was put out of the world.

Ganj Ali Khan, Chieftain of the Zik tribe of Kurds, Begler Begi of Kirman (and his more famous son, Ali Mardan Khan) became, in turn, governors of Kandahar on behalf of Shah Abbas I and Shah Sefi. In retaliation for the ill usage which the latter had meted out to the family of this chieftain, he delivered Kandahar to the Indian Government on 22nd March 1638. Ali Mardān Khan himself proceeded to the Court of the Emperor, Shah Jahan, and rose to high rank as a noble of the Indian Court.

While Kandahar was in the hands of the Indian Government, a retaliatory expedition entered Seistan. Malik Hamza-Khan was besieged in Kala Fath, and after breaking the bands, or weirs, in the Helmand, and doing a great deal of harm, the Indian troops returned to Kandahar.

Shah Abbas II very soon after his accession to the throne of Persia, began to make preparations for an attack on Kandahar. News of this movement was conveyed to India. Ali Mardan Khan, then Viceroy of Kabul, sent reinforcements and money to Kandahar; and orders were issued for the mobilization of troops in India, which were to protect Kandahar from invasion. Prince Aurangzebe was placed in command. The Indian nobles, averse to a winter campaign in Afghanistan, persuaded the Emperor that during the three winter months, hostilities were not possible, and that it was unreasonable to suppose that the Persians could take the field in the winter. At the same time reports were received that there was very great scarcity of grain and fodder in that country. The march to Kabul was postponed.

This false sense of security was, however, broken by a report, from the Governor of Kandahar, that Shah Abbas had made forced marches at the head of 50,000 horse, and with artillery, and had appeared before Kandahar on the 3rd January 1648. The winter had been selected for the attempt as, owing to the roads being closed by snow, no succours could reach the threatened city from India or Kabul. Orders were at once issued to collect troops, which were to march through the Bangash country (Kuram Valley), being the shortest route to Kabul; and the Emperor himself set out for Kabul. Where the Royal Cortege was crossing the Jhelum river, a mace-bearer arrived from Kandahar, and reported that news had overtaken him on the way, of the fall of Kandahar; and this report was shortly after confirmed by official messengers from Ghazni. The Governor of Kandahar finding no prospect of assistance, had surrendered the town on the 25th of February 1648. The Persians had lost 2,000 men, and a great number of animals, while the garrison had suffered to the extent of 400 or 500 men. On the third day after the surrender Mehrāb Khan, an Armenian (? Georgian), and a veteran of the Turkish wars, had been installed as Governor; and in a short time he had reduced all the outlying forts dependent on Kandahar, with a loss of 600 men, while the garrisons had lost the same number. A force of 10,000 men was left to hold Kandahar, and as his army was in a sorry plight, Shah Abbas retreated to Herat.

The Indian troops made their way painfully over snow-covered passes and in spite of the severe weather to Kabul, where they were forced to halt for a time to refit and to buy fresh animals for service and transport. The advance to Kandahar was resumed under very adverse circumstances, for in addition to a scarcity, the Persians had removed all supplies on the line of advance beyond Ghazni.

On the way to Kandahar, Malik Hasan (who is styled the "Zamindar of that country," that is the headman or chieftain of the inhabitants), deserted from Kandahar and joined the Indian Army. He was well received and obtained many tokens of favour. It would be interesting to know whether this man was Husen, son of Malik Yar, the Ghilzai, who was the father of Mir Weis, and whom Daulat Khan Abdali had made prisoner. Unfortunately the Indian chronicler (Khafi Khan) is silent on this point. There seems a probability that the Malik Hasan and Husen, son of Malik Yar, may have been one and the same person. His ill-treatment at the hands of the Abdali Chief may have been due to his desertion to the Indian side in this controversy.

On the 27th May 1648 Prince Aurangzebe, and his colleague the Vazier, Sadullah Khan, arrived before Kandahar and encamped at the Garden of Ganj Ali Khan; and siege operations were forthwith begun. Early in the same month Shah Jahan had arrived in Kabul to watch proceedings, and support his son and Vazier. It very soon became evident that the task would prove very difficult. A large force had been detailed from Herat to relieve Kandahar, and although the Persians raided and carried off bullocks and transport animals belonging to the besiegers, a force detailed to drive away the relieving force, was able to hold it off, and prevent further loss. The siege operations dragged on and the veteran Mehrāb Khan foiled every effort of the besiegers, and attempts to storm the fortifications were repulsed with heavy loss. Famine proved an effective ally, and the Emperor at last set out from Kabul in the autumn for India, after ordering the raising of the siege. Four months had been spent in fruitless efforts, and the losses of the besiegers were estimated to be 2,000 to 3,000 men; and from 4,000 to 5,000 animals perished in this time.

The loss of Kandahar, however, rankled in the breast of the Emperor Shah Jahan, and on his return to the capital of India from Kashmir, in 1650, orders were issued to raise an army for service in Southern Afghanistan. One division under Prince Aurangzebe was to advance on Kandahar from Multan, and the other under the Vazier Sadullah Khan from Kabul; and these were designed to unite near Kandahar, on the 15th of May 1651, which had been fixed as an auspicious date. The strength of the force was 70,000 horsemen, exclusive of sappers and other details, equipped with a powerful force of artillery of various calibres among which were twenty siege guns. Six hundred nobles and officers of rank served under the leaders. It was decided that Kala Bist and the outlying forts in the Zamindāwar should be reduced at the beginning of operations, in order to isolate and depress the garrison of Kandahar.

The Emperor again set out for Kabul, where he arrived after a journey of two months and four days, on the 14th of April; and the divisions of the Army of Kandahar united near that place on the 12th of April 1651; and siege operations were commenced in due course.

The valiant commander Mehrāb Khan, however, was undismayed, and all attempts to storm the works were repulsed with heavy loss. Sorties of the garrison were frequent, and inflicted great loss on the besiegers. On one occasion a strong body of Persian troops fell on the positions of the Vazier and Rustam Khan, disabling many guns, and returning to their defences with a large number of prisoners, under cover of a heavy fire from the walls. The superior marksmanship of the Turkish and Persian artillerymen rendered the progress of the siege operations very arduous. The capture of Kala Bist, and the forts of Zamindāwar, was frustrated by the differences of opinion that prevailed in the Indian camp, and the skill and constancy of the veteran commanders who held those places.

The siege dragged on, and ammunition was beginning to run short in the Indian Army, and in addition, the Uzbegs (? Hazaras) were ravaging the districts of Ghazni and inflicting great distress on the inhabitants. When these circumstances were placed before the Emperor, he issued orders recalling Prince Aurangzebe and the Vazier Sadullah Khan from Kandahar.

A third attempt to recover Kandahar was made under Prince Dāra Shekoh; and this time the invading force marched from Multan. The Emperor, who had gone to Multan to superintend the organisation of this expedition, set out again for Kabul; and an advance guard of 12,000 horse under Rustam Khan was despatched to Kandahar. This place was reached on the 24th of April 1653, and hostilities were commenced. The Prince, at the head of 104,000 men, marched by the Sangar Pass and Duki to Pishin, whilst his siege train and artillery were despatched by the easier route up the Bolan Pass. In the meantime the Persians had laid waste the country round Pishin, and had removed all the grain they could lay hands on. Prince Dāra Shekoh was unable to make a lengthy stop at that place and crossed the passes towards Kandahar. He encamped at the garden of Mirza Kāmrān, and once more siege operations were begun. On this occasion the fort of Kala Bist was captured, and the fort at Girishk was surrendered to the Indian troops. Malik Hasan, who was again in their camp, was detected in correspondence with the Persians in Kandahar, and was imprisoned.

Urged by repeated orders from the Emperor, and by his jealousy o his brother, Aurangzebe, Prince Dāra Shekoh made desperate efforts to capture Kandahar. The skill and constancy of Mehrāb Khan and the resolution and superior training of his men, once more proved too much for the Indian troops; and although one of the principal magazines of the place was exploded, the fire discipline of the besiegers and the blazing sheets (soaked in naphtha and grease), with which they repulsed assaults on the walls drove off the assailants with very heavy loss. Five great assaults were delivered and frustrated a with very great number of casualties.

After five months had been consumed in these unavailing operations, the ammunition of the besiegers again began to run short. The neighbouring country had been denuded of fodder and grain; and in addition cold and wet weather had set in: men and animals were dying in great numbers from hunger and exposure. Reports were made to the Emperor and an autograph rescript was issued recalling the troops from Kandahar, and on the 11th of October 1653, the siege was abandoned. Prince Dāra Shekoh took up a position to cover the retirement of his guns, and held it till the artillery had reached Ghazni. Then he broke up his camp and marched towards the Indus by the road by which he had advanced. The Persians and the tribesmen hung on the rear of his columns and harrassed his troops, till they arrived on the borders of the Multan Province. The fort at Pishin was destroyed by his orders.

For almost two hundred years, no Indian troops entered Southern Afghanistan.

The loss of Kandahar was never forgotten. The Emperor Aurangzebe taunted his son Shah Alam, when the latter was Viceroy of Kabul, with making no efforts to take it early in the eighteenth century. The Deccan ulcer, however, had made vast inroads into the vitality of the Indian Empire, and the effeminate and pleasure-loving nobility were no longer capable of enduring the hardships entailed by campaigns in Afghanistan. Notwithstanding the increasing disorders that were taking place in the Kandahar Province early in the eighteenth century, the Indian Emperors could make no attempt to take advantage of them to regain the lost dependency.

APPENDIX III.

Relations between Shah Mahmud of Kabul and the Persian Government, 1807-08.

Shah Mahmud had been an useful tool in the hands of the Shah, during the reign of Shah Zamān, by means of which the pretensions of the Shah of Persia in the direction of Herat and Afghanistan might be asserted. The cession of Ghurian to Persia was the price which Mahmud had agreed to pay for the countenance afforded him by the Shah. The place was handed over to Persia and a Deputy Governor had been installed.

When, however, Shah Mahmud had dethroned his brother, and Haji Prince Firuz-ud-din became Governor of Herat, he sent troops to take possession of Ghurian, having arranged with the Deputy Governor that it should be surrendered. The Persian troops however resisted the Afghans, and in the battle that took place the Afghan leader was shot dead in the golden howdah on the back of an elephant from which he directed the operation of his men.

The Governor of Khurassan marched on Herat to punish this breach of faith, and invested the city. Prince Firuz-ud-din was compelled to pay arrears of tribute for two years, and promised to discharge his obligations punctually in the future. He also gave his son as a hostage for his good faith.

APPENDIX IV.

Relations between the Afghans and Persians in the year 1232 A. H. (began Thursday 21st November 1816, ended Tuesday 11th November 1817), and the events which led to the downfall of Vazier Fath Khan Barakzai.

The turbulent chiefs of Khurassān needed a strong hand to control them, and Shah Fath Ali conferred the government of that Province on one of his sons. Hasan Ali Mirza, a Prince of a martial disposition and well calculated to reduce the rebellious chief in his government to obedience.

Haji Prince Firuz-ud-din had again invaded the district of Ghurian and the Prince Governor marched against Herat. The severe treatment meted out to the garrison of Mahmudābād, which the Prince had captured on his way, struck terror into the heart of Prince Firuz-ud-din, and he sent an envoy to the Persian camp, offering to give up Ghurian, and praying that Herat might be spared. The Persian Prince accepted Ghurian, but continued to advance on Herat (in 1232 A. H.)

This city, which at this time contained about 100,000 inhabitants, was besieged in due form; and the besiegers began to work their way up to the ditch by regular approaches, while the gates were watched by strong detachments. These preparations terrified Prince Firuz-ud-din into absolute submission, and on paying a fine of 50,000 tomans he was permitted to continue as governor of the city, and on condition that the Khutbah, or Public Prayers should be read in the name of the Shah, and also that money should be coined bearing the titles of the latter.

The Persians followed the treacherous governor of Ghurian, who had found refuge among the Firuz Kuhi tribes, into their fastnesses, where the Persians were very roughly handled, after which Prince Hasan Ali returned to Meshed.

In the same year, Hāji Prince Firuz-ud-din became apprehensive of his brother's displeasure, owing to his complaisant attitude with regard to the suzerainty of the Shah of Persia, and he asked for military aid to enable him to withstand the Persian troops. In compliance with this request, the expedition to Herat was undertaken, and, as has been already narrated, the Vazier Fath Khan advanced on Herat, dispossessed Firuz-ud-din of the town and the citadel, and in addition put the Vazier of Herat to death. Sardar Kohandil Khan, the Vazier's brother, was despatched to take possession of Ghurian.

Vazier Fath Khan wrote to all the chiefs of Khurassan exhorting them to make common cause with the Afghans, and to throw off the supremacy of the Shah. The Khan of Khiva and the Sardars of the Hazaras, and of the Firuz Kuhis were induced to come into this coalition. The sons of Ishak Khan Karai, of Turbat-i-Haidari (the father had been strangled in Meshed) joined this movement.

News of this danger to the Shah's authority was forwarded to Court, and the Motamid-ud-daulah was sent to Khurassan to exert himself to win back some of the warlike chiefs of that Province to their allegiance. Such troops also as were available were pushed on to Meshed as rapidly as possible, and the Shah prepared to follow after the celebration of the Nauroz festival. On the arrival of the reinforcements from Teheran, at Meshed, the Prince Governor Hasan Ali Mirza found himself able to take the field at the head of 10,000 men. He was uncertain whether to attack the Khan of Khiva, who was at Sarakhs with a powerful army, or Vazier Fath Khan, who was at the head of 40,000 men, on the borders of Persian Khurassan. Fearing that the Afghans would march on Meshed if he advanced on Sarakhs, the Prince determined to attack them first. He advanced in the direction of Ghurian; and soon came into touch with the Afghan forces in the Kohsuieh district. Vazier Fath Khan sent to inform His Highness Hasan Ali Mirza that he had no desire to fight, and that, if Ghurian was left in the possession of the Shah of Kabul, and his two allies, Muhammad Khan, and Ibrahim Khan Karai, were secured in their rights of Surbat and Bakharz respectively, he would engage to undertake no hostilities against the Persian Government. The Prince returned a taunting reply, and both sides prepared for battle. Fath Khan's immediate followers seem to have fought bravely, but the motley elements of which his army was composed, displayed their usual want of combination, which neutralized the advantages afforded by their greater numbers. In spite of their superior training, the Persians were giving way before the odds against which they were contending, when Fath Khan was struck by a spent bullet, and an impending defeat was converted into a victory for the Persians.

The Shah of Persia received the news of this decisive battle, while he was advancing from his capital towards Meshed; and he took advantage of it to turn aside and besiege the fort of Bam (held by a Ghilzai chief) of which he took possession. At this place he was met by an Ambassador, sent by Mahmud to assuage the wrath of the Persian Monarch, and to disavow the action of Vazier Fath Khan. The Shah, in reply, demanded that the Barakzai should be delivered to him in chains; or that Shah Mahmud should destroy the sight of the Vazier, as the only conditions on which he would suspend his intention of an immediate invasion of Afghanistan. (History of Persia—Watson, p. 192, *et. seq.*)

To have carried out the punishment of the Vazier, at the bidding of the Shah, would have caused an overwhelming outburst of popular feeling, and have estranged his staunchest supporters, and at once would have resulted in the loss of his throne on which the seat of Shah Mahmud was none too secure. It was necessary to find a pretext consonant with national usages and opinion, to carry out a plan which would appease the Shah of Persia, and remove a minister who was becoming too powerful. The violence offered by Dost Muhammad to the daughter of Shah Mahmud, the Rokiya Begum (of which there appears to be no doubt—as it was universally believed), the wife of Prince Firuz-ud-din, was just the opportunity which was desired. The Princess had sent her torn garments to Prince Kāmrān and called on him to avenge the insult she had suffered at the hands of Dost Muhammad, and Prince Kāmrān was provided with ample justification for the course he pursued, from an Afghan and oriental point of view.

APPENDIX V.

Relations between Dost Muhammad, Ruler of Kabul and the Persian Government, resulting in the Siege of Herat in 1837-38, by the Persians.

Dost Muhammad and his brother Nawab Jabbar Khan had always been desirous of entering into friendly relations with the British Government. The latter showed himself to be especially favourable to the Englishmen who visited Kabul during the earlier part of his brother's reign. The admiration of Nawab Jabbar Khan for the English, had led him to send his eldest son Ghias Khan to Ludhiana, to be educated in the Mission School at that place.

The overtures made by Dost Muhammad to the British Government were, however, coldly received. His inveterate enemy Shah Shuja, found an asylum in Ludhiana, which he used as a base of operations against the Barakzais, and the sympathetic attitude towards him of the Officials in Ludhiana was undoubtedly magnified by the astute Sadozai Exile into an actual alliance; and used by him to keep up the spirits of his adherents in Afghanistan, regarding the eventual restoration of this family. Dost Muhammad cannot be blamed if he turned towards Persia. The pretensions of the Shah with regard to Herat and Afghanistan constituted a standing menace; and an agreement or understanding with the Persian Government in his eyes would have had a two-fold effect of limiting the plans of conquest entertained by the Shah (thereby allowing to concentrate his efforts against an invasion by Shah Shuja and of obtaining assistance against the *ci-devant* Ruler of Afghanistan).

Haji Husen Ali Khan was despatched by the Amir to the Court of the Shah to negotiate a treaty of offensive and defensive alliance between the two governments, on the condition that a joint attack by Afghans and Persians should be made on Herat (held at this time by Kāmrān the Sadozai) and on the fall of that city, the territories dependent on it should be divided between the Barakzai Ruler of Kabul and the Shah of Persia. All the countries lying to the west of the river of Farah, excepting the district of Sabzawār, were to be the share of the Persian government and all the territory to the east of that river and including Sabzawār were to be made over to the Ruler of Kabul.

Haji Husen Ali Khan (Dost Muhammad's representative) appears to have doubted the utility of such a treaty, and to have been superseded by the arrival in Teheran of Aziz Khan, the Agent of the Kandahar Sardars who entered into an agreement with the Persian Government on the terms of a league against Prince Kāmrān, the Shah acknowledging the independence of the Kandahar Sardars.

These preliminaries having been settled, the Shah put his army in motion towards the east in the summer of 1836, but insuperable obstacles compelled him to postpone the fulfilment of his plans till the following year.

The Treaty of Turkmanchai had caused a complete reversal in the attitude of the British authorities in India towards Afghanistan, combined with the growth of the Sikh power in the Punjab, which had freed the Indian

Government from anxiety on the score of Afghan interference in the affairs of India. Every effort was made by the Representatives of Great Britain to restrain the Shah from attempting to forcibly assert his pretensions with regard to Herat, for by the provisions of the Treaty of Turkomanchai, if Herat had fallen into the hands of Persia, the Czar would have been entitled to place Consuls in that place for the protection of Russian Trade.

Muhammad Shah, the monarch of Persia, had been baulked of his prey when he had been compelled to abandon his projected operations against Herat in 1836. As soon as he had restored order in the internal affairs of his kingdom, he prepared to march into Khurassan with the capture of Herat as his ultimate object; and to enforce his pretensions with regard to Afghanistan, for he regarded the country between the boundary of Persia and Ghazni as belonging to Persia.

A more recent cause of quarrel, however, was the non-fulfilment by Prince Kāmrān (who had succeeded his father in Herat), of the terms of the three engagements he had entered into with Persia. The fortress of Ghurian had not been surrendered to Persia. Certain Persian families, who had been released from captivity and were to have been forwarded to Persia, had not been sent. The tribute, which the Prince had agreed to pay, had not been paid.

In addition there was the question of Seistan. This country had been over-run by Mir Weis, the Ghilzai, in 1715; and it had become a province of the kingdom of Afghanistan, in the time of Ahmad Shah. As the Kajar dynasty had become established on the throne of Persia its ambition had gradually become enlarged, and by the time that Muhammad Shah had ascended the throne of Persia, Seistan had come to be regarded, in Tehran, as an integral portion of the kingdom of the Shah, although the claims of the Shah had been asserted merely in countenancing a rival claimant to the chiefship of Seistan conditionally on the latter recognising the Shah as his Suzerain. Prince Kāmrān had been allowed by his Vazier Yār Muhammad to invade Seistan in 1836 and had established his authority in that country for the time being, thereby completing the displeasure of the Shah which had been growing against him.

While, however, the question of an advance on Herat was being debated between the British Representative at Tehran and the ministers of the Shah, Prince Kāmrān added fuel to the flame that had been already kindled by putting some Persians to death, and by driving others out of his city. This was due to the discovery of a plot against him, in Herat, which had originated with the Persian inhabitants of the city, who had agreed to rebel against him, whenever a Persian army should appear before Herat.

APPENDIX VI.

The events preceding the conclusion of peace by the Treaty of Paris, and the seizure of Herat by Dost Muhammad in 1863.

On the 25th of January 1853 an agreement had been concluded between Her Majesty's Minister at the Court of Persia, and the Shah's government, by which the latter had bound itself not to send troops to Herat, unless troops from Kabul or Kandahar should invade that principality.

In the meantime, however, a misunderstanding had arisen between Her Majesty's Representative and the ministers of the Shah, which culminated in the departure from Tehran, on the 5th December 1855, of the British Mission. As month after month passed by without a peremptory demand from Her Majesty's Government for apology and reparation, the Sadr-i-Azam began to entertain the idea that the action of the British Minister would be disavowed at Headquarters. Elated at his apparent success, he recklessly determined to gratify the national desire for the possession of Herat. In direct contravention of the agreement of 1855, orders were issued to the Prince, governor of Khurassān, to march on Herat.

Early in 1856 Prince Sultan Murād advanced on Herat. The city had fallen into his hands; and Prince Yusuf, the son of Hāji Prince Firuz-ud-din, had been surrendered to the Persians, by whom he had been deported to Tehran.

In the meantime preparations had been made in India for an expedition to Persia and on the 1st November 1856 war was formally declared with that country; the *casus belli* was declared to be the expedition against Herat.

The condition of Persia, and the political situation at that time, were such as to render it no easy matter to make war on that country without involving both the government and the country in utter ruin; and the war had to be conducted on the principle of doing only as much mischief, to the enemy as would suffice to induce him to make peace, on the terms required of him. The problem to be solved was, how to expel the Persian troops from Herat; and there were two courses open to the British Government, to effect this purpose. Either by an advance of British troops overland from Sind—the co-operation of both the Amir Dost Muhammad of Kabul. and the Khan of Kalat, had been bespoken; or by way of the sea, to effect a landing at Bandar Abbas with the permission of the Sultan of Maskat. This plan was finally adopted.

On the 4th December 1856, the island of Karak was occupied and troops were disembarked at Bandar Abbas. On the 9th of December the Persians were dislodged from Bushire. On the 27th of January 1857, Lieut.-General Sir James Outram landed at Bandar Abbas, and on the 8th February the Persians were completely defeated at Burasjun. On the 26th of March Muhamerah was captured.

The expedition to Persia was looked on with disfavour at Home, and before the fall of Muhamerah, a treaty had been signed; on the part of England by Lord Cowley, and on the Persian side by Ferrukh Khan, the Persian Ambassador to the Court of France, on the 4th March 1857.

By this treaty it was agreed that the forces of Her Majesty should evacuate Persian Territory when certain conditions had been fulfilled. The principal condition was the complete withdrawal of Persian troops from Herat, and from every other part of Afghanistan within three months from the date of the exchange of the ratifications of this Treaty. The Shah agreed to relinquish all claims to sovereignty over the territory and city of Herat, and the countries of Afghanistan, and never to demand from the chiefs of Herat, or of the countries of Afghanistan, any marks of obedience, such as the coinage, or the Khutbah[1], or tribute.

The Shah pledged himself to complete abstention from interference with the internal affairs of Afghanistan; and to recognize the independence of Herat, and of the whole of Afghanistan.

In case of differences arising between the Government of Persia, and the countries of Herat and Afghanistan, the Persian Government engaged to refer them to the friendly offices of the British Government, and not to take up arms unless those friendly offices should fail of effect.

The British Government, on their part, engaged at all times to exert their influence with the states of Afghanistan, to prevent any cause of umbrage being given by them, or by any of them, to the Persian Government; the British Government engaging, if appealed to by the Persian government in the event of difficulties arising to use their best endeavours to compose such differences in a manner just and honourable to Persia.

---

1 This is the public announcement of dependence on a Suzerain, by praying for him in the mosques.

In the case of any violation of the Persian frontier by any of the Afghan states, the Persian Government had the right, if due satisfaction were not given, to undertake military operations for the repression and punishment of the aggressors; but it was to be distinctly understood that any military force of the Shah which might cross the border for such a purpose, was to retire within his own territory as soon as the object should be accomplished, and that the exercise of this right was not to be made a pretext by Persia for the permanent occupation, or the annexation, of any town or portion of the Afghan States.

Such were the terms of the Treaty of Paris which referred to Afghanistan. The war had been forced on Great Britain, and she was willing to grant peace on the conditions that the independence of Afghanistan should be secured, and that suitable apology should be made for the affronts which had been offered to her Representative at the Persian Court. The outbreak of the Mutiny of the Bengal army, rendered it a matter of thankfulness that nothing had been allowed to retard the conclusion of peace. It also enabled the Shah's ministers to evade the fulfilment of some of the terms of the Treaty.

By the 8th article, the Persian government had engaged to set at liberty without ransom, immediately after the exchange of the ratifications of the Treaty, all prisoners taken during the operations of the Persian troops in Afghanistan. Among those captives was Muhammad Yusuf, the nephew (and heir) of the late Prince Kāmrān of Herat, who had been sent a prisoner to Tehran in the spring of the year 1856. He had been pardoned by the Shah and set free within the walls of the capital; but it was not the intention of the Persian Government to permit the Sadozai Prince to return to his principality. On the 10th of April 1857 a courier arrived at Tehran from Paris bearing despatches from Ferrukh Khan, in which his government was informed of the terms of the Treaty which he was about to conclude. The Sadr-i-Azam lost no time in deciding on the fate of Muhammad Yusuf (who naturally would feel should he recover his power, that he owed it to the measures taken by the English Government), and the former determined to place upon the throne of Herat, a ruler who would owe his advancement to the goodwill of the Persian Government, and who would be content to hold his position as a vassal of the Shah. On the 11th of April 1857, Muhammad Yusuf was handed over to the relatives of the late Seïd Muhammad, son of the late Vazier Yār Muhammad, and the unfortunate victim was dragged to a mound in front of the Kasr-i-Kajar Palace, and there clumsily hacked to pieces by the sabres of the relatives of the late Seïd Muhammad. Sultan Ahmad Khan, Barakzai, became ruler of Herat; where, of his own accord, he was to coin money in the Shah's name, and cause the Khutbah to be read in the Shah's name, in return for Persian support and Persian gold.[1]

The seizure of Farah by Sultan Jān, gave Dost Muhammad a pretext for action against Herat. On the 28th June 1862, intelligence was received in Tehran that Amir Dost Muhammad had reached Kandahar, with three regiments of infantry, two thousand cavalry, and five guns—and the Shah informed the British Ambassador that Sardars Amin Khan and Sharif Khan had invested Farah, which for its strength and importance may be called little Herat, with a powerful army. Farah surrendered on the 8th July. After the fall of this place the Amir marched on the same day towards Herat, which is 140 miles due north of Farah. On the 22nd July, the Amir took Sabzawār, which is seventy-five miles due south of Herat; on the 26th his cavalry defeated the Herati cavalry and killed Sardars Akram Khan and Yusuf Khan, Achakzais. On the 27th July, Dost Muhammad invested Herat, with sixteen thousand men and thirty-two guns. This naturally was the cause of deep anxiety to the Shah and he was anxious

---

1 History of Persia, from the beginning of the nineteenth century to the year 1858, by Robert Grant Watson, London 1866.

that a commission of a member of the British Legation and a Persian official of high rank, should be sent to the camp of the Amir to arrange the differences between him and his nephew, Sultan Jān. Mr. Eastwick was deputed from the Legation for this purpose. After leaving Meshed he came to the camp of the Hisām-us-Sultanah at Kalandarābād towards Herat. Here he met the Vazir of Herat Hasan Ali Khan—"He called himself a Kabuli, but he had a vile Uzbeg face, small, cunning eyes, high cheek bones, and a forehead "villainous low." On the 18th November Mr. Eastwick received a despatch from Lord Russell, appointing him Her Majesty's Chargé d'Affaires at the Court of Persia till further orders, and he was directed to return to Teheran as soon as possible. The Hisām-us-Sultanah, Prince Murad Mirza was informed that the policy of Her Majesty's Government was not to interfere with the Afghans.[1] Left to itself Herat surrendered to the Amir Dost Muhammad as already narrated. Sultan Jān deserved little at the hands of the English, as he had witnessed the murder of Sir Wm. Macnaghten in Kabul, if he did not take an active part in it.

1 Journal of a Diplomat's Three Years' Residence in Persia, by E. B. Eastwick, F.R.S., F.S.A. &c., 1864, II. 127, *et. seq.*

THE PRINCIPAL AUTHORITIES CONSULTED.

MSS.—Persian Text.

Rauzat-ul-Jannat-fi-ausaf-i-Madinati-l-Herat. Library of the Asiatic Society, Calcutta.

Tarikh-i-Salatin-i-Afaghinah. Library of the Asiatic Society, Calcutta.

Malfuzāt-i-Sahib Kirān ,, ,, ,,

Alam-ara-i-Abbasi ,, ,, ,,

Shah Jahānnāmah ,, ,, ,,

Tarikh-i-Khan Jahānkhan ,, ,, ,,

Husain Shahi ,, ,, ,,

Mirāt-ul-Abbasi. Library, Royal Asiatic Society, London.

Tahmāsnāmah.*

Khazānah-i-Amirah.*

'Alamgirnāmah.*

Majma'-ut-Tawārikh.*

Tarikh-i-Muhammadi.*

Tazkirah-i-Salatin-i-Chaghatai.*

Waqa'i-i-Zamānshāhi.*

Persian Text—Printed or Lithographed.

'Alamgirnāmah. Bibliotheca Indica.

Maasir-i-'Alamgiri ,, ,,

Badshahnāmah ,, ,,

Tarikh-i-Baihaki ,, ,,

Zafarnāmah ,, ,,

Muntakhab-al-Lubāb (Khafi Khan). Bibliotheca Indica.

Tuzuk-i-Jahāngīrī. Aligarh Edition. Litho.

Jahān Kushā-i-Nādiri ,,

Tarikh-i-Sultāni ,,

Waq'iāt-i-Durani ,,

Maasir-ul Umara. Bibliotheca Indica.

Seir-i-Mutākherin. Litho.

Dur-i-Nādiri ,,

The Second Afghan War, 1878-80, Abridged Official Account, 1907.

Treaties, Engagements and Sanads—Afghanistan. Vol. XI, 4th Edition, 1909.

---

* Translations and notes by W. Irvine, Esq., I.C.S. (Retd.), London.

Bactria. Professor N. G. Rawlinson, 1909.

Storia-do-Magor. Vols. I to IV., Irvine, 1908.

A Sketch of the Geography and Geology of the Himalaya Mountains and Tibet. Colonel Burrard, R.E., F.R.S., and H. H. Hayden, B.A., F.G.S., Calcutta, 1907-08.

Early History of India. V. A. Smith, London, 1908.

Baluchistan District Gazetteer Series, 1907:—Quetta-Pishin, Text and Statistics.

Loralai ,, ,, ,,

Zhob ,, ,, ,,

Sibi ,, ,, ,,

Makrān and Kharān. Vols. VII and VII (*a*): Text and Appendices.

Imperial Gazetteer of India. Provincial Series, 1908.

N.-W. Frontier Province.

N.-W. Frontier Province Gazetteer. Kuram Agency, 1908.

,, ,, ,, ,, Tochi ,, 1908.

Census of India, 1901. Languages.

Indian Antiquary. January, February and March, 1907.

Outlines of Punjab Ethnography. Ibbetson, Calcutta, 1883.

Settlement Report of the Karnal District. Ibbetson, 1872.

Journal of the Asiatic Society of Bengal. Vols. XLIV. and XLVIII.

Tabakat-i-Nasiri. Trans. Maj. Raverty.

Elliot's History of India (Dowson). Vol. VIII.

History of Persia. Malcolm, 2 Vols., 1829.

,, ,, ,, Watson (continuation of above), London, 1866.

,, ,, ,, Markham, London, 1874.

History of Armenia. Father Chamich. Trans. by Johannes Avdal. 2 Vols., Calcutta, 1827.

History of the Jews. H. Graetz, 5 Vols., 1891-92.

History of the Sikhs. Cunningham (Capt. J. D.), London, 1853.

History of the Afghans. Ferrier, London, 1858.

History of the Mahrattas. Grant Duff, London, 3 Vols., 1826.

Account of the Kingdom of Kabul. Elphinstone, 2 Vols., London, 1839.

Life and Adventures of the Revd. Joseph Wolff, D.D., LL.D., 2 Vols., 1845.

Journey from Bengal to England, through the northern part of India, Kashmir, Afghanistan, and Persia, and into Russia, by the Caspian Sea. George Foster, 2 Vols., London, 1798.

Travels into Bokhara. Burnes, 3 Vols., London, 1835.

Vigne's Travels, 2nd Edition. 2 Vols., London, 1843.

Moorcroft's Travels. Edited by H. H. Wilson. 2 Vols., London, 1841.

History of India, under the two first Sovereigns of the House of Timur, Baber and Humayun. 2 Vols., London, 1854.

Memoirs of Baber. Leyden. London, 1826.

Gulshan-i-Rehmat. Chas. Elliott. Oriental Trans. Fund. London, 1831.

Life of Ali Hazin, Text and Trans. by Belfour, Oriental Trans. Fund. London, 1830.

Kitab-i-Yamini, Utbi. Oriental Trans. Fund. London, 1858.

The First Afghan War and its causes. Sir H. M. Durand. London, 1879.

Narrative of the March and Operations of the Army of the Indus in the Expedition to Afghanistan, 1838-39. Major Hough. London, 1841.

Memoirs of Major-General Sir Wm. Nott. 2 Vols., London, 1854.

Life and Correspondence of Sir George Pollock. London, 1873.

Life of Dost Muhammad, Amir of Kabul. 2 Vols. Mohan Lall. London, 1846.

Journal of a Mission to Kandahar in 1857. Major H. B. Lumsden.

Asiatic Researches, Vol. I., Calcutta (1799).

,, ,, Vol. XI., Calcutta, the Roshanis by John Leyden.

History of the Reign of Shah Aulum. Francklin, London, 1798.

Military Memoirs of George Thomas. Francklin, London, 1803.

Pashtu Grammar, 2 Vols. Major Raverty. Calcutta, 1855.

Poetry of the Afghans, 16th to 19th Century. Major Raverty. London, 1862.

Khush Hal Khan Khatak; Afghan Poetry of the 17th Century. Biddulph. London, 1890.

The Caliphate, its Rise and Fall. Sir Wm. Muir, London, 1891.

Journal of a Diplomat's Three Years' Residence in Persia. By Ed. B. Eastwick, F.R.S., F.S.A., 2 Vols., London, 1864.

Account of the early Abdalis. Major Leech, Calcutta, 1840.

A Memoir of India and Afghanistan, Harlan, Philadelphia, 1842.

Journal of a Political Mission to Afghanistan in 1857. Bellew, London, 1862.

The Afghan Wars, 1839-42 and 1878-80. Archibald Forbes, 2 Vols., London, 1892.

INDEX.

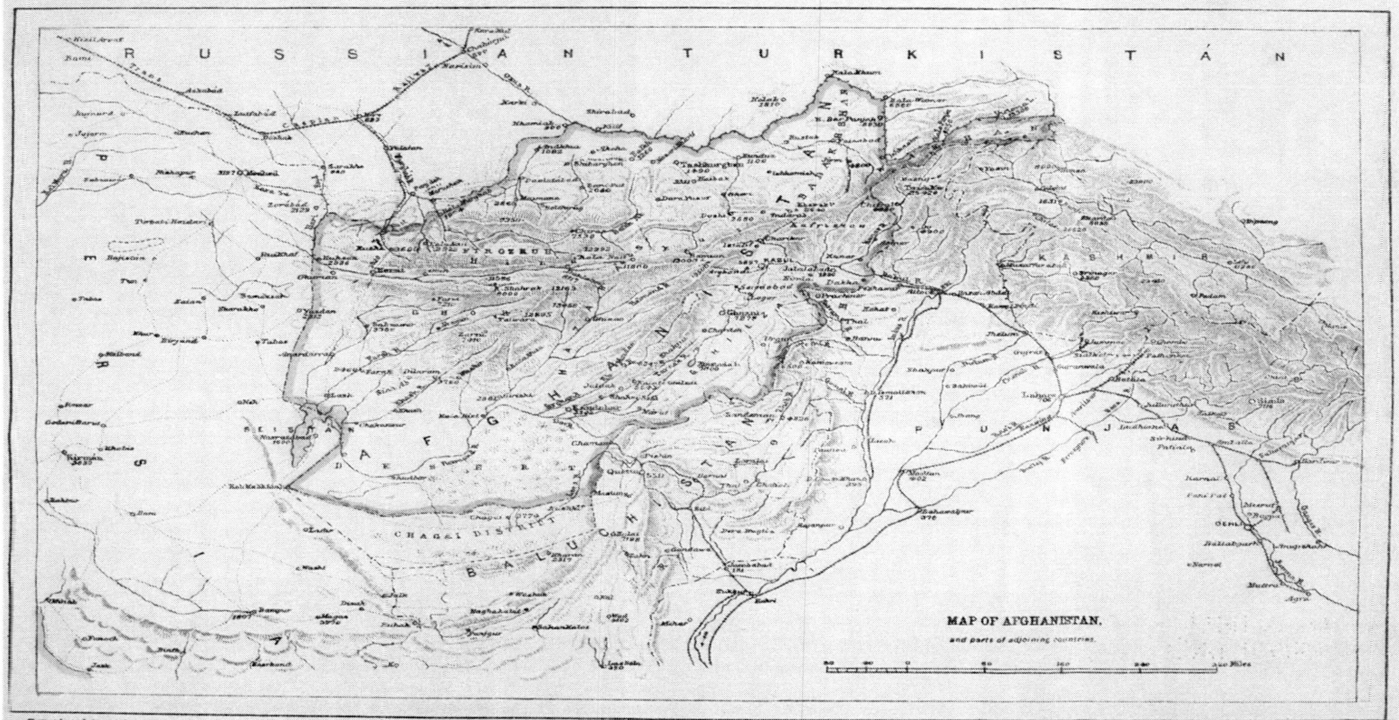

Reproduced direct from the original at the Photo.-Mechl. and Litho. Dept., Thomason College, Roorkee.

Zinco., August, 1910.—No. 6531-899